DYING

to

DRINK

DYING
to
DRINK

CONFRONTING BINGE DRINKING
ON COLLEGE CAMPUSES

HENRY WECHSLER, Ph.D.
DIRECTOR, HARVARD SCHOOL OF PUBLIC HEALTH
COLLEGE ALCOHOL STUDY

and BERNICE WUETHRICH

RODALE

To Joan
— H . W .

To my family
— B . W .

© 2002 by Henry Wechsler, Ph.D., and Bernice Wuethrich

Cover Photograph © Paul A. Souders/CORBIS

Printed in the United States of America

Rodale Inc. makes every effort to use acid-free ∞, recycled paper ♻.

Cover Designer: Christopher Rhoads
Cover Photographer: Paul A. Souders/CORBIS

Library of Congress Cataloging-in-Publication Data

Wechsler, Henry, date.
   Dying to drink : confronting binge drinking on college campuses / Henry Wechsler and
Bernice Wuethrich.
      p.   cm.
   Includes bibliographical references and index.
   ISBN 1–57954–583–1 hardcover
   1. College students—Alcohol use. 2. Alcoholism—Prevention. I. Wuethrich, Bernice.
II. Title. [DNLM: 1. Alcohol Drinking. 2. Alcoholic Intoxication. 3. Ethanol—poi-
soning. 4. Students—psychology. 5. Universities.]
   HV5135 .W397 2002
   362.292'088'375—dc21   2002006952

Distributed to the book trade by St. Martin's Press

2 4 6 8 10 9 7 5 3 1 hardcover

Visit us on the Web at www.rodalestore.com, or call us toll-free at (800) 848-4735.

WE **INSPIRE** AND **ENABLE** PEOPLE TO IMPROVE
THEIR LIVES AND THE WORLD AROUND THEM

ACKNOWLEDGMENTS

We gratefully acknowledge a number of individuals who made this book possible:

Mark Seibring, Toben F. Nelson, and Lisa A. Travis for their help in the preparation of this book and other members of the Harvard School of Public Health College Alcohol Study team: Meichun Kuo, Elissa R. Weitzman, Jae Eun Lee, Hang Lee, Karen Powers, and Jeff Hansen for their valuable contributions to the study of college binge drinking; and past team members George W. Dowdall, Jeana Gledhill-Hoyt, and Andrea E. Davenport.

Anthony Roman and his crew at the University of Massachusetts Survey Research Center for conducting the surveys.

Frank J. Chaloupka, Alexander C. Wagenaar, Ralph Hingson, Thomas C. Harford, and Lloyd Johnston for their outstanding contributions to the study of the drinking of young people.

Richard Keeling for his steadfast support and encouragement.

The Robert Wood Johnson Foundation for the early recognition of this major public health problem and continuing support, and to the outstanding staff—Seth Emont, Marjorie Gutman, Joan K. Hollendonner, Nancy Kaufman, and Mary Ann Scheirer—for their continuing support and advice.

Ellen Wilson and Andy Burness of Burness Communications for their insightful advice over many years about translating public health statistics into information that is meaningful for the general public.

Esmond Harmsworth, our agent, for his advice and enthusiasm.

Our editors and publishers at Rodale Books who believed in this book, most notably Stephanie Tade, Christopher Potash, and Marc Jaffe.

CONTENTS

PREFACE

As the principal investigator of four national College Alcohol Studies conducted for the Harvard School of Public Health, I have found that the number of students who binge drink has remained consistently high and that the style of drinking among the heaviest drinkers has become even more extreme.

Although our first study in 1993—and a mounting toll of alcohol-related student deaths—initially prodded university administrators to take action, the problem of college binge drinking has not abated. Why? Because the behavior is so longstanding and deeply entrenched that it requires long-term and comprehensive countermeasures. Unfortunately, the actions taken so far typically have been limited and off the mark. Focusing narrowly on the individual responsibilities of their students, some college administrators ignore the sea of alcohol in which their campuses swim. They allow cheap or free beer to flow at or near their schools and then blame the students for drinking.

I had already conducted three decades of research on binge drinking in New England when I launched our first national study. Only then did I grasp the full scope of the college drinking problem. Only after I went from campus to campus did I notice the ring of bars and liquor stores that surrounds each. Some schools have fifty, seventy-five, a hundred, or more alcohol outlets within a two-mile radius of campus. Yet those who are charged with solving the drinking problem have been looking right past the alcohol-saturated environment in which students live.

The alcohol industry is omnipresent on campus. Ads in college newspapers and on bulletin boards announce special promotions and reduced prices at local bars and liquor stores. Athletic departments, and sometimes other parts of the university, gratefully receive industry money. To top it off, industry money is behind most of the alcohol education programs adopted by colleges. With these funds, so-called social norms signs are posted on campuses and proudly state THE AVERAGE STUDENT AT THIS SCHOOL USUALLY ONLY HAS THREE DRINKS IN A ROW. Less than a mile away, larger signs off campus announce ten-cent beer specials or proclaim that here, ladies drink free. In this topsy-turvy world, the alcohol industry runs the programs aimed at "educating" students about "responsible" drinking—and proclaims success at every turn

Now, after just a few years of increased efforts to address student binge drinking, some school administrators and campus health professionals are giving in and lowering their expectations. Following the alcohol industry's lead, they are trying to put the problem back in the closet, trying to convince themselves and the public that college binge drinking is not such a serious problem after all.

This backpedaling has not been missed by our major media: "New Tactic on College Drinking: Play It Down," a *New York Times* front-page headline from October 2000 proclaimed; a *Wall Street Journal* headline a month later exclaimed: "On Many Campuses, Big Brewers Play a Role in New Alcohol Policies."

But partnering with the alcohol industry to play down the problem will not change the reality of the injuries, vandalism, sexual assaults, lost educational opportunities, and other ills that come with binge drinking. Alcohol is responsible for an estimated fourteen hundred student deaths a year and half a million unintentional injuries. The mess will not be cleaned up without the involvement of students and parents and civic leaders in a concerted full-scale effort to change the environment and culture of binge drinking on America's college campuses.

That is why I decided to write this book: because I could not turn a blind eye and allow this problem to be swept back under the rug.

—*Henry Wechsler, Ph.D.*

* * *

I was drawn to write this book for many reasons, reasons both personal and professional. As the daughter of a man whose dependence on alcohol undoubtedly contributed to his untimely death, I am keenly aware of the power of this drug. Now, as the mother of a young son whose life journey has scarcely begun, I am especially eager to understand the societal influences that can help or harm young people.

From an intellectual standpoint as a science writer, I am fascinated by the brain and its development. When I wrote about new insights into the effects of alcohol on the adolescent brain (*Discover Magazine*, March 2001), I also began to study the findings of Henry Wechsler and his College Alcohol Study (CAS). The volumes of data gathered from the CAS testify to the incredibly widespread nature of this problem. Other scientific and public-health research points to subtle but possibly long-lasting effects of heavy alcohol use on the development of young people.

Working on *Dying to Drink*, I interviewed dozens of students, administrators, health workers, and parents. I have talked to parents who have lost their children to alcohol and parents who daily balance their vigilance and love; and I've talked to students blind to their own drinking problems and to those who have lost friends and watched siblings in hospital beds, breathing on respirators after overdosing on alcohol. I know that these stories will continue, that they will fill pages and pages of the life scripts of seventeen- and eighteen-year-olds, of their parents and their teachers. But they need not.

It is my hope that this book will inspire courage and conviction and will help to improve the lives of young people as they find their way along life's journey as independent, competent, and compassionate people.

—*Bernice Wuethrich*

INTRODUCTION

At the core of this book are the results of the Harvard School of Public Health College Alcohol Study (CAS), an ongoing survey of more than fifty thousand students at 140 four-year colleges located in forty states. The study, supported through grants from The Robert Wood Johnson Foundation, has surveyed students at the same colleges four times: in 1993, 1997, 1999, and 2001. The participating schools were selected to represent public and private, urban and rural institutions of all sizes and academic competitiveness.

Administrators at each participating institution provided a random sample of more than two hundred undergraduates, to whom we mailed a nineteen-page questionnaire (see Appendix on page 274). The students answered the yes/no and multiple-choice questions and volunteered hundreds of pages of additional commentary on these topics as well. We then statistically analyzed all the results to compile a national picture of student drinking.

After examining problems associated with different levels of alcohol intake in the first study, we defined the term *binge drinking* for men as having five or more drinks in a row at least once in the prior two weeks, and for women as having four or more in a row. (We found that it took women only four drinks to reach the same level of problems that men reached at five drinks.) We classify as "occasional binge drinkers" those students who drank in this manner once or twice in the previous two weeks, and we classify as "frequent binge drinkers" those who drank in this way three or more times in two weeks.

Student responses to the CAS have established a strong relationship between binge drinking and the number and severity of problems that students face. For example, frequent binge drinkers are seventeen times more likely to miss a class, ten times more likely to vandalize property, and eight times more likely to get hurt or injured as a result of their drinking than are students who drink but do not binge. Therefore, we use the term *binge drinking* as a public-health tool to identify a level of drinking at and above which students are likely to experience and to cause a range of problems.

Students responded anonymously to the CAS questionnaire, and so the names used in this book are not their real ones. (At the same time, the names of some parents and citizens have been changed on their request to protect their privacy.) But their written commentary is real, and revealing, and exposes key issues in college alcohol use, including the tradition of heavy drinking on college campuses, the role of fraternities and sororities and athletics, the relationship of state alcohol control measures and college policies to this behavior, and the role that easy access to alcohol and low prices play. The CAS responses also provide insight into other high-risk behaviors, including tobacco and illicit drug use, unsafe sex, violence, and other behavioral, social, and health problems. Data on individual institutions, however, come not from the CAS—our data on specific universities is confidential—but from information that is publicly available.

Since the 1994 release of the first report on CAS findings, published in the *Journal of the American Medical Association*, the problem of binge drinking has captured national media attention and the public interest. The results of the study have been reported in more than fifty journal articles and innumerable newspapers and magazines. This book puts the major findings from the Harvard study into proper perspective and presents action plans developed from independent interviews with students, parents, administrators, campus health workers, advocacy organizations, and community leaders. Our one and only goal is to help solve what U.S. Surgeon General David Satcher called "the most serious public health problem on American college campuses today."

Part I
THE COLLEGE DRINKING ENVIRONMENT

CHAPTER 1

A CULTURE OF ALCOHOL

The Ramblin' Wreck
I'm a ramblin' wreck from Georgia Tech
And a hell of an engineer—
A helluva, helluva, helluva, helluva, hell of an engineer,
Like all the jolly good fellows,
I drink my whiskey clear.
I'm a ramblin' wreck from Georgia Tech
And a hell of an engineer.
—Frank Roman

In the university, we have entire generations that are learning to consume alcohol
in an institutional way.
—Gary, law school student

Cupid Week is an annual event at one Northeastern college. As its highlight, brothers of one fraternity take their shyest new member, get him completely wasted, and dress him up as Cupid. Then two brothers hold him up as he stumbles across campus. For every girl that he kisses the fraternity donates a dollar to the American Heart Association. The event draws hundreds of onlookers, both drunk and sober, and is bracketed by drinking parties at fraternities and sororities, in off-campus apartments, and in local bars.

On college campuses across America, alcohol-related culture takes many forms, from revered campus traditions to fraternity initiations, football tailgating parties, twenty-first-birthday "bar crawls" where the celebrant "drinks his age" with twenty-one shots, and more. Over many decades a culture of alcohol has become entwined in school customs, social lives, and institutions. Winked at for decades, this culture has its darker side.

One study estimates that fourteen hundred college students aged eighteen to twenty-four are killed each year as a result of drinking. They die from alcohol-related motor vehicle crashes, other unintentional injuries, and alcohol overdoses. At least half a million more students suffer an unintentional injury while under the influence.

College students nationally spend $5.5 billion on alcohol each year, more than they spend on soft drinks, tea, milk, juice, coffee, and schoolbooks combined. This represents more than just having an occasional beer with pizza. College binge drinkers drink to get drunk. They drink at least several times during the week and throughout the weekend, every weekend. Our College Alcohol Study has determined that two in five college students, including freshmen, can be called binge drinkers, consuming five or more drinks in a row for males, four or more for females, at least once in the past two weeks.

This culture of alcohol pervades too many American colleges. Whether it centers around the fraternity and sorority systems, among athletes and sports fans, or whether it has insinuated itself into all aspects of campus life—as it has at some colleges and universities—the problem must be acknowledged and addressed. In this chapter we look at the kinds of rituals, traditions, and myths that perpetuate a binge-drinking environment on and around college campuses.

SCHOOL RITUALS

Many universities host or at least tolerate high-risk rituals or events that are commonly known to involve heavy drinking. Some of these activities, such as Bonfire at Texas A&M University (now suspended), are student initiated and run, but so closely are they associated with the school's identity that administrators are often loath to interfere. Alcohol, goes the thinking, will help bond students to one another and to the school. Initiations and hazings are seen as serving the same purpose. But while participation in such rituals may help to forge friendships among some students and instill school loyalty that can later lead to alumni donations, in an unacceptable number of cases, participation in such rituals results in physical and emotional injury or even death.

NUDE OLYMPICS
and the NAKED MILE

The beginning and end of the academic year are often marked by drinking rituals. At Ithaca College in New York, seniors ritually jump into the campus's Dillingham Fountain on the last day of spring classes. Following the frolicking in 1999 about a hundred students were treated for alcohol-related injuries and illnesses. At the University of Michigan in Ann Arbor, students run the Naked Mile, streaking at midnight to mark the end of spring classes. Drunken students shed their shyness and their clothes, and the event draws spectators—including international pornographers—with cameras and video recorders.

At James Madison University in Harrisonburg, Virginia, the 2000 school year began with mass arrests as more than seven hundred partying students confronted riot police and state troopers. The students were celebrating school's beginning with an annual progressive party, drinking at seven different student apartments in a residential neighborhood. At least twenty students were arrested, many for underage drinking and public drunkenness, before police broke up the melee.

Other heavy-drinking rituals mark the changing of the seasons. Until recently Princeton students held their Nude Olympics on the midnight following the winter's first snowfall. This ritual started relatively modestly more than a quarter-century ago with about a dozen naked male students doing jumping jacks. In subsequent years other athletic feats were added, such as a naked wheelbarrow race. By 1999, the last year of the event, nearly four hundred students, many bolstered by alcohol, sprinted naked in front of the school's gothic dormitories. Nine students were either hospitalized with alcohol poisoning or treated at the school's health center. The administration was also alarmed by students who had sex or urinated in public at the outdoor sporting site.

College Student Drinking Facts

• 73 percent of fraternity and 57 percent of sorority members are binge drinkers.

• 58 percent of male athletes and 47 percent of female athletes are binge drinkers.

• Frequent binge drinkers constitute less than one-quarter of all students (23 percent) but consume three-quarters (72 percent) of all the alcohol college students drink.

• A ring of bars and liquor stores surrounds most colleges. At one college we found 185 alcohol outlets within two miles of campus.

KEG JUMPS, CARNIVAL, *and* HOMECOMING

In the fall of 2000 the University of Dayton administration indefinitely suspended Homecoming. President Raymond Fitz cited the reason as "extensive and excessive drinking and trashing of the student neighborhoods." Homecoming the previous year had attracted some seventy-five hundred people to a weekend-long party that had neighbors complaining about drunken, lewd behavior, fires set by students, and young alumni who burned several couches in the street.

Dartmouth College in Hanover, New Hampshire, has three annual rituals, each tied to the seasons and to alcohol: Homecoming in the fall features a giant bonfire, Winter Carnival features "keg jumps," and the spring's Green Key is all and only about getting trashed, according to Jason, a recent Dartmouth graduate. During the Carnival keg jumps, students flood a fraternity lawn forming an ice pond on which they line up a row of beer kegs. Emboldened by alcohol, students take turns skating downslope and then leaping over the kegs to land on mattresses, blankets, and pillows piled on the other side. The spring ritual, Green Key, "is based purely on drinking. There's nothing special going on and we don't build anything. You get a day off and go to parties all weekend. The majority of campus is drunk by Friday night," Jason said.

Since becoming president of Dartmouth, James Wright has addressed alcohol abuse at the university:

> I assure you that my concern about alcohol does not grow out of a desire to be telling students what to do with their spare time or a desire to ruin their fun. I have no secret goal of stopping drinking and harbor no illusions that we could do that. Colleges are about

choices and freedom—and responsibility. But there is a difference between having fun and potentially harming oneself or someone else. My concern is with what is called binge drinking—which seems to have increased here, and increased upon an already worrisome base. And I am concerned about the impact that alcohol has on the educational experience Dartmouth provides.

Despite Wright's concerns and efforts to bring the binge drinking under control, Dartmouth drinking traditions remain entrenched.

A SLIPPERY SLOPE

For students at Cornell University, nestled in the rolling hills of central New York State, Slope Day marks the end of the spring classes and graduation for seniors. Thousands of students congregate on the university's Libe Slope. If it is raining, the slope becomes a mudslide. The tumble of students careening downhill has resulted in dozens upon dozens of injuries—from fractured bones to dislocated joints and lost teeth. This tradition has persisted for years.

In 1996 Cornell police responded to 114 incidents and made dozens of arrests, most for liquor law violations. Police confiscated more than two hundred cases of beer, including a hundred cases brought by a fraternity for free distribution. Three students were taken to the local emergency room for alcohol poisoning; twenty were treated at the on-campus health center for fractured bones, torn ligaments, dislocated joints, cuts and bruises, and knocked out teeth; and another forty—too drunk to know where they were—were treated on the hill.

The administration and students have argued over the best ways to make the annual ritual a safer one. In an open letter to the campus in 1997, university president Hunter Rawlings wrote, "Each year, the health-care services of our community are overextended, students become dangerously ill, broken bones are commonplace, and criminal instances of vandalism, assault, public lewdness, and the destruction of property occur regularly. It is one thing to party; it's another to endanger your own safety and that of others." He appealed to students to take steps to improve their personal safety and sought the enrollment of faculty and sober student volunteers to act as monitors on the Slope for those in need of medical assistance.

The administration subsequently limited the number of beers students could bring to the Slope to six, and the university offered an alternative, nonalcoholic program across campus with live music. Although many students attend the alternative event, a large number go back and forth between the sodden Libe Slope and the dry alternative festival, undermining its effectiveness.

BONFIRE

They call it Bonfire. It stands on its own. Every year since 1909, when a group of student cadets razed furniture from around campus and set it ablaze, students at Texas A&M University in College Station have built Bonfire. They burn their creation before the season's final football game, played between Texas A&M and archrival University of Texas, or TU, as it is called. For Aggies, Bonfire represents "the burning desire to beat the hell out of TU."

By 1999 Bonfire had grown to be a student-managed project of massive proportions. From a simple tepee structure it had evolved into a layered wedding-cake design with thousands of logs piled together, stack upon stack. It reached a height of sixty feet and weighed close to two million pounds, about as much as two 747 jets. Students passed down instructions for building Bonfire by word of mouth, year after year, as older students instructed younger. There was neither blueprint nor systematic professional engineering oversight.

Students cut down the five-hundred-pound oak trees, stripped their branches, and heaved them into trucks. On site, they stacked the logs, one by one, until Bonfire was six stories high. The students would be muddy and sore as they strapped each log to a chain and caught their breath as, lifted by a crane, it broke free from the ground and swung momentarily, a lethal weapon belonging neither to the Earth nor the stack.

On the night of November 19, 1999, as Bonfire neared completion, the unthinkable happened. At 2:45 that morning, with seventy young men and women working on the structure, something shifted at its base as a restraining wire wrapped around several logs in the bottom-most tier snapped. Then another wire snapped, and another. Suddenly all that had been holding the mammoth structure together, every safeguard assumed to be in place, failed as the structure collapsed like a house of cards. Logs began to fall away from the bottom stack's southeast side. Second-stack logs followed, shifting sideways and hurtling into the gaps below. Students screamed and scrambled for safety as their friends plunged down with the logs.

Then, with a shuddering boom like a cannon salute, the center pole snapped between the first and second stacks. The third and fourth stacks shifted radically and, with a single sickening roar, the whole thing collapsed as the center pole, momentarily restrained by ropes, cracked again and whipped through the air. It broke at ground level and smashed into the hard-packed earth.

Twelve students were crushed to death, and twenty-seven were injured, retrieved from the twisted pile of logs and wire. Disbelief and grief were as tangible as death was intangible. The loss reverberated throughout the university and the state. When alumni heard the news, some are reported to have wept.

"IRRESPONSIBLE BEHAVIOR"

In the tragedy's aftermath the university appointed an independent special commission to determine the cause of the collapse. The Commission report ultimately found that the collapse was due to a number of physical and organizational factors. Structural failure was the result of "excessive internal stresses driven primarily by aggressive wedging of second stack logs into the first stack [and] . . . inadequate containment stress." The students had failed to use strong enough baling wire and had skipped the use of auxiliary cables to contain the enormous pressures generated on the bottom stack.

But the physical failure was driven by an organizational failure in which decisions and actions by both students and university officials over many years "created an environment in which a complex and dangerous structure was allowed to be built without adequate physical or engineering control."

What role did alcohol play in this college tradition? The report found "considerable evidence of irresponsible behavior in Bonfire. Alcohol use was substantial, although student leaders prohibited alcohol. Also, evidence of hazing and harassment by student workers and student leaders as well as unnecessary horseplay and fighting was significant." Investigators documented dozens of examples of these behaviors over the years, some of which led to accidents in which students were hurt or hospitalized. The report also concluded, however, that these incidences did not contribute materially to the collapse itself.

The university released some 2,300 Bonfire documents under the Texas Open Records Act. Among them are photographs that show empty beer cans in a truck parked near the stack and bottle caps strewn around. An unopened beer was found stuffed between the cushions of a sofa on the grounds. Two of the victims, one younger than twenty-one, had high levels of alcohol in their systems when they died. While their actual blood alcohol levels may never be known because of conflicting test results, one test registered a BAC of .392.

Laban Toscano, a sergeant with the Texas Alcoholic Beverage Commission who helped investigate the Bonfire tragedy, said, "You've got people drinking beer while putting together a complex structure. You have to wonder if, over the years, that isn't what caused the change in structure, the hand-me-downs of instructions from students getting convoluted while under the influence."

JUST AVERAGE, *or* UNIQUE?

Some students argue that it is unfair to criticize the use of alcohol at Bonfire, saying that it is part of a whole college culture of heavy drinking and partying. Indeed, a university-commissioned study the previous year had found that 65 percent of students under age twenty-one reported using alcohol within the thirty days prior to completing the survey, and 44 percent of students binge drank in the previous two weeks—putting Texas A&M right at the national average for binge drinking.

In fact, Texas A&M is no stranger to alcohol-related tragedy. The year before Bonfire collapsed, two students died in alcohol-related incidents. One inebriated eighteen-year-old student fell off a third floor stairwell in the parking garage. A second student died after celebrating his twenty-first birthday. "The last place he drank was a shot bar," Toscano said. "He was drinking from four-ounce shot glasses, and most of the concoctions didn't even have juice or water, just combinations of different liquors, some as much as 180 proof." (Pure alcohol is 200 proof.) After the young man passed out, his friends got him home and put him to bed. When his mother called the next morning to wish her son a happy birthday, his roommates could not rouse him. Emergency medical personnel arrived shortly thereafter and pronounced the young student dead.

Given Bonfire's history and the campus alcohol culture, many now say that the A&M tragedy was inevitable and that it is fortunate more lives were not lost. Commenting on the alcohol consumption, hazing, and horseplay associated with Bonfire, the Special Commission wrote, "Texas A&M is unique in allowing this level of irresponsible personal behavior in and around a construction project of this magnitude." Although the magnitude of the construction project was indeed unique, the Texas A&M administration was not unique in its willingness to turn a blind eye to campus drinking problems.

Bonfire is now permanently suspended.

DRINKING GAMES

In addition to "wet" school rituals, drinking games add a kick to the campus alcohol culture. Some drinking games mandate that players down a certain number of shots in a set amount of time. Other games call for drinking whenever the rules dictate—for instance, when a television character says something predictable. In a kind of forced march to intoxication, students playing drinking games are more likely to ignore their own limits and continue drinking in a stupor after the point where they would have normally passed out.

BEER PONG

Students at some schools identify their college experience with the most popular campus drinking games. At Dartmouth many students, particularly members of fraternities, are adherents of beer pong, played on a plywood table with ping-pong paddles stripped of their handles and gripped in the hand. The object is to lob the ping-pong ball into your opponent's cup of beer on the other side of the table. When you do, he or she must chug it down. If you miss, you chug. The game is over when the beers—or the players—are finished off.

Lisa said that as a freshman she became somewhat of an expert. "My drinking experience is colored by the fact that I have good eye-hand coordination, so I'm good at beer pong," she said. Because she won more often than she lost, Lisa rarely had to play until she was falling-down drunk, the fate of many a freshman who eagerly try their hand at beer pong.

At the end of her sophomore year Lisa learned that she had a mild heart condition that could be aggravated by drinking alcohol, so she switched the beer to water. "Even though I was playing in a frat where I was very comfortable, people would still say, 'Why aren't you drinking beer?'" she recalled. For most players the game and the drink are inseparable.

QUARTERS *and* JELL-O SHOTS

Anheuser-Busch recently capitalized on the popularity of quarters, a well-known college drinking game in which players bounce quarters into a glass and make others drink until they can't see straight. Bud Light sponsored a version of the game in which a group of players in participating bars around the country bounced quarter-sized tokens off a miniature tabletop basketball court into shot-glass-sized nets. They competed for prizes that included a trip to the finals of the NCAA men's basketball tournament in 2002. Commercials on the cable sports network advertised the "event" as the Bud Light/ESPN Quarter Bouncers Tournament.

The Internet provides yet another way for students to access drinking games and to centralize their experiences. Sites like PartySchool.com list hundreds of drinking games. The Ultimate Drinking Game home page specializes in media-based games, listing 663 at last count. Internet sites give students a forum in which to reinforce each other's drinking while connecting socially, albeit superficially, during what can be a lonely time, especially for freshmen.

Corresponding about Jell-O shots on PartySchool.com, one student wrote, "Yes, I've had jello-shots and . . . they're awesome!!! I just moved to Austin (I'm about to start UT) and I don't really know anyone or of anything to do so if anyone has any suggestions, please e-mail me."

Socializing with drinking games is most popular among binge drinkers and further encourages the practice. Our study found that while only 14 percent of non-bingers play drinking games, 57 percent of bingers do, and a full 72 percent of frequent bingers participate.

THE FRESHMAN EXPERIENCE

Our surveys show that more than half of freshmen arrive at college to find their first bingeing opportunity within the first week of college—often before purchasing even one textbook.

Alicia, arriving as a freshman at a university in Pennsylvania, described the drinking scene she found:

> The thing that blew me away was that people were on the street, pouring out of houses with beer, drunk, and the police stand

there doing nothing. The truth is, in twelve hours, from dark to light, you wouldn't be able to arrest or stop every person that's drunk in public. There are too many people. It can't be done.

Although every school is different—and we found that binge drinking rates vary from 1 percent to 83 percent of students—first-year students at many schools find themselves influenced by a culture and environment that promotes alcohol consumption. They enter this culture at a point of major transition in their lives: teeming with excitement, filled with doubt, knowing what they are leaving but not what they are going to find. Breaking from parents and home may be the most exhilarating and frightening thing they have experienced.

Many freshmen are eager to test their limits and to prove that they can handle themselves in adult situations. But all too frequently in a pro-drinking college culture, alcohol overtakes them. Students who regularly binge drink may be scarcely aware that they have entered dangerous territory, as the following first-person accounts illustrate.

LORIANNE: DRINKING WHENEVER, WHEREVER

The opportunities to party are everywhere, all the time. The first few weeks of school there was a party nearly every night of the week. They were all-campus parties at the fraternities where *everyone* is welcome. Especially freshman girls like me. I could go wherever I wanted, whenever I wanted.

I knew there would be a lot of alcohol, and that I would drink more than I did in high school. But I watch my weight. I don't want to gain the freshman fifteen [pounds]. So, after the first month I limited myself to drinking one, two, or maybe three times a week, never more than three. My friends and me buy hard alcohol, Bacardi rum, or Bacardi Limón, and sometimes people would have these ten-dollar handles of vodka that taste like rubbing alcohol. It makes me sick just to smell it. There's a lot more hard liquor than in high school, but it's expensive, so we go to all-you-can-drink fraternity parties for five dollars. That's fun, as long as the beer isn't too gross.

I rely on my friends—we all rely on each other, to take care of each other. If you drink too much, it's much better to have a friend with you to watch you.

Once I was taking medication for a spider bite; my whole leg was swollen up. I didn't realize that it wouldn't take too much alcohol for me to get drunk. In my dorm room we had a few shots of vodka before going out to the party. Later, my stomach felt queasy, so I ate some of the nachos and peanuts and things, but it just felt worse. I figured the food was making me sick and had more to drink. It kept happening, I kept feeling worse, so I kept drinking more to feel better, until I could barely stand up. Then my girlfriend took me home on the shuttle. But I had to get off. I was totally nauseous and threw up on the side of the road. I don't understand why nobody stopped me from drinking so much. I could have really hurt myself.

CATHY: FINDING FAKE IDS

My daughter has had three fake IDs. My husband found the first. I promptly cut that up. Then she came in with the second. She said she was going downtown for St. Patrick's Day and that she was going to be careful of what bars to go to because her friend wasn't of age. I said, "Neither are you." I took the ID from her. Then I consulted with a couple friends. They asked if taking the ID was going to stop her. I had to admit it wasn't. So it seemed to me a better approach to talk about how she could prepare herself and be safe, rather than for me to be punitive.

I talked to her about bar safety, being with friends, watching out for each other, and designated drivers. I asked her if she knew her limit. She said four or five; maybe six drinks in an evening. I said, "Then do you understand that you're a binge drinker? Think about the side effects that come from over-consumption." We talked about keeping an eye on your drink, moderation, and the bottom line that what she was choosing to do was still illegal and she was going to have to pay the consequences if she got caught. I wasn't going to rush to New York City and bail her out of jail.

She's grown up in a university community and was at an age where she understood deaths from alcohol, and I consumed a fair amount of alcohol in college and probably easily would have been classified as a binge drinker. So we talked freely about situations I had found myself in and don't want to find her in—the risk you take.

I'm concerned because my daughter has a sense that if she intellectually understands something, it will translate into practice. But that's not always the case.

GARY: KISSING *away* FALL SEMESTER

I was definitely appalled when I got to school. I had had one beer in four years of high school. The university had a rule against kegs in fraternities. I was appalled at the number of cans; I had an environmental response. A regular practice would be to go out and get 30, 40, 50, 60 cases of beer cans, the cheap stuff.

I lost my virginity at college and it was with a girlfriend of five years so it was very purposeful. But we would have drunken weekends. We would start at four o'clock Friday afternoon and not stop until six on Sunday. We wouldn't even eat. The best way to get over a hangover is to drink it off. For a weekend we would drink a case of MGD longnecks, a bottle of vodka and of schnapps, 750 ml each. That would be the weekend—pretty heavy stuff.

I struggled during the fall, particularly of my freshman year. It had to do with other things as well as the alcohol—as an African-American I was dealing with racism and trying to fit in socially. It was hard to handle the workload and to be away from my parents for the first time. Fall semester, basically, you just kiss it away.

ALCOHOL CULTURE MYTHS

College life is rife with myths about alcohol and drinking on campus. Understanding the reality of those myths or putting them into context can help students make sound decisions that ultimately allow them to be true to themselves.

MYTH: Work hard, play hard.

Students may pride themselves on their "Work hard, play hard" ethos, but our research has found that those who play hard are less likely to work hard. Binge drinkers are more likely to miss classes, to fall behind in schoolwork, and to have poor or failing grades than students who drink but do not binge (non-binge drinkers). Our survey revealed that:

- Drinking reduces the number of hours spent studying per day. Each additional drink per occasion is associated with fifteen minutes less studying per day.

- Drinking is associated with lower grades. Approximately five drinks per occasion are associated with a GPA lower by half a grade.

- Each additional drink consumed per occasion increased the probability of missing a class by 8 percent and getting behind in school by 5 percent.

Similarly, the Core Drug and Alcohol Survey, conducted by the Center for Alcohol and Drug Studies at Southern Illinois University-Carbondale, found that students who reported D and F grade point averages consumed an average of eleven alcoholic drinks per week, while those who earned mostly A's consumed only three drinks a week.

One student described his take on this prevalent myth:

"Work hard, play hard" is so killer. It becomes a motto that people live by and want their college to be known by. They want to be champions of that saying. It is the ultimate vindication for a student who feels like he's worked hard his whole life. He could have been a nerd all through high school. Now he can say, "You know what, I work hard, but I play hard too." They think they're taking that approach in everything, but it hyper-exaggerates when they're alcoholing. The people who are playing the hardest in drinking aren't playing the hardest in after-school activity, because drinking is their after-school activity.

MYTH: As an individual, it's up to me to drink responsibly. I'm in control. I can handle my liquor.

This sounds good, but it is not the way alcohol works. With alcohol, the more you drink, the less control you have over how much you drink, regardless of your original intentions. It has nothing to do with how good a person you are; it is in the nature of alcohol. Many people who start out as responsible drinkers become irresponsible drinkers.

This is the danger of the alcohol industry's mantra "Know when to say when" or "social norms" campaigns that tout "moderation." They obscure the reality that alcohol is an addictive drug that actually changes your brain chemistry in a way that can make you dependent on alcohol. The younger you are when you begin to drink heavily, the more likely it is that you will have alcohol problems later in life.

Our data show that 6 percent of college students have already acquired an alcohol dependent diagnosis (a term similar to alcoholism). Nearly *one-third* of students would be given an alcohol abuse diagnosis under psychiatric criteria. Forty-four percent of students reported at least one symptom of either abuse or dependence.

The more you drink, the more difficult it is to be objective about your drinking. In our survey, 86 percent of the women and 78 percent of the men who were frequent binge drinkers considered themselves to be moderate or light drinkers.

MYTH: Everybody does it.

Students often hear that everybody in college binge drinks. They may feel pressure to binge drink in order to fit in. But our research shows that the majority—56 percent—do not binge drink, including 20 percent who abstain from alcohol altogether. For the vast majority of black, Hispanic, and Asian students, drinking is *not*, and has never been, a strong tradition.

Nor is binge drinking a major problem at all schools. It is not present on every campus. In 2001, at one in four of the schools surveyed, binge drinking rates were 33 percent or lower; and at one in three schools, the rate was 51 percent or higher.

If you do not binge drink, you're not alone. Not only can you find friends who don't binge, but you could have a positive affect on others who do. A female student said:

> There are people in my school who don't drink at all and don't do any sort of drugs and I think that these people have their reasons. It is very individual. You shouldn't do things that you don't think are good to do and the more you think about why you do or don't do things, the happier you'll be. I don't think that I'm going to drink forever. I respect the people around me who don't drink just as much as I respect those who do. I respect them as adults. The fact that there are people who don't do it at all makes me think about why I constantly drink.

MYTH: Smart people don't binge drink; academically demanding schools are safe from binge drinking.

SAT or IQ scores do not protect one from binge drinking, and neither does the academic status of a college. Binge drinking goes on at almost all colleges, including Ivy League schools. The tragic death of Scott Krueger from an alcohol overdose at an MIT fraternity in 1997 made it clear that attending a top school provides no protection from a binge drinking culture. In our study we found that the level of binge drinking at a college was not related to that school's average SAT score.

At some Ivy League schools, students cite academic stress as a reason for drinking. One Ivy League student wryly noted:

> Everyone is working so hard academically, they're busting their ass academically, and when Friday night comes, you've got to let

the lead out. That's a spaz. It teaches that extremes are good in life, and they're not. Contrasts are healthy, but not extremes.

MYTH: Alcohol is not that harmful; there are lots of things that are worse. After all, it's only beer.

We have found that the heaviest drinkers—those who binge frequently—account for 72 percent of all the beer college students consume. And, unlike its somewhat innocent image, beer can be just as dangerous as hard liquor. It accounts for 80 percent of dangerous drinking.

If you drink heavily, you are more likely to make poor decisions. You could get into a car in which the driver has been drinking and end up in an accident. You could get behind the wheel yourself. Our study shows that 59 percent of frequent binge drinkers report driving after drinking, compared to 18 percent of students who drink but don't binge.

It is unsafe to drive after drinking *any* amount of alcohol. Nearly eleven hundred college students die every year in alcohol-related motor vehicle crashes. If you are caught driving under the influence, you may end up with your license suspended and your insurance canceled. You could be at a party that is raided by the police and end up being charged with underage drinking or public drunkenness. In 2000 there were 42,455 campus-related liquor arrests. With repeated offenses, you may find yourself suspended or even expelled from school.

Further, alcohol can be harmful, both in the short and the long run, as it can derail your emotional and intellectual development.

MYTH: My drinking is my own business; it doesn't hurt anyone else.

Three-quarters of all students report having had bad experiences due to someone else's drinking. Secondhand effects range from being assaulted, insulted, or humiliated to having your sleep or study time interrupted. We estimate that a staggering number of students—more than six hundred thousand a year—are hit or assaulted by another student who has been drinking.

The more you binge drink, the more likely you are to have serious problems related to your drinking. Ultimately those problems can affect your family, especially your parents and brothers or sisters.

We know this is not a one-way street. The parents of many college students are drinkers themselves; and like some nineteen million children in the United States you may have grown up in a family in which at least one parent abused alcohol. Whether you are a student or a parent, alcohol problems are family problems.

Costs to society for alcohol abuse are also high—even more costly than tobacco or illegal drugs. The total bill to the nation for alcohol abuse in 1995 was estimated at $166.5 billion; in 1999 the cost of underage drinking was nearly $53 billion. Most costs were productivity losses associated with illness and death. If you are a full-time student, productivity losses translate into missed classes and study time. Sometimes missed educational opportunities cannot be made up.

MYTH: Alcohol increases sex drive—and sex appeal.

Shakespeare's Macbeth put it this way: "[Drink] provokes the desire, but it takes away the performance." Alcohol lowers blood levels of the sex hormone testosterone, which regulates the male sex drive. Although less common among college students than in older men, impotence is the combined result of this reduction and alcohol's interference with the conduction of nerve impulses necessary for an erection. A single binge can cause such a downfall; habitual bingeing can shrink the testes, lower sperm count, retard sperm maturation, and ultimately lead to permanent impotence.

For women, as for men, alcohol in small doses may increase their sexual desire. But alcohol at larger doses may decrease their ability to have an orgasm. Even moderate drinking may increase the risk of spontaneous abortion and contribute to infertility. Women who become dependent on alcohol may stop menstruating altogether.

What most definitely does increase with moderate to heavy drinking is the incidence of forced and nonconsensual sex. Female students who binge drink are more than three times as likely to be forced to have intercourse than students who do not binge drink. Based on responses to our surveys, we estimate that each year more than a hundred thousand, or 3.7 percent of college women age 18 to 24 years old, are forced to engage in sex while they are intoxicated and therefore unable to give consent. One in eleven women who are frequent binge drinkers are victimized in this way.

A young man said of alcohol and sex:

> Alcohol is certainly present at every party; it colors every interaction between men and women on any given Friday night. It adds to what's been called a "hook-up" culture, where long-term relationships just aren't really fostered. Alcoholic judgment plays a role. The problem to me is it's gender interaction without much meaning or substance, being physical rather than intellectual or social. College seems like a good time to interact with the opposite sex on different levels, not necessarily physically.

MYTH: Most students are dead set against any college efforts to restrict alcohol on campus.

The majority of college students in our study supported a series of strong measures to deal with binge drinking. These policies include holding hosts responsible for problems resulting from alcohol use at their parties, cracking down on drinking at fraternities and sororities, banning kegs on campus, and enforcing rules more strictly.

The strongest opposition to these measures comes from a small but vocal minority of the heaviest drinkers. Our surveys show that while only 35 percent of frequent binge drinkers think existing rules should be enforced more strictly, a full 75 percent of non-bingers do. Unfortunately, college administrators may be more timid than their students about enacting and enforcing campus alcohol policies. Administrators will often listen to the strident voices of the heaviest drinkers and fail to act strongly to deal with this real problem.

MYTH: Drinking is a rite of passage. Boys will be boys. They'll grow out of it.

For years people have used these lame refrains as a rationale for ignoring the problem of binge drinking. The truth is that while many students will grow out of it, a significant minority will grow into it. They will establish long-term drinking patterns that harm their health and well-being for years to come. An even larger number will suffer injuries, trauma, and considerable losses in educational opportunities, and many will eventually die from alcohol-related causes.

It is time to reject these excuses and think more deeply about how to raise both young men and young women. What does it mean to be a man? To be a woman? The macho characters in beer commercials, the sex stereotypes that we all too easily buy into, cannot be the role models for our children. They deserve better than that.

HAS IT ALWAYS BEEN THIS WAY?

Historians have noted that alcohol has been around since the first American colleges were founded, but prior to 1950 most reports of drinking on college campus were anecdotal. In the eighteenth century wines, beer, and liquor were sold in student canteens called butteries. Harvard passed a resolution in 1734 that stipulated that no college resident should drink or serve distilled spirits or mixed drinks, and that no undergraduate should "keep by him brandy, rum or other distilled spirituous liquors." The school apparently wanted to supplant the use of strong liquor with beer or wine, which were sold in college dining halls as well as in the butteries.

Former Harvard president Neil Rudenstine described in the *Boston Globe* why the sheriff preceded the academic procession at Harvard Yard at graduation. He noted that by the early nineteenth century commencement had evolved into a festival of gambling, drinking, swearing, and fighting that required the involvement of the sheriff, constables, and two special judges.

The nineteenth century saw frequent eruptions of alcohol-fueled rowdiness on college campuses. In 1832 the faculty at the Southern and Western Theological Seminary in Tennessee (later Maryville College) expelled student James Ewing for "acts of immorality most nefarious and unbecoming," drinking and rioting among them. Ewing appealed to have his honor and that of his family restored and the decision overturned. After dozens of students appeared on his behalf, the school president relented.

At the University of North Carolina in October 1840, a hard-drinking clique stole two horses and rode them around the campus until one died from exhaustion. The cabal went on to cut off the tails of two professors' horses and assault a black woman.

Thomas Jefferson complained about drinking at the University of Virginia in the 1820s. His protests, however, apparently fell on deaf ears—beginning in 1825 and continuing for nearly 165 years, UV students threw a spring fling called Easters to roughly coincide with Jefferson's April 13 birthday. The university administration cut off official support for the bash in 1983 after being increasingly overwhelmed by the task of containing the thousands of revelers who would jam the streets, making it impossible for fire trucks or ambulances to get through.

But old ways die hard, and UV students continued with other drinking rituals. These include the Fourth-Year Fifth, in which fourth-year students mark Homecoming by tossing down a fifth of liquor. In 1997 that ritual led to the tragic death of twenty-one-year-old student Leslie Baltz. Her parents and some of her contemporaries have since marked the day with an alternative tradition, a five-kilometer Walk for Life.

COMPARING *and* CONTRASTING GENERATIONS

But looking back on one's own experiences is not necessarily a good gauge by which to evaluate today's campus drinking scene. Alcohol is America's drug of choice, and that can make it difficult to view objectively. Our College Alcohol Study was the first in nearly half a century to systematically assess the use and abuse of alcohol on America's college campuses.

The only prior such effort was in 1949. That year, Robert Straus and Selden Bacon of Yale University initiated a survey of more than six thousand students on twenty-seven campuses. The results from the Straus and Bacon survey provide an interesting counterpoint to today.

We asked Straus what the main changes have been in the fifty-plus years since his study. He noted three: "First, the women have caught up with the men. That's pretty dramatic. Second, it's pretty obvious that the numbers of students drinking in larger amounts have gone up significantly for men, and even more so for women. Third, the reasons for drinking have changed. The percent of students who say they drink to get drunk is way up. We had very few in 1950."

A review of Straus and Bacon's work reveals that in 1949 only 17 percent of the men and 6 percent of the women reported drinking more than once a week. Today 26 percent of the men and 21 percent of the women drink at binge levels more than once a week. Since 1949 the percent of male abstainers has remained the same (20 percent), but the percent of female abstainers has declined by half (from 40 percent to 20 percent).

Another interesting contrast is found in where students drank. In the 1949 study only 3 percent of male users customarily drank in their college rooms, and less than 3 percent drank in their fraternities. Among female users only 1 percent drank in their rooms and, about 5 percent drank in fraternities or sororities. Most college students drank in private homes or public places such as restaurants, taverns, bars, or nightclubs. Today fraternities are a center of campus alcohol consumption.

The year of the Bacon and Straus study saw the deaths of two students during drinking parties and the near-death of a third while being initiated into a drinking club. These events provoked a public outcry, condemning the laxity of college administrators. A *New York Times* article headlined "Drinking Blame Put on College Rulers" quoted the head of an intercollegiate fraternity criticizing universities for their tolerance of excessive drinking and moral laxity. Clearly, things *have* changed.

In 1949 the era of *in loco parentis* was still in force, with universities expected to act in place of parents, legally charged with being both moral tutor and supervisor over the personal lives of college students. Rules and regulations mandated curfews, classroom and dining dress codes, and relations between men and women. Undergraduate women in the 1950s lived in separate, supervised housing. Male visitors had to sign in and out with the dorm supervisor, and dorm room doors remained open during the visit.

After World War II, the Korean War, and the Vietnam War, as more veterans became students under the GI Bill and college students assumed a more adult role, they increasingly challenged this doctrine. Veterans objected to being told that they could go to war, shoot at the enemy, and get shot, but when in college they could not choose their own wardrobes or order a drink. The upheavals of the civil rights movement, the women's movement, and the antiwar movement all contributed to students' rejection of the paternalistic *in loco parentis*, and by the 1970s it was history.

ALCOHOL *as* ENTITLEMENT

Campus drinking norms began to change radically in the 1960s and 1970s. One of the largest contributing factors came from off campus: The drinking age was lowered to eighteen. By the time it was reraised to twenty-one by the mid-1980s, the cat was out of the bag; underage students had developed a sense of entitlement to alcohol.

In the meantime, colleges themselves had changed in pertinent ways. They relaxed restrictions and supervision of dormitories, which became coed as colleges attempted to accommodate rising enrollment and the attendant housing crunch. Fraternities began to more actively cultivate their party images, and university administrations welcomed Greek residences as one solution to the lack of student housing.

In recent decades college sports have become increasingly big business for higher education, and alcohol is ingrained in them—from industry sponsorship of sporting events to tailgate parties, from team hubris to hazings. Our survey showed that athletes are 50 percent more likely to binge when they drink. Student athletes both drink more often and report more alcohol-related harms such as injuries and police run-ins than nonathletes. And sports fans follow closely on athletes' heels when it comes to heavy drinking.

Another change in higher education over the past twenty-five years has been increased competition among universities for students, and some colleges are reluctant to dispel an image that many students desire: that of a fun-loving party school. And thus universities find themselves balancing a need to fill dorms and classrooms against the potential liability that could arise from harmful or lethal drinking episodes—and against the damage to intellectual life that heavy drinking produces.

Are students today more hedonistic or nihilistic than in the past? We think not. Students have a wide range of values, and for many, college is a time when they are shaping those values into committed philosophies. College students have an enormous range of interests, personalities, emotional states, and family backgrounds—all of which play into their decision-making about drinking.

Regardless of these differences and the individual reasons students give for drinking alcohol, it is a practice established and enabled by the culture. Colleges and their surrounding communities provide the setting for students to binge drink, and students do so significantly more than their non-college peers. College cultural traditions and norms often encourage heavy drinking, and schools that fail to enforce the minimum legal drinking age insulate students from the effects of the law.

SOCIETY'S INEBRIATED CHILD

Finally, college drinking cannot be separated from the presence and role of alcohol in society at large. An estimated fourteen million to twenty-five million Americans are addicted to alcohol or suffer from serious problems related to its use. Every year more than one hundred thousand deaths in the United States are caused by excessive alcohol consumption. Despite the alcohol industry's conflicting claims, men who consume more than two alcoholic drinks a day are at increased risk for cancer, cerebrovascular disease, accidents, and violence, and long-term heavy alcohol use is the nation's leading cause of illness and death from liver disease.

Americans are painfully aware of the toll that alcohol takes. More than half of American adults have a close family member who has or has had alcoholism. It is no surprise, then, that an overwhelming number of Americans are concerned about underage drinking, and a majority support measures that would help reduce teen drinking, such as stricter controls on alcohol sales, advertising, and promotion.

This concern needs to be extended to include the college campus, where two out of every five students binge drink, causing daily harm to themselves and to others. It is time to challenge the culture and environment that encourages this practice.

CHAPTER 2

WHERE'S THE PARTY?

The newer fraternities at my school were designed so that all the partying could be done in the basement. The stereo and electrical equipment is waterproofed. The floor slightly slopes toward a huge center drain, and the basement is equipped with a hose. In the course of one party, together you consume, say, seven hundred cans of beer. In the end, you have all this waste and stench, and all you have to do is spray the hose. It goes down the drain and it's like it never happened.
—Clay, former fraternity member at a private Southeastern university

Adrian Heideman pledged the Pi Kappa Phi fraternity in the fall of 2000. A freshman at California State University, Chico, Heideman had avoided heavy drinking in high school. He was fond of writing poetry and composing music, and he had performed in plays for ten years at the Palo Alto Children's Theater. Heideman's mother, Edith, told the *San Francisco Chronicle*, "Adrian was not a drinker. He was a vegetarian, he didn't smoke, he didn't really drink. . . . He was always the designated driver."

Heideman kept an online diary during his first weeks in school. He wrote about his classes and about joining Pi Kappa Phi. Although initially hesitant to get involved with an organization associated with heavy drinking and partying, he wrote, "But the fraternity I'm pledging to is a lot nicer than that."

Only too late did Heideman learn the extent to which alcohol dictated life at Pi Kappa Phi. The house designated Sunday through Tuesday for study, Wednesday through Saturday for drinking. Wednesday was Forties Night, so-called for the forty-ounce bottles of beer consumed; two open party nights followed; and Saturday was Keg Night. House members were divided into groups identified by their preferred drink. Heideman belonged to the Foul Pups, whose drink was blackberry brandy.

One Pi Kappa Phi tradition common among fraternities was a night when pledges are formally introduced to their "big brothers." Heideman's life ended that night. An initiation ceremony culminated when pledges were given a bottle of brandy and a pitcher of beer and told to finish the brandy. Of the twenty-four pledges, twenty-one were minors, and all but three got drunk. As typical of such fraternity rituals, the purpose of the event was to bond pledges to their big brothers, who would supposedly take care of them—no matter what.

A lawsuit later filed by Heideman's parents alleged that by 10:30 P.M. the seventeen-year-old freshman was too drunk to walk, and two fraternity brothers took him to a basement room to lie down while they went back upstairs to watch a strip show. At 1:00 A.M. they found him dead.

Police reports later said that Heideman had choked on his own vomit, and an autopsy determined that he had a .37 blood-alcohol content when he died.

Seven months later, Adrian's parents, Michael and Edith Heideman, filed a lawsuit against the fraternity. While wrongful death suits that claim negligence against fraternities are not uncommon, the Heideman case relied on California's unfair competition law. It claimed that fraternities that illegally permit widespread alcohol consumption have an unfair advantage over those that follow the law. "When some frats comply with the law and others don't, there's a competitive advantage," said the plaintiffs' attorney, Michael Von Loewenfeldt.

Unfortunately, many if not most fraternities fail to follow the law. "The Greek system is the single largest unregulated industry that provides the use of alcohol to underage drinkers," Douglas Fierberg, an attorney who has litigated dozens of fraternity hazing cases, told us.

THE GREEK SCENE

For college students, the single strongest predictor of binge drinking is fraternity or sorority residence or membership. Our 2001 survey showed that three-quarters of fraternity or sorority house residents (80 percent and 69 percent, respectively) are binge drinkers; amazingly, this constitutes a recent improvement in the situation, as the binge drinking level of fraternity and sorority house residents in 1993 was up at 83 percent. As for Greek members, 73 percent of the men and 57 percent of the women binge drink. While some fraternities may not be so heavily steeped in alcohol, our statistics indicate that most are.

Participation in fraternity initiations and events heightens the risk of excessive drinking. Over the years, fraternity culture has become identified with heavy partying. Alcohol consumption is the fraternity's social lubricant and badge of belonging. Most students who join fraternities expect alcohol to be central to their experience, even though they are likely to be legally underage; they believe they are entitled to drink. Most universities have complied with these expectations. There is little incentive for individual fraternities to chart a "dry" path; when they do, they can expect to have a hard time competing for members. Prospective pledges go where the beer flows.

One fraternity member wrote to us:

> I am not an advocate for responsible college drinking; in fact I am quite the opposite. I party hard and I party a lot, but what the 1980s labeled as a "party animal" has now taken on the label of "binge

drinker." So what if I bong three beers at a time and often play drinking games that drain a case of beer between four people in less than seventy-five minutes? I drink often and a lot, but I know my limits and I don't wake up each morning needing a drink. If you look hard and ask students, you'll see that alcohol has become an institution at parties. A party is not a party without it. . . . By the way, I am only twenty years old and my parents know full well how much I drink. In fact, more than 90 percent of the parents of the men in our fraternity know how much their kids are drinking and they aren't worried about it.

A FRATERNAL DIS-ORDER

Fraternities and sororities, also known as Greek societies (they take their names from the Greek alphabet), are single-sex student organizations that hold out the promise to members of lifelong friendships, intense camaraderie, and some added meaning to the college experience—as well as access to the opposite sex and career-enhancing networks. Fraternities say that their core values include such aims as the pursuit of truth and justice and the promotion of philanthropy and scholarship. In fact, most early fraternities began as reading and study clubs. The very first fraternity was founded as a forum for debate in 1776 at the College of William and Mary in Williamsburg, Virginia. Students today may still join fraternities to experience brotherhood, but the meaning of that word on campus has become twisted. Many fraternities operate as party houses awash in a sea of alcohol. They increasingly struggle with risk management policies and fend off lawsuits that stem from the many harms associated with binge drinking.

Nationwide, approximately 400,000 students belong to fraternities, in more than 5,300 chapters on more than 800 campuses;

250,000 belong to sororities. Fraternity alumni are an even bigger constituency. The North-American Interfraternity Conference represents almost 4.5 million alumni. The vast majority of fraternity members are white, although African Americans, Hispanic Americans, and Asian Americans have founded their own Greek societies.

Each fraternal order, designated by two or three Greek letters, has its own symbols, traditions, and secret rituals, often accompanied by heavy alcohol consumption. To join a Greek society, students participate in a process called rush. During rush they attend fraternity events and choose to apply for membership in one or more. Each fraternity reviews its pool of applicants and offers invitations to join to those deemed worthy. After accepting this bid, the student pledge endures weeks of experiences meant to build loyalty and instill an abiding regard for house history, values, and rituals. This process often includes heavy alcohol use and some form of hazing.

George Kuh, a researcher at Indiana University, explained how fraternities use alcohol to socialize newcomers. During pledgeship, pledge educators, who are active members of the fraternity, alternatively provide or withhold alcohol to teach newcomers how to behave and their proper place in the organization hierarchy. Alcohol use becomes "a privilege, symbolizing full membership in the group, an important goal for most newcomers, given what they had to endure to attain such status."

ALL HAIL ALCOHOL

For students who do not already drink heavily when they begin college, joining a Greek organization is a sure way to start. Over three-fourths of fraternity residents who had not binged in high school became binge drinkers in college, as did three of four sorority house residents. Mark Nason, a prevention consultant with the Prevention

Research Institute, a nonprofit organization that develops curricula to reduce the risk of alcohol and drug problems, told us:

> Our organization has worked extensively with Greek groups over the past twenty years and has found some chapters to report that more than 70 percent of their members consume thirteen or more drinks per occasion. We frequently hear from other professionals on campuses that fifteen to twenty drinks per occasion, though not the norm, is not uncommon among some groups of students.

The high place of alcohol is readily apparent in the interior decorating of fraternity houses: neon beer signs, beer mugs, shot glasses, novelty beer cans, pitchers, posters related to drinking—all of this and more, sporting the name of one beer or liquor company or another. Fraternities usually own or lease their houses, and these are party headquarters.

One sorority member wrote on her survey:

> The reason I started to drink so much at college is due to pledging a sorority. As a pledge during first semester, we would have "pledge parties" with a fraternity's new members at least four times a week. We would all get drunk before we knew it and it's because it's fun for me and my friends . . . I only do it to have fun, not because I have problems.

DATE RAPE CENTRAL

Binge drinking affects many aspects of college life. Our study shows that nearly twice as many fraternity residents as non-fraternity residents fall behind in schoolwork, argue with friends, damage property, have unprotected sex, or suffer injuries. Frat house residents are also more likely to drink and drive or ride with a high or drunk driver.

One of the most disturbing problems associated with binge

Jeremy: A Student Takes a Stand

I pledged a fraternity in my freshman year, and I de-pledged, dropped out of my pledge class, three weeks into it. During rush period, the fraternities entice you to join. They are wooing you with free food, games, bowling, playing pool. There was a smash-a-car dinner. After dinner we went to the fraternity's top floor and threw old appliances down on an old car below that they had purchased just for that night.

Rush was alcohol-free. Totally dry. But after you accept the bid to join the fraternity, you drink. It's understood.

I ended up getting a couple of bids, to my great surprise. I was kind of flattered and decided to accept it, even though I had rushed for the pure sake of rushing. I figured, Why not, they like me, I don't dislike them.

But a few weeks later I de-pledged. I don't agree with everything that goes on in fraternities. The treatment of women, for one thing. People talk down upon women and I didn't want to be a part of that. The attitude to people not in the fraternity was not good. And there was a dangerous element. There was so much alcohol at the parties that it was possible an accident could happen with regard to overdrinking.

If you're officially going to become somebody else's brother then you better really respect and like him. You have to pay to be in a fraternity. It's putting money there, contractual. You represent it, contribute to it, and support it. Whatever one of your brothers does reflects upon you. Being in a fraternity means that you are complying with what goes on there. I did not want to do that. So I decided I should get out before I full-heartedly invested myself.

It was very, very hard to de-pledge. It made me define my values. I had to say, I do not stand for this. I wrestled with it for a few days and nights. As much as those guys had their faults, I did respect some of them, all of them in some ways. I didn't want to let them down. I felt I was somehow betraying them. And I felt I was throwing something away myself. Being in a frat is your ticket to having a strong group of friends forever, or at least in college.

I wanted to return the friendship, but it wasn't going to be that way. It took deep thinking. A self-reflection and re-evaluation, what I was doing in college and with my life. Who I wanted to be. I kept asking myself that: Who do I want to be? I had a long think with myself.

drinking in fraternities is sexual abuse. Alan, who joined a fraternity at his high-binge school during his sophomore year, recalled the Monday night dinner at the house:

> We'd go around the table, talk about who got laid, who hooked up. We'd drink to that. It was funny, harmless. In one house it's a game for the pledges, to find out who slept with who. That makes it a little more important. A certain idea about women gets perpetuated at house parties. Pledges and freshmen that are there get influenced. Parties are sketchy, scandalous. They encourage drinking. Brothers are forward in trying to hook up with women. It's not a bad thing. If you have a guy who is forward like that, life will bite his ass. But when you have a whole house that condones that kind of behavior, it's bad. Younger folk are very malleable. Girls see it. They feel like they have to start catering.

Clay, a student at another school who quit his fraternity in his junior year, described the scene in his house:

> There was a lot of date rape; sometimes people had intercourse after the girls were passed out. There was a lot of nonconsensual sex in the fraternities. The way that most frats are designed, there's a party room downstairs, and then there are bedrooms. It's not like you go to a ballroom, where there aren't beds.

Unlike fraternities, sorority houses have traditionally been dry. But that doesn't keep sorority sisters from drinking. When sorority members, especially freshmen, drink, they put themselves at risk. The combination of female students trying to "keep up" with the drinking of male students and their own increased susceptibility to the same dose of alcohol puts women at greater risk of alcohol-related problems.

Our study indicates that sorority sisters differ from their fraternity brothers in another way as well. They are less likely to enter sorority life as experienced binge drinkers. Typically they are no savvier with alcohol than are non-sorority freshmen. The opposite is true of fraternity members, who enter college with much more alcohol under their belts than do non-fraternity male students. As a result, sorority house residents are nearly twice as likely as nonmembers to experience an unwanted sexual advance and are more frequently the victims of sexual assault or date rape. A student at one college wrote in our survey, "Many of the frats here have the nickname 'date rape' frat."

A sorority member wrote on our survey,

Being Greek and living in a sorority house has, believe it or not, cut down on my drinking. I don't need it to socialize because I live with all my friends; I see them all the time, whether I want to or not! Therefore, I don't have to go to the bars or parties to interact with them. However, I am currently seriously considering deactivating. While I don't need to go to the bars and parties, that's what everyone's life centers around. All anyone talks about is who got how drunk and who they "accidentally" got it on with because of this. All our events are based on the consumption of alcohol. I don't go to them because I don't want to be tempted to drink. Because I don't go, I don't know what went on. Because of *this*, I am basically alienated from the house.

PRESSURE FOR REFORM

The year was 1997. Before he fell into a coma, Scott Krueger and eleven other Phi Gamma Delta fraternity recruits at the Massachusetts Institute of Technology had spent a mandatory night drinking beer and Jack Daniel's and watching the 1978 film *Animal House*, a college "classic" that details the exploits of a fraternity. According to the Commonwealth's Statement of the Case filed in Suffolk Superior Court by the office of the Suffolk County District Attorney, Krueger also reportedly received a bottle of spiced rum from his big brother. The video event was a tradition, part of welcoming new members to the fraternity house. When Krueger was found in a coma early the next morning, his blood alcohol level was a toxic .41. He died two days later.

As early as 1992, two students had warned the administration about out-of-control fraternity drinking. The students, Scott R. Velazquez and Robert Plotkin, had pledged—and then depledged—Pi Lambda Phi. They wrote a fifty-page booklet describing the fraternity's alcohol abuse, peer pressure, and hazing practices and sent it to top administrators. A year later, frustrated by university inaction, Velazquez and Plotkin again wrote to university president Charles M. Vest. "When a student is killed or dies at an MIT fraternity, how will MIT explain its full knowledge of dangerous and illegal practices persisting unchecked over a period of years?" they asked.

Three years after Krueger's death, MIT and Mr. and Mrs. Krueger announced a $6 million out-of-court legal settlement. In a letter to the Kruegers, President Vest wrote, "Despite your trust in MIT, things went terribly awry. At a very personal level, I feel that we at MIT failed you and Scott. For this you have our profound apology."

Krueger's death was a wakeup call to universities and fraternities, who fear the multimillion-dollar settlements that can follow wrongful death suits. Yet such tragedies continue, and every year thousands of students are asked, cajoled, or coerced to drink to excess in fraternities.

INSURANCE RISK

But the stakes are rising for individual fraternity chapters, their national affiliates, and their host universities. By the late 1980s the Na-

tional Association of Insurance Commissioners had ranked fraternities and sororities among the top ten risks for insurance companies, along with asbestos contractors and hazardous waste disposal
companies.

An internal alcohol-abuse task force appointed by the national
fraternity Alpha Epsilon Pi issued a report in 1999 that said, "Undergraduate brothers, alumni, and the International Fraternity as a
whole are placed in jeopardy each and every time a chapter hosts
an event with alcohol." The fraternity worried that underage members typically plan, execute, and monitor events where alcohol is
distributed.

The task force cited a study by a Kentucky insurer of more than
twelve hundred insurance claims filed against fraternities between
1987 and 1995. The study found that underage drinking occurred
in 61 percent of the alcohol-related insurance claims. Of all the fraternity claims reviewed, alcohol was involved in:

95 percent of roof/window falls

94 percent of fights

93 percent of sexual abuse incidents

88 percent of fatalities

87 percent of automobile incidents

78 percent of psychological injuries

In addition, our most recent study showed a slight drop in the
number of students that belong to fraternities, choose to live in
them, and attend their parties. Just as a significant minority of students now choose to abstain and to live in substance-free dorms,
student aversion to a heavy-binge lifestyle may be beginning to reflect itself in a turn away from fraternities.

SCHOOLS WAKING UP

Some universities, for their part, are finally beginning to take the binge-drinking problems at their fraternities seriously.

Following Scott Krueger's death, MIT reviewed its alcohol policies and enforcement and housing options. "Scott's death galvanized us to action," President Vest wrote to the grieving parents. "It impelled us to greatly intensify our consideration and accelerate our actions with regard to alcohol, our housing system, and other issues of student life and learning." Krueger's fraternity, Phi Gamma Delta, was banished in perpetuity.

In addition, MIT finally broached the glaring problem of its undergraduate housing shortage. Like many other schools, MIT had relied upon its fraternities—thirty in all—to help make up the housing shortage. Only after Krueger's death did MIT design a new 350-bed freshman dorm and decree that upon its opening all freshmen will be required to live in residence halls for their first year. The school also mandated that all fraternities and sororities have graduate resident advisors living in their houses.

Some schools are abolishing or fundamentally restructuring their fraternity systems. In what may have been a preemptive strike against tragedy, Santa Clara University in California decided to end its Greek system beginning in June 2003. The university framed its decision as largely financial. It provides the Greek system with thirty thousand dollars annually from student fees and decided that the funds could better serve the entire student body. The university wants to be sure "there are other outlets for students on campus," said Jeanne M. Rosenberger, dean of student life and leadership at the university.

The trustees of Hamilton College in Clinton, New York, decided to close the houses owned by fraternities and required all fraternity members to live in college-owned housing but allowed the student associations themselves to continue. The decision initially met strong resistance. Students demonstrated in protest, and town businesses that supplied products and services to the fraternity houses were equally upset. Alumni also registered their objections.

Eugene Tobin, president of the college, wrote in the *Chronicle of Higher Education* that he received a letter from Representative Robert Livingston, a fraternity supporter and then-chair of the House Appropriations Committee, in which Livingston implied that the school's "federal funds would be in jeopardy if we did not change course in our dealings with fraternities." According to Tobin, the congressman sent the same message to the presidents of Bowdoin, Colby, and Middlebury Colleges, which had taken similar steps to control Greek influence on their campuses.

It has now been seven years since Hamilton College closed the fraternity houses. The results: As might be expected, fraternity members at first had difficulty adjusting to the more supervised environment of residence halls, and alumni participation in the annual fund did indeed take a hit, falling from 55 percent to 52 percent the year after the decision. But since then alumni support has rebounded to an all-time high of nearly 59 percent. Tobin wrote in the article, "Viewed in its entirety, social life at Hamilton has greater balance, is more diverse, and is no longer dominated by Greek organizations. . . . Most important, the academic profile of the Hamilton student body is the best in more than two decades. . . . Students who prefer little or no Greek life on campus have combined SAT scores 60 points higher than those of students who prefer fraternities and sororities."

Emory University in Atlanta has invested more than $3 million in renovating and constructing Greek houses. Emory undertook the renovation as part of an innovative fraternity management program, called the Phoenix Plan, designed to help university administrators and fraternity members to work together on many aspects of Greek life. One result of the plan was seen in 1999, when Emory's non-alcohol fraternity, Phi Delta Theta, received the largest number of pledges among all Emory fraternities. In fact, nationally there is a small but growing trend among fraternities to go dry.

Schools have also expelled or suspended individual fraternities for violating alcohol rules. Colgate University, Louisiana State University, Ohio State University, San Diego State University, the University of Arkansas, the University of Vermont, Washington State University, and the University of Michigan are among the schools that have taken such actions in recent years. For example, in the last ten years the University of Michigan has closed ten fraternities and two sororities for alcohol and hazing violations.

Other universities and fraternities have delayed rush, either for a semester or a year. This allows freshmen to have some time to settle down and adjust to university life before entering a culture of alcohol that they are often ill prepared to handle.

EFFORTS *from* WITHIN

There are some efforts within the fraternity system to reform. In the winter of 2001 the first-ever Greek Alcohol Summit brought together 134 fraternity and sorority student leaders from twenty-eight campuses to discuss how to reduce the damage caused by excess drinking. The conference noted that eight of fifty-two national fraternity organizations have committed to having alcohol-free houses for their local chapters in the next three years.

One Greek society member described for us how his thinking about fraternity drinking changed:

> A friend of mine who was a big brother brought his little brother to my [fraternity] house to play beer pong. They're playing, and my friend's little brother is throwing up and trying to swallow it so he can keep playing. He couldn't even see the ball. Every time

(continued on page 50)

Alcohol, Hazing, and the Greek Industry

Attorney Douglas Fierberg is a partner at the Washington, D.C, law firm Bode & Grenier. He specializes in representing students and the families of students in high school and college who have been seriously injured or killed. Most often, the precipitating misconduct involves the crimes of hazing, alcohol misuse, sexual assault, or other violations of school codes of conduct. He has worked on more than fifty such cases. Visit his Web site at www.hazinglaw.com.

Daniel Reardon, a freshman at the University of Maryland in College Park, died last February after taking part in the Phi Sigma Kappa bid night celebration. Do you believe Reardon died as a result of hazing?

Maryland's law defines hazing as doing any act, or causing any situation that recklessly or intentionally subjects a student to the risk of serious bodily injury for the purpose of initiation into a student organization, school, college, or university.

While I presently have only limited public information about the incident, I understand that Reardon was going through a ritual related to the first step of gaining entrance into the fraternity and that fraternity brothers and officers were present. The introduction of alcohol into any portion of that initiation process is about as high-risk as you can get in the area of misuse of alcohol. That placed Dan Reardon in a situation that recklessly subjected him to the risk of serious bodily injury.

Many people would say that Reardon drank voluntarily. How can that constitute hazing?

First, there is not yet a lot of publically available information about what exactly happened to Daniel Reardon. Maryland law says that the implied or expressed consent of a student to hazing may not be used as a defense. This is reflective of the unique type of crime and wrongdoing we are talking about. It is recognition that the situations created by hazing are often of such a coercive nature and involve so much pressure to join, to make the grade, to pass the test that as a matter of public policy, a

(continued)

Alcohol, Hazing, and the Greek Industry—cont.

student's supposed consent to drinking or to being branded or to being part of a kidnapping event is irrelevant.

This is true in Maryland and in many states and many university codes of conduct. And it is true in terms of the risk management policies of fraternities.

How does the Greek system regulate alcohol use?

The Greek system is the single largest unregulated industry that provides a means for the use of alcohol by underage drinkers. All bars, restaurants, and stores that sell alcohol are regulated by the state. They have investigators that go in and try to do buys with fake IDs, liquor licenses come up for review. Flying under that radar screen on virtually every college campus are Greek entities.

They know that the presence of alcohol in their houses or at their events is widespread. They also know, have reason to know, or should know, that those same chapter houses are filled with underage people who have no lawful right to be drinking. If you're pledging as a freshman or a sophomore, you're not twenty-one.

This industry is tacitly involved in providing locations for illegal underage drinking across the country. I'm not going to say whether it is by way of intention or default. It just is. And who's going through all the frat houses making sure all IDs are checked? Fraternity members. What other industry regulates itself using twenty-year-old kids who answer to nobody? We don't rely on liquor stores to be self-regulating. For the most part, that is the risk management strategy for many fraternities.

Chapter house residents include seventeen-, eighteen-, and nineteen-year-olds. If the Greek system isn't regulating their use of alcohol, who is?

When the national fraternities get sued, they would tell you that it's the responsibility of the local chapter house, and of the university. They say, "We educate our members about alcohol use, we're not there to supervise." I believe they have more obligations than they seek to portray.

If you ask the university if they're responsible, they say, "We can't be in every nook and cranny of the campus. The fraternities are responsible for managing their own conduct, because we require that they do it."

The central question is this: What structure has been set up to regulate this industry, which is a delivery system of alcohol to the group at highest risk of binge drinking? There's presently none that is adequate to regulate these groups.

Why do you consider fraternities an industry?

The average person who goes to college sees a row of frat houses. They never sit down and ask what they're all about. Yet, as an example, the national fraternity Tau Kappa Epsilon has something like three hundred chapters across the country and operates in numerous localities through a three-corporate structure: The national fraternity is a nonprofit corporation with hundreds of thousands of dollars in annual revenue; the housing corporation has purchased real estate in prime areas of the country; and a chapter corporation has about 165,000 dues-paying members and refers in its internal documents to its members as customers.

In the court's Hernandez opinion in Arizona, a case in which a young man got hurt, the court says that the modern day fraternity is essentially an organization sponsoring a series of drinking clubs across the country. This opinion is generally accurate. Their corporate structure channels income to the top. That is the Greek industry. Its products are all types of social events, paraphernalia, membership, housing. Alumni continue to pay dues. The funds are used to pay for boards of directors, for trips, and benefits. The entire organization benefits.

What should be done?

I think the states should take control and the fraternities should go dry. University responsibility should be considered on a case-by-case basis, but they should be aware of how little the fraternities are doing to prevent the harm caused by their operations.

the ball went off [the] table, this kid had to drink another beer. And I'm watching this kid. I'm like, "Game over, dude, game over. This kid is throwing up. Take care of him. He's your little brother."

Watching that, something changed for me. I joined the Alcohol and Other Drugs Committee. I worked on alcohol education and planned alternative activities. In the end, I think the biggest problem is that there is not enough of a commitment from colleges to be part of the process that slows drinking down. They'd much rather turn their cheek and hope nothing goes wrong, hope people have a good time, finish their four years, and leave.

OBSTACLES TO CHANGE

Despite efforts toward reform from the various parties involved, obstacles to changing the fraternity drinking culture are still formidable. One of the most significant roadblocks is the universities' fear of alienating alumni who give money to their colleges. Research by the North-American Interfraternity Conference and the National Panhellenic Conference in 1998 found that 11 percent of Greek alumni donated between one thousand and five thousand dollars to their schools, compared with 1.4 percent of non-Greek alumni.

Some alumni still view the past through beer goggles and think that the current generation should have the same access to alcohol they did. School presidents have told us that some of the most vocal opposition to cracking down on fraternity drinking comes from influential alumni. It is time for alumni and parents to encourage rather than hinder change.

Equally difficult to overcome is the entrenched attitude toward the place of alcohol in fraternity culture. Students join fraternities expecting to experience frequent and rip-roaring parties. While individual members may oppose the binge drinking of Greek societies, they lack the support of most of their peers and thus the clout to change the culture to "dry."

"It's very difficult to maintain a substance-free fraternity when others are not," said Dick McKaig, vice chancellor for student affairs and director of the Center for Study of the College Fraternity at Indiana University in Bloomington. "There's a disadvantage in recruitment, campus image, social life, and a disadvantage in socializing with women's sororities," he told us.

McKaig is skeptical of the effectiveness of temporarily closing fraternity houses. In the early 1990s he closed a fraternity chapter because of an alcohol incident. It reopened several years later. "The first seventeen members held substance-free housing almost as a badge of honor," he said. The pledges they recruited also by and large supported the fraternity's decision to be dry. But the recruits that followed the next year began to view it as a restriction, and the class after that saw it as an impediment to their success as a group. "It lost all meaning," he said.

Yet another obstacle to reform is the overwhelming access on many campuses to a cheap and plentiful alcohol supply. According to Cathy Solow, a member of the Stepping Up Coalition at the University of Iowa, "The amount of advertising directed at the Greek community by the city's bars is incredible. They leaflet the Greeks about all their specials, they have special rooms for the Greeks so they could host parties in the back of the bar. They typically employ a number of Greeks as bartenders and bouncers, and this is seen as cool. They very much targeted the fraternities and sororities."

Another way fraternities avoid major reform is by planning for change sometime in the future, say two or three years down the road. The danger is that reform measures will be put off indefinitely. We refer to this tendency to postpone reform as NIMBY—Not In My Baccalaureate Years.

Of course, simply writing new rules will not ensure that they are followed. In the spring of 1998, when Washington State University banned alcohol at fraternity social functions, hundreds of students rioted, throwing beer cans and rocks at officers who fired teargas in return. At Dartmouth College, where roughly 50 percent of the student body belongs to a fraternity or sorority, a commission to reimagine student life was set up in 1999. But, as a recent graduate told us, "When the average student tries to imagine what they would do on a Friday or Saturday night if there weren't a Greek system, they imagine going and drinking somewhere else."

In 2001 the National Panhellenic Conference, an association of twenty-six national sororities, attempted to address the problems associated with fraternity binge drinking by passing a rule prohibiting its members from attending fraternity house parties where alcohol is served. But many sorority members see the rule as a challenge to overcome. Laura, social chair of her sorority, explained, "If a fraternity has an open party, I can go as an independent student rather than as a member of my sorority." In other words, as long as she is not there with a large group of sorority sisters identified as such, she can drink alcohol at fraternity house parties. Laura is ambivalent about the new rule. "I guess something needed to be done," she said. "But I understand the resistance a lot of people feel. I see both sides."

CURING THE CULTURE

The fraternity drinking culture is so entrenched that only the united will and action of university administrators, students, parents, alumni, and fraternities themselves will change it. The time is ripe. Every passing semester brings more tragedies on Fraternity Row.

Change will take enforcement of alcohol policies, restrictions on the cheap-and-easy alcohol supply, and in some cases, more lawsuits and new legislation.

Hazing is illegal in many states; let's make it illegal everywhere, with stiff penalties. Fraternities and colleges that countenance this type of behavior should be put on notice that they will be prosecuted through the criminal justice system. Individual host liability suits have been used against fraternities; the threat of such civil suits against colleges is a powerful motive to change.

It is unconscionable to have fraternity and sorority rush in the first semester of freshman year. This should be postponed until the sophomore year. Freshmen should not live in fraternity houses; an administrator should. And at least two-thirds of frat-house residents should be upperclassmen. All fraternity parties should be dry. The real benefits of brotherhood and sisterhood would begin shaping the college experience of Greek members if fraternities truly returned to the more enlightened aspects of their founding principles.

Changing the fraternity culture will mean ensuring that local chapters, national organizations, and universities stop passing the buck. Only then will the steady stream of student injuries, rapes, and deaths cease.

CHAPTER 3

COLLEGE SPORTS AND ALCOHOL

I have conversations with my sons—I'd think athletes would tend to take better care of their bodies, but it's not necessarily the case. They have a lot of parties and tend to live together off campus in these houses—unsupervised places. It's very much like life in a fraternity. The team is the group they hang out with; one tries to outdo the other in everything, including drinking.
—Adele, mother of two college athletes

The Mavericks hockey team of the University of Nebraska at Omaha celebrated its winning season in 2001 by giving away two thousand team photos to its proud and loyal fans. The photo, eagerly grabbed up by children and teens attending the last regular-season game, pictured the team on the home ice at Omaha's Civic Arena—under a looming Budweiser sign. The juxtaposition of the sign and the team was an "unfortunate coincidence," said Brad Haynes, director of marketing for the school's athletic department. It wouldn't happen again.

Alcohol promotion and consumption have become an expected part of the college and professional sports landscape. Alcohol advertising is on display around athletic fields, at tailgate parties in stadium parking lots, and during the commercial breaks of broadcast sporting events, both college and professional. To attract attention to their brands beer companies are involved in everything, from printing up sports schedules imprinted with their logos to buying space in game programs and on scoreboards to flying planes and blimps overhead. They have struck sponsorship deals with university athletic departments and employ famous former athletes as commercial spokespeople on sports programming viewed by millions, including underage college students and teens.

Student athletes are at greater risk for alcohol abuse than the overall student population, and sports fans also binge drink at rates that far surpass non-fan students. Although you would expect student athletes to pride themselves on their physical condition, in our surveys 57 percent of the male athletes and 48 percent of the female athletes are binge drinkers and experience a greater number of drinking-related harms than other students. We have found that college athletes are more likely than other students to binge when they drink and more likely to say that getting drunk is an "important reason" for drinking. In their 2001 Study of Substance Use Habits of College Student Athletes, the National Collegiate Athletic Association (NCAA) found that nearly 80 percent of college athletes drink.

There is no doubt that college athletes are at a statistically higher risk for alcohol abuse and exposure to its secondhand effects than nonathlete students. Listen to the experience of a student who joined the lacrosse team at her small Southwestern college. Like all the school's teams, hers planned a night to initiate new members. Luna doesn't drink, so she was the team's designated driver. "The whole point of the night was to get the rookies as drunk as possible before running them through a gamut of games," Luna explained. "Around midnight, everyone went to a frat house," she recalled. "The guys sat each girl down in a chair in turn and poured liquor down her throat and sprayed canned whipped cream in her mouth, and then held her face in their hands and shook her head violently back and forth." The initiation lasted five hours. By the end of the night, one girl was lost, wandering around a strange neighborhood, another was sobbing hysterically, and others were throwing up and falling over. After that night, Luna knew she would never really be a part of the team.

Or take Evan. A skier since age five, Evan knew he had a good shot at becoming the next captain of his university's ski team—if he could just keep standing. Psyched at the possibility, Evan braced himself. The day of the competition he had an early pasta lunch to settle his stomach, and then he went for it. Evan and twelve other members of his ski team gathered that night around a keg in a fraternity basement while friends and girlfriends stood by. At countdown, they began chugging—one beer a minute. The last one to throw-up would become captain. Evan lost it at seven beers. He didn't even make junior captain.

ATHLETES AND BINGE DRINKING

Although the more conscientious student athletes may avoid alcohol during training season and before games, when they do drink, they do so intensively. "If the average eighteen- to twenty-year-old thinks that nothing is going to affect them physically, imagine an athlete who is in wonderful condition," said Murray Sperber, an American studies professor at the University of Indiana in Bloomington who has written extensively about college sports. In addition, athletes are particularly prone to peer pressure, to "team think," and bonding. Athletes spend their time in intensely social settings. Just being part of a team provides them with an instant and large circle of friends with whom to party.

Jeremy is on the cross-country track team at his school and considers himself a light drinker:

> The cross-country athletes don't drink on Friday nights before meets. But there is considerable drinking among other sports teams.

The basketball team parties really hard. So does lacrosse. A lot of sports team members are in fraternities, and in fraternities there's more drinking. People who play sports are social and driven and engage in activity, and drinking is just another activity that doesn't take much thought. And alcohol makes you feel good.

As in fraternities, athletes use alcohol to "bond" teammates, often through hazing. In the fall of 1999 freshman goalie Corey LaTulippe filed a federal lawsuit against the University of Vermont hockey team for hazing during an alcohol-saturated initiation ceremony. The suit said that veteran hockey players had coerced the new players into parading naked while holding each other's genitals. They ordered the young players to do push-ups, dipping their private parts into glasses of beer, then ordered the initiates to drink the beer. LaTulippe also alleged that the new players were blindfolded and fondled by strippers to amuse the older players.

The disclosures provoked an outpouring of public outrage, leading the university to cancel the second half of the hockey season. Enrollment in the university dropped about 5 percent the following year. The case ended with an eighty thousand-dollar settlement. When the hockey team picked up its sticks again in fall 2001, most of the players returned—still on scholarship. LaTulippe was playing for a junior team in Cleveland.

As in any hazing or initiation ceremony that involves alcohol, the personal risks to participants are high, regardless of their athletic prowess. In April 2001 Ken Christiansen, a nineteen-year-old University of Minnesota-Duluth student who had just made the rugby team, attended a team initiation party where students drank heavily. Walking home after the party, Christiansen fell down a ravine. His body was found the next day. At the time of death his blood-alcohol level was twice that of the legal limit to drive in Minnesota. Although the coroner's report determined that hypothermia was the cause of death, three university students were later charged with providing alcohol to a minor. The three had hosted the party and supplied kegs of beer for the event.

FUELING THE FANS

College sports teams don't only compete against one another, they also compete for fans. In 2001 Al Bohl, the newly hired athletic director for the University of Kansas's down-and-out football program, decided that the key to winning weekly sellouts of the 51,000-seat school stadium would be bringing back the beer. The Associated Press reported in *Sporting News* that Bohl told a gathering of football coaches and players, "This year, right now I'm working on making an atmosphere that includes tailgating. . . . [T]he attitude has to be that Lawrence on a Saturday afternoon of a home football game, it is the place to be in this state." Bohl was challenging Kansas's ban on alcohol on campus. "That's something I know must get done," he told the gathering, according to the *News*.

KU's archrival, Kansas State University, typically had thousands of tailgaters every game day. Although alcohol was banned at Kansas State as well, the restriction was not enforced, and parking lot revelers commonly downed beer and hard liquor. Bohl apparently thought it was time to level the playing field. It was a startlingly frank admission of the importance of alcohol to attracting fans.

Our surveys show that among students who drink alcohol, some 53 percent of sports fans usually binge when drinking, compared to 41 percent of male and 37 percent of female non-fans. In addition, fans are more likely to have drunk on ten or more occasions in the past thirty days and to drink "to get drunk."

Alcohol and the Athlete's Body

Alcohol prevention programs should take advantage of athletes' motives for limiting their drinking. A major reason athletes give for not drinking is that it interferes with their sports activity. Just as many athletes have chosen to avoid tobacco, they can steer away from alcohol. Here are some ways alcohol can affect athletic performance:

• Alcohol promotes water loss by depressing production of the antidiuretic hormone. This increases urination and loss of body fluid, increasing thirst. For each ten grams of alcohol consumed (about one drink) four ounces of body fluid is lost.

• Water loss caused by alcohol consumption involves the additional loss of important minerals such as magnesium, potassium, calcium, and zinc. These are vital to the maintenance of fluid balance and to nerve and muscle action and coordination.

• Alcohol interferes with the metabolism of fat and glucose. Fats and glucose are diverted into making body fat that accumulates in the liver cells. Fat can accumulate in the liver after a single night of heavy drinking.

• The presence of alcohol alters amino acid (protein) metabolism in the liver cells. Protein deficiency can develop in heavy drinkers.

• Heavy alcohol use can interfere with the intestines' ability to absorb thiamin, folacin, and vitamin B_{12}. Nutrient deficiencies are almost an inevitable consequence of heavy drinking.

• Alcohol use can raise blood pressure.

• Two-thirds of the calories in beer are alcohol derived (seven kilocalories/gram). These calories are used primarily for heat and are not stored as muscle glycogen, needed for energy.

• Alcohol use results in decreased exercise time to exhaustion and decreased performance in middle-distance running events.

• Metabolism of alcohol can result in buildup of lactic acid in the blood when alcohol is consumed right before or after strenuous exercise.

• Alcohol is a vasodilator: It causes blood vessels near the skin's surface to expand and thereby promotes heat loss and lowers body temperature.

Conversely, fewer sports fans than non-fans abstain from drinking alcohol.

One student wrote:

> Our football games are way out of control. It is not safe to be in the lower part of the student section because you're mauled by your own team's fans with whatever can be thrown from above. Seems more and more non-thinkers are running amuck on campus.

Our study also found that a larger proportion of student fans (38 percent) take advantage of low-priced drink specials at bars than non-fans (24 percent) and of special promotions by beer companies (19 percent versus 11 percent).

As a result of their heavier drinking, fans are more likely to experience a full range of problems related to drinking, from academic problems to sexual violence. For example, among students who drank any alcohol in the previous thirty days, 15 percent of fans reported having had an alcohol-related injury, compared to 10 percent of non-fans.

Tailgating parties during the fall football season often start early in the morning and go all day. They pose special dangers to students, especially freshmen who may be less-experienced drinkers. Many tailgaters never make it in to the game, preferring to spend the day drinking outside the stadium gates.

One student related how her brother's tailgating affected her family:

> When my older brother, Rick, started college, and had all that freedom, he went a little too crazy at first. He started tailgating a lot. He wound up in the hospital one of his first days there. Because he was eighteen, my parents didn't find out about it till they got the medical bills. They told him to stop drinking and he agreed. Then

it happened again. After a football game he wound up in the hospital again. This time for three days. I think he had a .35 BAL. I went to visit him and he was unconscious. And just seeing my older brother lying there really helpless—I was kind of hopeful that he would regain consciousness, but you can never be too sure. He has a small frame, smaller than me, and he can't drink a lot. He looked so pale and he didn't move; it really scared me. I didn't know what to think.

THE ALCOHOL–SPORTS CONNECTION

Wherever there's a sporting event, look for the logo of an alcohol company. Professional racecar drivers sport Anheuser-Busch–brand logos on their clothes and cars. The Bacardi bat symbol formed the prominent backdrop for the rap halftime show at the 2002 Orange Bowl. The cartoon-character image of Captain Morgan and his sponsor's product, Seagram's rum, were omnipresent at 2001's U.S. Ski and Snowboard Association competitions in Vermont. Contestants, many of whom were teenagers, wore official Captain Morgan bibs. A black-bearded Captain look-alike worked the crowd while a ten-foot-tall inflatable Captain bobbed on the racecourse.

In addition to its hard sell, the alcohol industry is very adept at a soft sell, wooing women, for example, by sponsoring campus activities that they value, such as women's fun runs or breast cancer awareness programs. While this presence may be a minor aspect of the campus environment, it presents the alcohol industry as a friend of amateur athletes and of women in general.

Other countries are way ahead of the United States in recognizing that the use of logos is a form of advertising that can powerfully influence even the youngest sports fans. In 2000 the Supreme Court of Norway heard a case about the use of brewery logos on athletes' shirts and unanimously agreed with the government's view that such use of logos on athletes' clothing constitutes alcohol advertisements and is thus prohibited in that country—where all advertisement of alcoholic beverages is forbidden by law.

CORPORATE SPONSORSHIPS

College sports mirrors the broader society in which professional sports is closely tied to alcohol. For one thing, alcohol companies outright own many athletic teams. Recent ownership of major baseball teams includes Anheuser-Busch (the St. Louis Cardinals) and Labatt (the Toronto Blue Jays). Miller Brewing Company is a major partner with the Milwaukee Brewers, who play in the new Miller Park, a $300 million retractable-roof ballpark. The logo on the Brewers' caps (a script *M*) looks a lot like the *M* in recent Miller Genuine Draft advertisements.

Anheuser-Busch (A-B)—the "official beer sponsor" of the National Basketball Association (NBA), the National Hockey League, the Women's World Cup, and major league baseball—has agreements with 84 percent of the major professional sports stadiums and arenas across the United States. A-B's Budweiser brand name appears in twenty-six of thirty-one National Football League stadiums. A-B recently competed for and won an exclusive beer sponsorship deal at Invesco Field in Denver. The deal makes A-B the only alcohol company whose advertisements can be seen from the 76,125 seats at the football stadium. The stadium's VIP party area is now called the Budweiser Champions Club since A-B also purchased the naming rights to that elite enclave. While A-B has a monopoly over beer advertising in the seating bowl, other alcohol companies advertise elsewhere in the stadium, and fans can buy a variety of major brands and microbrews. College athletic teams often play in professional stadiums (including Invesco Field) that are plastered with beer advertising, further cementing the connection between alcohol, sports, and fans.

A-B milks its sports sponsorships in numerous ways. When it took over the NBA sponsorship from Miller Brewing Company, it launched a promotional under-the-cap, instant-win contest for Budweiser called "Get Some Game." Winners received a trip to a future All-Star Game and cologo'd Bud/NBA apparel. Only large, single-serve twenty-two- and thirty-two-ounce bottles were topped with winning caps. And Bud could expect beer in these packages to appeal to college students and African Americans, as reported in *Brandweek*.

THE SUPER BOWL
and MARCH MADNESS

Young male sports fans are the beer industry's biggest customers. Brewers advertise across ESPN's college football schedule, and A-B dominates television advertising during the Super Bowl. The greatest advertising platform in the world, the Super Bowl, is watched by as many as thirty-three million underage viewers—some 40 percent of all underage persons in the United States. In 2000 the Super Bowl was the only broadcast in which ratings for commercial breaks beat out those for the actual programming. During the 2002 Super Bowl telecast, A-B aired ten thirty-second commercial spots, including for Budweiser and Bud Light. Pepsi, in contrast, ran only two spots (one ninety-second spot that featured Britney Spears and one thirty-second spot). Other Super Bowl advertisers included Blockbuster, M&M/Mars, Taco Bell, and Monster.com.

Alcohol companies also advertise heavily on the single-most viewed college sports event, the basketball championships known as March Madness. "It's not simply beer," Sperber told us, "but a whole new group of alcohol products aimed at college students, including a new malt liquor by Smirnoff. They can't advertise their vodka, but they know there's a lapover when students see the Smirnoff brand."

The NCAA has an arrangement with CBS to telecast March Madness basketball tournaments. "The NCAA will receive $6 billion from CBS through this decade to the next," Sperber said. "The NCAA is allowed to tell CBS that they don't want alcohol ads on any college's sports programs." Sperber said that the NCAA disallows other types of ads, for instance those that encourage gambling through the promotion of casinos or special packages to Las Vegas. "If they do that, why can't they do the same for alcohol advertisements? You better believe they would have to take less money on their TV contracts."

Our surveys show that more college sports fans than other students report spending at least two hours a day watching television. This heavy viewing could be associated with their higher levels of drinking since television sports programming contains many more alcohol commercials than other television programs.

SMILING CELEBRITIES
and ENDEARING MASCOTS

Further cementing the identity of professional sports and alcohol, companies sign up former sports celebrities to pitch their products.

(Active players are prohibited by the industry's voluntary codes from endorsing alcoholic beverages.) In one beer commercial, Earvin "Magic" Johnson holds a six-pack of Original Coors and says, "Here's the real triple-double." Johnson was known for triple-doubles during his pro basketball days.

During the 2002 college basketball championships, Anheuser-Busch found a new way to raise its profile—in the good company of beloved college mascots in front of millions of television viewers. The beer company paid for a thirty-second "responsible drinking" spot in conjunction with the National Association of State Universities and Land-Grant Colleges (NASULGC).

The spot opened with a coach addressing his off-camera team: "As you all know, winning is a great feeling, and it's okay to celebrate," he says. "The way you celebrate says a lot about you. So keep up the good work. Being responsible, respecting the law, celebrating safely—it's all about having a good head on your shoulders—figuratively speaking." Then the camera cuts to reveal the coach talking to a team of school mascots in full costume, one with a really big head. The spot ends with the logos of Anheuser-Busch and the college association.

The spot did a lot of work for Anheuser-Busch: It created a benign image for the industry, making it seem almost like part of the university—friendly and concerned, even cool. "On the other hand, there is nothing in the message that suggests any possibility other than winning, celebrating, and celebrating by drinking," said Richard Keeling, M.D., editor of the *Journal of American College Health* and former health director at both the University of Virginia and the University of Wisconsin-Madison. "The ad cleverly equates the coach with the industry and in some ways with the bartender, serving up a 'good head' (on a beer) and saying it's possible to drink responsibly. Neither are students likely to miss the sexual connotations of 'good head,'" Keeling said.

Alcohol prevention experts roundly criticized the ad. The *St. Louis Post-Dispatch* reported that Lisa Erk, spokeswoman for the college alcohol prevention program A Matter of Degree, called it a "tacit endorsement of drinking." On the other hand, Francine Katz, vice president of consumer affairs for Anheuser-Busch, said it "delivers a clear message to fans of personal responsibility and respect for the law." Was the ad effective in that? Not based on the behavior of some drunken fans.

POST-GAME SPREES

Following the University of Maryland's 2002 win over Indiana University during the NCAA men's basketball championship game, besotted fans rioted on both campuses. Indiana University fans torched couches and hurled bottles at police, leading to three arrests. In Maryland, rioters—many of whom had been drinking beer—damaged six police cars and set at least sixteen blazes. About two dozen people were injured, including an off-duty but uniformed Metro bus driver who required surgery on his eye.

The University of Maryland riots were a repeat performance. Terrapins fans had also rioted in 2001 when their team lost to Duke University's Blue Devils. Marauding drunks set more than twelve bonfires, the tallest of which they fed anything they could lay their hands on, including four sofas and a chair ransacked from a nearby home and boxes of food. The flames sizzled an expensive fiber optic utility line, knocking out cable service to thirty thousand homes and causing damage worth at least a quarter-million dollars. Rioters kept fire trucks at bay until police marched in with riot gear to disperse the crowd.

Earlier in the day, some sixty-five hundred drinkers, including many college students, had participated in a "pub crawl," visiting thirteen bars in nearby Washington, D.C. Budweiser, a local radio station, and Lindy Promotions—a company that runs bar crawls in East Coast cities—sponsored the event. Advertisements reached local college campuses. The crawl featured two-dollar pints of Bud and Bud Light and three-dollar Captain Morgan drinks. The Metropolitan Police made fifty arrests, many for underage drinking, open containers, and fake IDs. Many of the students who rioted following the Terrapins' loss were drunk too.

ALCOHOL BANS
AND DRY FANS

Nationally, universities and college athletics have only begun to address these problems. In 1998 Donna Shalala, then-secretary of the U.S. Department of Health and Human Services, called on the National Collegiate Athletic Association "to sever the tie between college sports and drinking. Completely. Absolutely. And forever!"

Since then, a small but growing number of school athletic departments have begun to break with Big Alcohol. Some Division I schools have opted not to accept financial support from the alcohol industry. These include the University of Minnesota, the University of North Carolina, Brigham Young University, Baylor University, the University of Rhode Island, and the University of Kentucky.

Kentucky came to its decision after two of its star football players were killed in a drunk-driving crash, and the driver, a fellow athlete, was charged with drunk driving and two charges of felony manslaughter.

The University of Wisconsin-Madison agreed not to sell alcohol at any sporting events at its Kohl Center arena, christened in 1998. With that decision, the athletic department forfeited approximately a half-million dollars in alcohol sales each hockey season.

In fall 2001 the University of Rhode Island banned alcohol from its Homecoming football game, which it said had become a "fenced-in alcohol bash." The year before, six thousand people in eight hundred cars had packed into the tailgating area. Ten people were treated for alcohol or drug poisoning, two students broke their ankles, and there were two assaults with dangerous weapons and one carjacking. URI President Robert Carothers wrote in an editorial, "Each year I hold my breath that it [Homecoming] will not include preparation for a funeral and each year I count myself lucky that we have been spared at least that."

In an even more dramatic action, the University of Dayton indefinitely suspended Homecoming itself. President Raymond Fitz explained the action by saying that at Homecoming, "There is extensive and excessive drinking and trashing of the student neighborhoods." The fall 2000 Homecoming had attracted up to eight thousand revelers; eight people were arrested, and at least two couches were set on fire in the street. According to school officials, many of the partiers were younger alumni who didn't even attend the football game.

THE WINNING EDGE

If your son or daughter is an athlete, you've cheered them on for years, through hundreds of practices, at game after game. Or maybe, afraid to disturb their concentration, you've stayed away and listened to their stories later. In either case, you've celebrated their vic-

Go, TEAMS!

Among several national efforts to change the relationship of college sports to the alcohol industry is TEAMS: Time to End Alcohol Marketing in Sports. Its members include high school coaches, public health professionals, youth advocates, and substance abuse prevention groups. As a project of the Center for Science in the Public Interest, TEAMS seeks to:

• Eliminate alcoholic-beverage sponsorship of college and Olympic sports.

• Extend the current NCAA restriction on alcohol advertising to all collegiate sporting events, including pre- and post-game sports shows.

• Prohibit alcohol advertising in sports broadcasting when 15 percent, or two million persons (the lesser of the two), in the viewing or listening audience are under the age of twenty-one.

• Eliminate alcohol sponsorship and promotion of youth sports events, athletic teams and leagues, and individual athletes.

tories, suffered their defeats, soothed their pride, and nursed their injuries. Now you need to help guide them when it comes to the one substance most likely to undermine their collegiate success.

Through its advertising, promotions, and sports sponsorships—on campus and off—the alcohol industry has tried to equate the enjoyment of sports with the consumption of alcohol. That connection is a beneficial one for the beer business and helps owners and administrators to fill stadiums. For college students and young people in general, this equation fosters binge drinking and alcohol abuse.

While special alcohol education and prevention programs have targeted student athletes, they have barely made a dent in the problem. Breaking the cement bond between alcohol and college sports requires challenging basic assumptions about how we as a culture enjoy sports. It requires that universities and their athletics associations sever their ties with Big Alcohol. And it requires adult perspective so that young people who track the fortunes of sports teams and idolize professional athletes can understand that there's much more to winning and losing, both on the playing field and off, than a fist pumped in the air and a drunken chant.

CHAPTER 4

THE PROBLEM OF UNDERAGE DRINKING

Incoming freshmen vomit during the summertime advising session, their parents in tow. They come into town and immediately head to the bars that evening. It is of considerable concern.
—the director of orientation services at a Midwestern university

Groups of teenagers drink alcohol and smoke marijuana at a lounge on the west side of Charleston, South Carolina. On at least one occasion nearly 150 teens, some as young as twelve years old, reportedly joined in the "fun." It is a scene played out, to one degree or another, across the country. In bars and liquor stores, underage people can too often purchase alcohol directly or have an older friend or acquaintance buy it for them. Children drink alcohol they find at home and alcohol purchased by their friends' parents. A frightening number of young people begin drinking years before they reach college age. And those that make it to the university bring their drinking with them.

Today, more than half of all eighth graders and four of five high school seniors have tried alcohol. Thirty percent of high school seniors report binge drinking—consuming five or more drinks in a row. Even among eighth graders, 15 percent report bingeing. And the gender gap in alcohol use has closed: Ninth-grade girls binge drink just as much as the boys in their class.

When underage students drink, they typically do so with abandon. For some the results are devastating:

- Alcohol is a factor in about one-third of the car-crash deaths involving teenagers.

- More than 40 percent of individuals who start drinking before the age of thirteen will develop alcohol abuse or alcohol dependence patterns at some point in their lives.

- Among children age nine to fifteen, 28 percent of suicides and 46 percent of homicides can be attributed directly to alcohol.

- Twelve- to sixteen-year-old girls who drink are four times more likely than their nondrinking peers to suffer depression later in life.

- Those who start drinking before age twenty-one have an elevated risk of unintentional injuries and involvement in alcohol-related motor vehicle crashes as adults.

- The total cost attributable to the consequences of underage drinking is about $53 billion per year.

While disturbing, it is not surprising that young people drink alcohol and suffer as a result. They are growing up in a society where the average adult drinks more than thirty-two gallons of beer (compared to twenty-three gallons of coffee) a year. Furthermore, alcohol marketing messages greet young people when they turn on the television, go to the movies, or attend sporting or almost any other public event.

For example, Anheuser-Busch pays some forty-five thousand dollars a year for the right to promote and sell its products at the family-oriented festival that draws hundreds of thousands of people to Whittier Narrows Park in East Los Angeles for the Mexican-

American holiday *Cinco de Mayo*. The event is now officially called the Bud Light Cinco de Mayo Festival. For several years community members—both parents and youth—have protested A-B's cooptation of their holiday, declaring that *"¡Nuestra Cultura No Se Vende!"* (Our culture is not for sale!).

The *New York Times* predicted in 2002 that America's brewers and distillers will spend more than $350 million that year to sell young people new "designer" drinks—sweet, fruity, alcoholic beverages called alcopops that are packaged and marketed like beer—such as Smirnoff Ice.

This is the icy reality that parents and children alike face. And of course, the temptations that lead teenagers to drink do not end with high school graduation. At that point, if anything, it grows stronger.

THE "WET" COLLEGE ENVIRONMENT

Colleges inherit the behavior of young people who binged in high school, and a "wet" college is likely to induce people who were previously non-bingers to take up the habit.

College environments can be more or less "wet," depending on how students socialize, where they live, school policies, state and local laws, and how local retailers and distributors market alcohol in the community. Drinking is not restricted to bars and sports arenas. Off-campus parties, dormitory social events, fraternity parties, and on-campus dances all provide ample opportunity for underage students to drink.

ALL-YOU-CAN-DRINK

Former high school star wrestler Jared Drosnock was eighteen and a freshman at Bloomsburg University in Pennsylvania when he drank himself to death at an off-campus party on January 28, 2001. The vodka he consumed was furbished by a twenty-one-year-old, who was later charged with involuntary manslaughter, recklessly endangering another person, and furnishing alcohol to minors. Earlier in the evening, Drosnock had been helping some fraternity brothers fix up their house. When the work was done, the party moved to an apartment next door.

Many parties in off-campus apartments or fraternity houses offer all-you-can-drink beer for a fixed fee—the equivalent of selling alcohol without a license. If laws against this practice were implemented and enforced, an important source of alcohol to underage drinkers would be cut off.

Shelbi, a senior at a Northeastern university, described the scene at her school:

Campus administrations are useless. They need stronger punishment, especially for those underage. They need to punish the upperclassmen who have parties just to make money off freshmen. They can make three hundred to four hundred dollars per night. You charge three dollars per person and have a couple kegs. Boys especially will have parties because they don't care if their houses are messed up.

We call the underage students the "freshmen herds," because Friday and Saturday night at 10 P.M. you can look out the window and see herds of ten to fifteen people just walking away from campus. We look out the window and say, "Oh, the freshmen herds, they're out already." They're going to look for a party. For underclassmen, it's the thing in college to drink, but they can't buy liquor or beer, so where are they going to go except to an upperclassman's house? Police don't do anything. Campus security don't do anything. They need to bust the houses that are having a party just to make money.

EASY ACCESS

The wetter the environment, the easier it is for underage students to obtain alcohol. In our latest College Alcohol Study, one in four underage students reported that they were able to purchase alcohol either without proof of identity or with a fake identity card. About 54 percent of underage students said it was very easy to obtain alcohol. Underage students were more likely than of-age students to get free drinks (25 percent versus 5 percent) and to pay a set price for unlimited drinks or less than a dollar per drink (32 percent versus 11 percent). Students who usually paid less per drink or got them for a set price were more likely to binge.

Even in so-called dry environments it can be relatively simple for underage students to get alcohol. One nineteen-year-old student in an officially dry college town described how easy it is for her to obtain alcohol:

> There's a little disco club where you can buy beer; it's part of the student union. You need to have ID, but it's easy to drink there if you don't. Just ask someone who does to buy you a drink. You can also get alcohol from a restaurant/bar that delivers alcohol like pizza. Not hard alcohol, but beer and hard cider. If you go inside they won't serve you without an ID, but if they deliver it's pretty easy to get them to bend their rules. They get a lot of money from their liquor sales. That's how I get alcohol, because I'm underage.

A STUDENT'S "RIGHT" TO DRINK

As one Lehigh University student put it, "If you can vote for your elected officials, if you can die for your country, if you can be executed for crimes—you should be able to drink a beer." Of course, the fact is that based on Minimum Legal Drinking Age (MLDA) laws, the sale of alcohol to a person under age twenty-one is illegal. For many students this is cause enough not to drink. Others will argue passionately that the law is unfair and illogical.

But is it? Not all rights are granted at the same age. A person can obtain a hunting license at age twelve, a driver's license at age sixteen, vote and serve in the military at age eighteen, serve in the U.S. Senate at age thirty, and run for president at age thirty-five. We have an age of legal consent for sexual intercourse and for the purchase of tobacco products.

"There is no one perfect age to first drive a car, get married, or run for senator," Alexander Wagenaar, a public health expert at the University of Minnesota, told us. "We set these standards based on risk and judgments of maturity. For alcohol, we tried a drinking age of eighteen, and we saw significant problems, especially high car crash rates. Also, we're a democracy, and three-quarters of the population supports the age-twenty-one legal drinking age."

CHALLENGES *to the* MLDA

Some argue that a twenty-one minimum drinking age makes alcohol the forbidden fruit and that if intoxicating beverages were legal for eighteen-year-olds (or younger), they would be less appealing. Similarly, some argue that a lower drinking age would help teach responsible use of alcohol, but our studies suggest that the opposite is true. For instance, students between twenty-one and twenty-three years of age drink and drive more frequently than underage students. It seems that as soon as they cross the legal threshold to drink they think they can drink and drive. Reducing the legal drinking age may replicate this behavior at an even lower age and further increase the teen fatalities on our roadways.

Despite all the evidence of the protective effects of the Minimum Legal Drinking Age, critics keep up a steady chorus. Whether well-meaning people or self-interested representatives of the alcoholic drinks industry, they periodically challenge and constantly undermine the law.

Some suggest a "provisional drinkers license," replacing the minimum-age law with a system of gradual access to alcohol for teens. More directly, at a National Beer Wholesalers Association conference, August Busch III, CEO of Anheuser-Busch, floated a trial balloon challenging the MLDA. "We need to listen to those who say that a law that makes it illegal for college students to drink beer is wrong and that it results in the very behavior that we are trying to fight," he said.

Lowering the Minimum Legal Drinking Age would be far from the quick fix that some hope and others guarantee. On the contrary, it would be a grave mistake. Those who want to lower the MLDA often point to Europe as an example of the benefits of legalizing alcohol for teens. But the facts tell a different story.

LESSONS *from* EUROPE

As one student at an East Coast university argued, "Drinking is a problem only because America's drinking age is so high. If the legal

(continued on page 80)

"Society Is a Network"

Alexander Wagenaar, a pubic health expert at the University of Minnesota, has studied the effects of Minimum Legal Drinking Age (MLDA) laws. In 1976 individual states began to raise their minimum legal drinking ages. Then, in 1984 the United States Congress passed the National Minimum Purchase Age Act, which encourages states to enact a minimum legal standard of twenty-one years for the purchase of alcohol. Here Wagenaar shares his insights into the effects and implementation of these laws.

What is the value of the Minimum Legal Drinking Age being set at twenty-one?

The MLDA reduces the death rates among teenagers—that is the bottom line. It's the single most effective prevention effort that we have implemented in the United States in the last few decades. The National Highway Traffic Safety Administration estimates that the MLDA saved more than twenty thousand lives since the 1970s.

We could choose a society that would allow younger people to drink, but the cost is these deaths, and the deaths are the tip of the iceberg. For every one death there are ten serious injuries and an additional one hundred more or less serious injuries.

What evidence is there that the MLDA works?

In the early 1970s, when the voting age was reduced from twenty-one to eighteen, there was an effort to reduce the drinking age to eighteen. Between 1970 and 1976 the drinking age was lowered in twenty-nine states.

Then in the mid-1970s, studies began to show a significant and sudden increase in alcohol-related deaths and injuries among teenagers, setting off the debate on whether to raise the drinking age again. In 1976 Maine was the first state to go back, raising the age to twenty. By the end of the 1970s the trend had completely reversed. No states were lowering the age, and many were moving back up toward twenty-one.

I started research in the late-1970s, looking at those states that had returned the age to a higher level. I found that when a state returned to twenty-one, it reversed the previous increase in the death rate. In state after state I saw very clearly that when the age went down to eighteen, the death rates bounced up, and when the age went back up to twenty-one, the death rates bounced back down. It is incontrovertible evidence that the policy has had a significant effect on drinking rates and deaths.

Can anything more be done to render the MLDA even more effective?

The MLDA has been only partially implemented. One of the surprising things is that we've seen this magnitude of an effect simply by passing it as a law and without really implementing it. Early on, it was virtually not enforced at all.

We need regular compliance checks on outlets. We do compliance checks to make sure that restaurants aren't selling contaminated food. Alcohol is a risky thing. It's appropriate to sell it in a safe and legal manner. Without regular compliance checks we know that many of those outlets will sell to kids

Where citizens are activated, where there are local coalitions, where parents are making it an issue and putting pressure on local police, typically that is where you see enforcement.

There have to be penalties that the outlets notice. There doesn't have to be jail terms, just an administrative penalty on the license holder who has the privilege to sell alcohol. They're obligated to follow the law in how they sell it. We need a noticeable penalty that is graduated up. A second time, the license is suspended for a few days. If an outlet is caught four times in a row, we take its license away. They are not fit to sell this product if they can't follow a basic standard. It's easy to enforce—it just needs to be a priority.

Car crashes are still the leading cause of teen death, and alcohol is involved about one-third of the time. One strategy has been to reduce these deaths by lowering the legal Blood Alcohol Concentration (BAC) for driving from .10 to .08. Some industry groups opposed this vehemently. They argued that laws should focus on high-BAC repeat offenders. What do you think?

(continued)

"Society Is a Network"—cont.

This is a classic argument. But when we shape the environment to lower risk, it lowers the whole risk distribution. If something is risky and you lower the risk curve by 10 percent, everyone's risk goes down 10 percent—the death rates and problem rates go down for the whole population. Lowering the BAC for everyone would have this type of effect.

There are several dimensions to this. The extremely high-BAC drivers aren't the only ones creating risks on highways. We know that with every drink consumed on any given occasion the risk accelerates exponentially. So, at a BAC of .04 or .05 there is already several times the risk of someone not drinking at all. At .08 the risk is several times more than that. This is particularly true for people who are not addicted to alcohol but who maybe drink a little bit much on Friday night. College students who have four to five beers have a dramatically increased risk of causing a car crash. So it's not only people with a BAC of .2 that are a danger.

It is an artificial dichotomy to think that some people drink a lot and cause problems and others who drink less don't cause any risk. When we shift the environmental conditions, we lower the risk among those who drink a little, a fair bit, and a lot. We shift that whole curve down.

Additionally, sometimes the only way to get to really heavy drinkers is to change the drinking environment around them. If middle-level drinkers drink less, it's part of the environment that causes really heavy drinkers to drink less.

Society is a huge network; everybody is influenced by everybody else.

drinking age were lower, like in Europe, people would become responsible drinkers at a younger age."

The reality of youthful drinking in Europe runs counter to this myth. In many European countries, where people under age twenty-one legally drink, binge drinking is a growing problem along with alcohol-related deaths, disease, and other problems.

Recognizing just how critical the problem had become, in February 2001 the World Health Organization (WHO) sponsored a conference on young people and alcohol in Europe. Health ministers from across the continent attended the gathering. Dr. Gro Harlem Brundtland, the director-general of WHO, told attendees that alcohol was responsible for the deaths of fifty-five thousand Europeans between the ages of fifteen and twenty-nine in 1999. In addition, "One in four deaths of men in the age group fifteen to twenty-nine are related to alcohol. In parts of Eastern Europe, the figure is as high as one in three."

A study of thirty countries in Europe found that binge drinking by fifteen- and sixteen-year-olds has increased in half of the countries. In no country has it decreased. The biggest increases have been in Poland and Slovenia, although it is also on the rise in Denmark, Iceland, Ireland, Malta, Norway, and the United Kingdom. The largest proportions of teenage beer drinkers are in the Nordic countries, the United Kingdom, and Ireland.

Myths about European drinking abound. France is often touted as a country where children grow up drinking wine, with little ill effect. If only it were true. Alcohol-related causes claim the lives of nearly forty-three thousand French people every year—a death rate twice that for Americans. French youth, who can legally drink at age sixteen, are especially at risk. Roughly 65 percent of twelve- to eighteen-year-olds consume alcohol in France.

But contrary to their national image, the French prefer beer and liquor to wine, and frequent binge drinking by twelve- to fourteen-year-olds has contributed to a five-fold increase in consumption by youth since 1996. This has prompted a new government war against drugs that, unlike in America, includes alcohol.

GLOBAL MARKETS, GLOBAL PROBLEM

As in America, not only are European youth in general binge drinking more, but also girls and young women have noticeably increased their consumption. Britain's chief medical officer, Professor Liam Donaldson, released a report in December 2001 showing that twice as many eighteen- to twenty-four-year-old women in England drink at or in excess of danger levels than their male peers. This has led to a sharp increase in cirrhosis deaths for women. This disease, which causes permanent scarring and damage of the liver, now kills sixteen hundred British women a year, compared to twelve hundred seven years ago.

Meanwhile, Irish health workers note that "the drinking habits of the Irish are becoming more like those of people in the United Kingdom. In other words, there has been a marked increase in binge drinking." Only 8 percent of Irish sixteen-year-olds consider themselves abstainers, whereas 32 percent of both boys and girls binge drink three or more times a month. And, alarmingly, young women are matching young men drink for drink, with all the consequent dangers.

Why is binge drinking by young people on the rise across Europe? Participants in the Stockholm conference noted that the alcohol industry is aggressively marketing alcohol, including alcopops, to teenagers. In addition, economic changes that have extended the free market have eroded public health safety nets and weakened social structures in many countries. In Ireland, for example, deregulation of the alcohol industry has meant longer opening hours for alcohol outlets.

Easier access and more aggressive marketing—some of the same factors at work on American youth—are encouraging dangerous levels of alcohol consumption in Europe.

Dr. Brundtland called for "a concerted review by international experts of this issue of marketing and promotion of alcohol to young people." The conference's Declaration on Young People and Alcohol called on governments to work harder to protect youth from aggressive alcohol marketing. It advocated controlling alcohol availability by addressing access, minimum age, and economic measures—including pricing—which influence underage drinking.

Far from being the model of responsible drinking that many young people imagine, where sensible young people drink sensibly, Europe is increasingly plagued by youthful alcohol abuse, and the industry is having a field day, legally targeting their products at teenagers.

DRINKING AND DRIVING

Parents are painfully aware of the potential dangers of driving while under the influence. Said one father, "Parents' greatest fear is drunk driving. Every time your children go out you're scared to death. There's nothing you can do except wait for them to come home. It's a randomness that's very frightening. They could be in the wrong place at the wrong time. Kids on Highway I-93 wrap themselves around trees. Every parent worries."

How prevalent is drinking and driving among college students, and among underage students in particular? Why do they do it? Here's the perspective of one high school senior in Washington, D.C.:

Fatal Crashes and the Young Driver

• The number of young people who died in a crash where an intoxicated young driver was involved has declined by almost 63 percent since 1982, from 2,763 to 1,033, largely due to Minimum Legal Drinking Age laws.

• For every one hundred thousand licensed drivers, young drinking drivers are involved in fatal crashes at approximately twice the rate of drivers aged twenty-one and older.

• Per mile driven, sixteen-year-old drivers have the highest rate of fatal crash involvement by a wide margin.

• Approximately three times as many young people die in alcohol-related crashes, per day, on weekends than on weekdays.

• In 1999 the state of Hawaii had the lowest youth alcohol-related fatality rate at 2.3 fatalities per one hundred thousand population, followed by Rhode Island at 3.1, and New York at 3.6. No other state had a fatality rate less than 4. The highest rates (more than 20) were found in the rural Western states. The national rate was 9.5.

• In 1999 about 7 percent of licensed drivers were ages fifteen through twenty. However, approximately 15 percent of drivers involved in fatal crashes were in this age group, and 13 percent of drivers involved with alcohol in their system were in this age group.

• As of June 1998 all states and the District of Columbia have set a BAC limit of .02 or lower for drivers under the age of twenty-one (a so-called zero-tolerance law).

When I was in junior high school, this person was killed in a drunk-driving accident. We all signed a piece of paper that said we will never drink and drive—that we will never get in a car with a drunk driver. That was when there was no alcohol around. Now it is around. We've all gotten into a car with a drunk driver. Even some of my friends that really care, they get in the car—maybe it's their only ride. Or they do it without thinking.

Our research shows that while students over twenty-one years of age are more likely than underage students to drive after drinking, underage students ride with a drunken driver just as often as their older classmates. In any one year, drinking and driving claims the lives of approximately eleven hundred college students.

Because they are preventable, drunk-driving deaths seem especially cruel. The loss of innocent life is staggering, as on a stretch of a two-lane highway outside of Laramie, Wyoming, in September 2001. A southbound pickup truck drifted into the oncoming lane. The driver, a member of the university's rodeo team, was on his way to see his girlfriend. His pickup collided head-on with an SUV carrying eight members of the university's cross-country running team. All eight college athletes were killed, and the survivor who was pulled out of the pickup was charged with vehicular homicide and being drunk at the time of the crash.

Our research shows that the best way to prevent alcohol-impaired driving is to reduce alcohol consumption. And for this, "wet" environments—such as high-binge schools—need to dry out.

We also found that in states with tougher alcohol laws, students were less likely to drive after having five or more drinks. Laws that specifically prohibit the use of fake IDs for underage people, punish attempts to purchase alcohol under the legal drinking age, require keg registration, prohibit home alcohol delivery, enforce a .08 BAC limit for drivers, and restrict alcohol billboard advertisements all contribute to an environment that cuts down on drunk-driving incidents by students.

Similarly, Wagenaar found that when states passed laws that lowered the BAC limit for underage youth to anywhere from 0 to .05, they enjoyed a much lower rate of drunk driving by teenagers.

In the United States, as in Europe, public policy has a huge impact on underage drinking. As widespread as underage drinking and its consequences are today, the Minimum Legal Drinking Age is the strongest deterrent we have to teenage drinking. Lowering the MLDA would be a disaster.

Part II
BIG ALCOHOL

CHAPTER 5

SELLING ALCOHOL TO STUDENTS

The pressure to drink is high; the daily bar specials are published in the campus newspaper, and there are at least ten bars in a two-block area downtown. I'm sure there are other things to do besides drink, but no one really knows about them.
—Denise, a student at a Midwestern university

Four Bud Girls walk up to a bar, ready to work the student crowd inside. Dressed in white miniskirts and tank tops with BUDWEISER emblazoned in red on their chests, the girls anticipate a good night. "They look like cheerleaders, but for a beer product rather than a football team," said Karla, a bartender on door duty the night when the Girls arrived on the Tennessee Strip in Tallahassee. The Strip is the epicenter of drinking for students from Florida State University. Just doing her job, Karla asked to see the Bud Girls' IDs. "One said, 'I'm here for Budweiser. I'm working.' She didn't have an ID." Later that night Karla noticed the same Bud Girl drinking a beer. She told the night manager that the girl had no ID and was probably underage. He passed the problem on to the general manager. "She said she didn't know what she could do," said Karla.

The sole distributor of Anheuser-Busch beer—including Budweiser and Bud Light—in Tallahassee and nine counties in Florida's Panhandle is Tri-Eagle Distributing. Tri-Eagle sells more than three million cases of beer a year and controls 71 percent of the market share. In 2001 Florida governor Jeb Bush honored Tri-Eagle with a

Business Leadership Award, identifying the company as an "active leader in many community-based organizations."

The Bud Girls chat up customers as they promote Bud products in Strip bars, where even underage students find it relatively easy to get served: Nearly half—47 percent—of the underage underclassmen surveyed said it was unlikely they would be caught trying to purchase alcohol in an off-campus bar. One game the Girls play to keep their audience engaged is to have the guys impersonate farmyard animals. "Baa like a sheep," they might command before rewarding willing followers with a Budweiser T-shirt. On the night before home football games, said Karla, the Girls pass out mini-footballs sporting Bud logos. But even the Bud Girls have competition—sometimes they run into the Miller Girls or the Bacardi Girls working the same bars.

And the action is not just at the bars. FSU students can bargain-hunt for their binge beverage of choice at restaurants, convenience stores, liquor outlets—at a total of 185 different establishments within a two-mile radius of the university. In 2001 posters around campus even promised free beer at the annual summer shoe sale of a local athletics store. That's another effective way to market alcohol to students: low price. Draft beers go for less than a dollar around FSU, and convenience stores sell individual cans for fifty-one cents each. The typical admission fee to a private student party near campus is three dollars and includes all the beer you can drink.

The bottom line is this: At hundreds of universities, the college environment encourages students to binge drink.

BIG ALCOHOL

While most attempts to curb heavy drinking thus far have focused on changing the attitudes of individual students or on pointing out alcohol's harms, far less attention has been paid to changing the environment that promotes, facilitates, and perpetuates heavy drinking. Simply urging students to drink "responsibly" is not enough. In fact, that message can be interpreted as a pro-alcohol message because it omits the option of abstaining altogether. It's time to take a hard look at how the multibillion-dollar alcohol industry shapes the drinking environment on our college campuses.

The industry shapes that environment through its aggressive efforts in three primary areas: sports connections, alcohol "education," and advertising. Alcohol companies, particularly the beer brewers, have spent many years and millions of dollars to forge a link between alcohol and college sports in the minds of young fans. Now, when college football—or hockey, or baseball, or skiing—enthusiasts think of their favorite game, they reach for their favorite beer. It's no surprise that fans and athletes are among the heaviest drinkers on campus.

Next, the industry actually *raises* its profile among students through its alcohol education efforts and the campus organizations that it supports. While professing to do a good deed, alcohol companies are in fact increasing brand recognition by promoting self-serving and largely ineffective—if not downright counterproductive—alcohol education messages.

Retail alcohol outlets that surround colleges, and the distributors that service them, set the stage for heavy drinking with their low prices and high-powered promotions. A high concentration of bars in a small area breeds competition that forces owners to reduce prices or stage irresponsible promotions in order to survive economically. Two-for-ones, twenty-five-cent beers, and ladies'-night specials are common pitches. Advertisements circulate in campus fliers and in campus newspapers. Students know that, one way or another, alcohol is available, and often for less than the cost of a soft drink. A binge may be cheaper than a movie.

BIKINI NIGHTS, BAR PARTIES, AND PUB CRAWLS

As part of the 2001 College Alcohol Study, we interviewed bar owners, servers, and student patrons about industry variables such as drink prices, carding policies, and the many "creative" enticements bars offer to encourage students to drink the night away. Here is a sampling of what we found:

• One bar near a college in New York State beckons with bikini bartender nights. Another offers oil wrestling competitions, a boxing ring in the corner, and volleyball outside. A local bartender at another bar told us that people under twenty-one are not marked as underage because the bouncer keeps an eye on them.

• The biggest student bar near a university in Oklahoma holds from four hundred to five hundred patrons. No food is sold. Beer is free on Wednesdays and Thursdays, and on Fridays it's ten cents a glass. Saturday nights are ladies' night, with free beer for women. A "wall of shame" is covered with confiscated IDs.

• Hundreds of bras hang from the ceilings and walls of a bar near a Texas university. Six Slurpee machines each have two flavors of frozen alcoholic drinks with names like Call a Cab and 911. Another bar sells a bucket of six longneck bottles of beer for five dollars. A third charges a six-dollar cover, then two cents for a twenty-ounce pitcher with unlimited free refills.

• At a favorite university hangout in Oregon, a ten-dollar cover buys one-cent bottles of beer and a live musical performance. T-shirts with the nightclub's logo are available in school colors.

• A California watering hole decorated with both Miller Lite and college banners has GO TROJANS GO painted on the side of the bar.

These examples illustrate typical tactics bar owners use to court a college crowd. Promoting school colors and athletic teams suggests a bond between bar and college. Drink specials bring in the students, and the cheaper the drinks, the more students consume. Free drinks for women have the added benefit of drawing the heavy-drinking men. Bikini-clad servers sell sexual fantasies along with beer. These and similarly effective selling practices can encourage binge drinking.

AGAINST *the* ODDS

Bars advertise their parties and specials widely on college campuses—on radio, in newspapers, and on fliers hung on dorm room doors, posted on university kiosks, and scattered to the winds—regardless of the fact that their messages are reaching largely an underage audience. Alcohol ads generate about 35 percent of all college newspaper advertising.

The Catholic University of America (CUA) in Washington, D.C.,

BAR DENSITY WITHIN 2 MILES

University	Enrollment	# of Alcohol Venues
University of Colorado at Boulder	20,436	152
University of Delaware-Newark	14,908	32
Florida State University (Tallahassee)	22,241	185
University of Iowa (Iowa City)	16,884	85
Louisiana State University (Baton Rouge)	22,965	83
University of Nebraska at Lincoln	15,714	117
University of Vermont (Burlington)	7,230	156
University of Wisconsin-Madison	33,014	156

finally drew the line on such activity, becoming perhaps the first university to initiate an investigation and prosecution of a bar in cooperation with an alcohol licensing department and city attorney's office. "The Odds Bar hosted a 'CUA all-you-can-drink' night and got hundreds of undergraduates. We got the bar suspended and fined, leveling the largest fine in the history of the Alcohol Beverage Control Board in the city," said Craig Parker, general counsel and assistant secretary at CUA.

In December 2000 the Odds Bar printed fliers for campus distribution and paid one student a finder's fee for each fellow freshman he got to show up at the party. It also hired student bartenders and bouncers, all of whom were underage. After the party a number of students returned to campus intoxicated and physically ill, and several had allegedly been assaulted. One student was transported to the hospital via ambulance for alcohol poisoning.

The university's dean of students charged the students who had worked at the bar with violating its alcohol provisions stated in the Standard of Student Conduct. While conducting its own investigation, the campus administration requested and received the involvement of the ABC licensing investigators. The ABC Board conducted a hearing, prosecuted by the District of Columbia Corporation Counsel, in which CUA and other area universities testified. In exchange for a temporary loss of its license, the Odds Bar entered into an agreement in which it agreed to cease promoting all-you-can-drink parties to known underage persons, cease hiring underage persons to work as bartenders, and cease serving alcohol to underage and intoxicated persons. The bar was fined ten thousand dollars and put on probation for one year, and its liquor license was suspended for a total of sixteen days. It also agreed to comply with the following conditions of operation:

1. No admittance of persons under age twenty-one without parent/guardian.

2. No all-you-can-drink parties.

3. No solicitation of college/university students by any means, including fliers.

4. Formal training of bartenders.

5. Assignment of all these conditions with any future transfer of license.

Kathryn Bender, the associate general counsel for CUA, later made the following statement: "This proves that colleges and universities are not powerless against bars who continue to prey upon underage students. It also goes to the heart of the problem, identified in the Harvard School of Public Health 1997 study, which found that the critical factor for heavy episodic drinking of college students is the supply . . . of cheap alcohol in large volumes to underage drinkers."

Although the Catholic University of America's successful action was an important step, college campuses in and around the nation's capital remain bedeviled by alcohol promotions, including "pub crawls" advertised in local school papers. During the crawls, thousands of drinkers, including a large percentage of college students, go from bar to bar to imbibe cheap drinks. The reality is that schools in a region need to ally with each other and with the larger community to impact the broader drinking environment. This is a step that five Washington, D.C., universities have already taken.

SPRING BREAK

Spring break vacations in exotic places provide the ultimate drinking environment for college students. Advertisements promise unlimited opportunities to imbibe. According to Murray Sperber in his book *Beer and Circus*, in the year 2000 at least 1.25 million students spent more than $1 billion at spring break festivities, and corporations spent approximately $50 million promoting themselves and their products to this valued demographic. Needless to say, these free-for-alls are times of exceptional risk, especially for underage students less experienced with heavy drinking.

FLORIDA "FUN"

Besides the real physical danger to individual students attending spring break events, the general atmosphere of rowdiness and lawlessness pose what some see as a greater threat: that spring break drinking will raise the bar for students' expectations of year-round cheap bingeing. This became an issue in the winter of 2001–2002, when spring break plans caused a "brew-ha-ha" between two communities more than a thousand miles apart. A twelve-page advertisement in the student newspaper at the University of Nebraska in Lincoln invited students to a weeklong spring break sex-and-sand drinking fling in Panama City Beach, Florida. The insert promised "beer parties up the wazoo," a "beach club party pass," and "the world's largest and longest keg party" with free beer all day long. It also implied that underage drinking would be winked at: "Local police are pretty cool," read one message.

And that is what set off Lincoln Police Chief Tom Casady. He mailed a letter to Panama City Beach's police chief, Robert Harding, writing, "The publication in general and the characterization of your law enforcement approach in particular undermines my department's efforts [to discourage high-risk drinking] and appears to give tacit approval to underage drinking."

Casady, cochair of NU Directions, a campus-community coalition to reduce high-risk drinking by college students, is particularly conscious of the forces that encourage student drinking. He knows that although students may spend their spring breaks thousands of miles from their campuses, they bring the experience and drinking expectations back with them. "These young people come back to the Lincolns and the Lansings and the Iowa Cities somewhat conditioned to expect the same laissez-faire attitude by the local constable. . . . And a few of them are willing to fight for their right to party."

Harding responded by saying that his policy had been portrayed inaccurately and that the city police force does not tolerate drunken behavior or underage drinking during spring break. He assured the distant chief that he would have a beefed-up police force, including thirty-six state troopers, and extra agents from the state's beverage and tobacco division. In 2001, however, more than half-a-million students converged on Panama City Beach, and as many were expected in 2002. And they mostly come anticipating a week of nonstop drinking.

The Panama City Beach Visitor's Bureau sponsored the twelve-page spring break ad, and travel agencies regularly promote all-inclusive packages directly to students. "A lot of travel agencies, especially around campus, they'll distribute flyers, sell you a package—your flight, hotel, an all-you-can-drink and all-you-can-eat rate," said Shelbi, a college senior. Some alcohol companies directly promote spring break bashes. A 1999 report by the Federal Trade Commission noted, "One alcohol company . . . sponsors Web sites for tour operators that promote spring break trips to Mexico and elsewhere for college and high school students. One Web site notes that the legal drinking age in Mexico is lower and asks whether the crowded bars at one U.S. destination (South Padre Island, Texas) will be able to keep 18- to 20-year-olds from drinking: The bad news is that the drinking age in Texas is 21; the good news is that most of the clubs allow 18-year-olds in for fun but no alcohol.

Is this practical? Can they really keep 18- to 20-year-olds from drinking in a jammed bar? You be the judge."

GOING SOUTH

Every year students are injured or die during spring break. In March 2002 Michael Norman, a twenty-year-old college student from the University of Hartford, died after falling from a second-floor mall in the heart of the party district in Cancun, Mexico. In 2001 a nineteen-year-old Rutgers University sophomore, Michael Santiago, died after trying to jump from a third-floor balcony into a motel swimming pool while "vacationing" in Fort Lauderdale, Florida. In Puerto Peñasco, nineteen-year-old Ross Hunter White, a freshman at the University of Arizona, died when his sport-utility vehicle rolled in what was apparently a drunk driving accident. His friend, twenty-year-old student Derek Dominic Sharecky, was critically injured in the accident and died the next day.

An ambulance driver who transports Americans across the border to local hospitals told the *Arizona Republic* that clinics in some Mexican beach towns become overwhelmed with students during spring break. "We get everything from fights, stabbings, shootings, car wrecks, cut fingers, somebody stepped on a sea urchin. It's a wild party down there for a month." Up to ten thousand American students jam the area.

MTV is also in on the act, sponsoring parties and hosting camera crews at popular spring break destinations. "MTV puts spring break on TV," Shelbi said. "They go to Cancun and show the concerts, all the drinking and partying. They popularize spending all day on the beach, getting a tan, seeing big stars, then at night go out and party. Just by the way they portray it on TV, they're promoting this lifestyle."

PRICE MATTERS

Whether at Daytona Beach on spring break or back at their regular campus watering holes, students are quite aware of the price of alcohol, and our studies show a direct effect of price on binge drinking. One student who attends a Jesuit college told us, "On Tuesdays there are twenty-five-cent drafts. My friends go for cheap beer and get hammered. I'll ask, 'Are you going out?' They'll say, 'Like, duh, *twenty-five-cent special.*' I have a 9:30 A.M. class on Wednesday, so I don't go. The bar serves a no-name brand, something gross. It tastes crappy, so you drink as fast as you can, then need another one in your hand. People take advantage of the bar deals. I don't think they'd be consuming as much, they may not even go out to the bars, if not for the specials."

Our studies show that access to an unlimited amount of alcohol for a flat fee increases the number of drinks in a sitting by 1.6 drinks. On the other hand, a dollar increase in the price of a drink decreases the number of drinks consumed in a sitting by almost one drink. Students who have to pay more for alcohol, therefore, are less likely to become heavy drinkers if they currently drink moderately or to become moderate drinkers if they currently abstain.

Increasing the price of alcohol—for instance, through eliminating price specials and promotions—would almost certainly reduce moderate and heavy drinking by college students. But this is easier said than done.

BARS *and* PAR

Campus and community members in Tallahassee have been fighting an uphill battle to change the heavy-drinking environment that sur-

(coninued on page 102)

Easy as ABC: The Alternative Break Corp

Not all students choose to spend spring break drinking themselves sick. Although still relatively few in number, a growing cadre of students participate in alternative spring breaks. Break Away is a national nonprofit organization that connects campuses and communities to promote quality alternative break programs. Britt Holderness attends Florida State University, where she is a leader of the local Break Away chapter, called the Alternative Break Corps (ABC). Britt attended a magnet high school for ballet and joined a sorority as a college freshman. She went on her first alternative spring break in her junior year and is now on the ABC executive board and applying to medical school. The following is her experience with the ABC.

I only signed up because I was going to work with HIV patients, and it was going to look good for medical school applications. I was in a sorority, all of my friends were going on a cruise, and they were like, You can't drink for a whole week, that sucks. I was totally bummed—I did not want to go.

Then we left for New York. We worked with an organization that cooks and delivers meals to homebound people with AIDS. It was so different. It's like, you get in the van with these twelve people you don't know—and I didn't really like it at first. We slept on the floor of a dorm lobby. We got up at four in the morning, in order to get to Soho. I got to see every aspect of the project—got to cook, prepare food, bag food, deliver food. It was just an amazing experience. I met my best friend in the whole world on that trip. She was my site leader, I knew of her, she was pre-med too, but we had never really hung out until after we went on this trip. We've been inseparable since then.

On alternative break we had a strict alcohol policy; the whole Alternative Break Corps has one. The question of drinking came up a couple of times. We said that we're having so much fun we wouldn't even really want a drink. It would just mess things up.

It's so funny because before then I had been a pretty big partier. On spring break in my sophomore year, when we went to Key West, we bought cases and cases of beer. There were ten of us and we had two hotel rooms and both bathtubs were filled up with beers. We got up in the morning, started drinking, and we were like, this is great.

My best friend at the time and I got in this huge fight; we were horribly, totally drunk. We had gone to Duval Street, the big bar street in Key West.

One of our friends had wanted to stay with this guy that she had just met. I was like, I don't think we should leave her. My best friend was fighting me on it. She was like: Britt, it's fine. We were in this huge, horrible, screaming fight. We didn't go out the next day. We watched a movie. On the way back to school we went up to Daytona. It was just gross hotel rooms, nasty guys. It's just a waste of time.

I joined the sorority my first semester in college. It was really fun for a couple of years. It was a great time. Suddenly you had a million friends and everyone wanted to be super-duper nice to you and invite you to do everything. But once I started to get more into my major and school and made my own friends, things changed. You get fined if you don't go to certain things, attend certain events, and I was just busy with other things. And they didn't like my new friend from ABC. They were like, Why do you hang out with this girl who isn't in the sorority? They slowly alienated me. I went inactive in my last semester. The sorority is just a silly concept. Every summer I'd get a list of clothes and the brand names that I need to buy for rush. If you didn't pass dress inspection, they'd take you to the mall. They don't encourage any kind of individuality.

Alternative Break Corps affected my values, or took what I used to have and expanded on them. I think diversity in groups is a good value. I never was around it in the sorority. It's really cool to meet people with different types of majors, from different cultures, sexual orientations, all kinds of things. And ABC has definitely increased my value in learning and travel. All the traveling I've done, I've done through this program. I've been to Salt Lake City, New Orleans, Ukraine, and we're going to Panama in May. When we went to Ukraine, it was the first time I had left the country. We worked in orphanages and a children's hospital. It's like nothing I can explain. I feel like I'm still learning something, not stagnating, wasting time.

Now with ABC, we have about eighty people going on trips from FSU. We have our recruitment process in fall. People that do it once are very dedicated, but it's hard getting people to do it the first time. Our trips cost three hundred dollars per person. That much money deters students that may not have it and would just go home or stay here. Other groups get money from their schools; we don't get any money from FSU. We're working really hard on corporate sponsors. We don't have any right now. It's a great, great, great program and I wish more people would do it.

rounds Florida State University. In 1999 concerned individuals and organizations created a coalition to reduce alcohol abuse among the city's college-student population. The Partnership for Alcohol Responsibility, or PAR, adopted what is called an environmental approach to its work. PAR is part of the national Robert Wood Johnson Foundation-funded A Matter of Degree program, which works with ten university-community coalitions to reduce alcohol abuse among college students. Its vision: "An environment in which alcohol is less available to underage youth, more responsibly promoted and served, and less of a threat to the health and safety of the community."

By 1999 it was clear that the threat was large and growing. From the rowdy atmosphere of the Tennessee Strip to drink specials advertised in the school paper, alcohol consumption seemed to be encouraged at every turn. PAR's 2002 strategic plan noted that, 51.1 percent of FSU students binge drink. Out-of-control parties are a related problem. Neighbors made nineteen hundred calls to Tallahassee police for noise complaints alone in 2000. Crashes related to drunk driving in Tallahassee have steadily risen over the last several years too: 446 were reported in 1996, 515 in 2000. Drunk driving deaths are not uncommon, as when in October 2000 a nineteen-year-old lost control of his car, killing a friend in the passenger seat.

Alcohol-related sexual abuse is a frequent problem on campus and in the neighboring communities. On one winter night in 2001, two women were allegedly raped in two different nightclubs on the Strip. One victim told police that when she went outside to look for her sister she was attacked from behind, forced to the ground, and raped. In the second case a woman reported being raped in the men's room as the bar was closing at 2:00 A.M. In yet a third attack that winter a woman claimed to have been gang-raped by five university students. Because the young woman admitted that she was drunk at the time, a state attorney refused to prosecute. During that same winter FSU suspended the fraternity Tau Kappa Epsilon due to sexual misconduct and alcohol consumption at a "dry" social event.

Recently the FSU administration has strengthened its alcohol policies. It has increased the number of substance-free housing units, limited alcohol advertising on campus, banned open house parties at fraternities, and implemented a parental notification system for high-risk students. These are all important steps, and they have helped to reduce the secondhand effects on the FSU campus, said Dan Skiles, the FSU project director for PAR. "As long as students can walk across the street and drink free beer all night, however, we're still going to see high rates of binge drinking and associated harms in the community."

IT'S *about* ACCESS

The PAR steering committee is made up of the director of Mothers Against Drunk Driving (MADD), the FSU administration, city officials, and local law enforcement. Their strategy focuses on promoting policy change at the institutional and local levels. Their goals include reforming Tallahassee's alcohol-service practices, increasing the penalties for underage drinking, and strengthening the enforcement of alcohol abuse violations in neighborhoods. "Reducing access to alcohol is the most important thing," Skiles told us. To that end, PAR has proposed an ordinance that would sanction problem bars—those that have excessive code violations—by reducing their hours of operation, which is one of the few things the city can regulate. This primarily affects the bars with lower beverage service standards since those tend to be the ones that have the most calls to police for underage sales, noise, trash, fights, and other related problems.

But passage of such an ordinance will require strong public backing, and given the influence that Big Alcohol exerts in Tallahassee, as in other college towns, that will be no easy feat. "Our plan was endorsed by the PAR steering committee and the majority of the coalition," said Steve Meisburg, a Tallahassee city commissioner and PAR chair. "But the alcohol industry has lined up against it."

In an early effort to undermine PAR, alcohol industry representatives released a draft of the coalition's strategic plan to the media. They also sent an eleven-page document listing their objections to members of the city commission, said Diane Leiva, who is the PAR program evaluator at Florida State University for the Harvard School of Public Health. What ensued was a very public debate between Meisburg and another commissioner who crafted a widely circulated letter that opposed policy change and instead emphasized teaching "responsible behavior."

Susie Busch-Transou, vice president of Tri-Eagle and the daughter of Anheuser-Busch CEO August Busch III, holds seats on the Tallahassee chamber of commerce and the local board of education. When the Busch-Transou family took over the local distributorship and moved to Tallahassee in the late 1990s, "they almost single-handedly got the city commission to vote to change the ordinances that allow advertising and service in our public parks," Meisburg told us. One event that followed and that served to increase access to alcohol is the Downtown Getdown, held before home football games.

The Getdown is one huge open party. Several blocks of downtown are closed; and bars sell drinks to visitors in front of their establishments. The city of Tallahassee picks up the event's security costs.

Meanwhile, Tri-Eagle has maintained a high philanthropic profile. Susie Busch-Transou reportedly convinced the Anheuser-Busch

Foundation to donate $1 million for a sculpture outside the state capitol and has arranged an annual spot for the company's iconic Clydesdale horses in Tallahassee's spring parade. Tri-Eagle's parent company, Anheuser-Busch, has also thrown its weight behind an alternative to PAR's environmental approach: an alcohol "education" campaign called social norms. Why? It could be because Florida, recently ranked third in per capita beer consumption in the nation, plays host to a college crowd that has been known to drink more than its fair share.

CHAPTER 6

ADVERTISING TO GENERATION NEXT

*Everyone always talks about what they are drinking. Nobody talks
about the taste. A drink can make you streetwise, sophisticated, athletic.
It's a huge factor in what you're consuming.*
—college senior

Like marketers of everything from Nike shoes to the nightly news,
those who push alcohol speak of courting Generation Next. The
exact age of this prized demographic is often left vague, but the alcohol industry's intention is clear: It wants to catch the attention of
the next generation of drinkers.

Big Alcohol strategizes about how to reach college students.
And why not? College students drink more than their non-college
peers and often have money to burn. And there are other excellent
reasons to pursue these young consumers. Drinkers tend to stick
with the brands they try first, so competition for new drinkers is
fierce. In addition, people tend to drink less as they get older, so
new blood is needed to grow sales. According to one study, the
vast majority of adults (87 percent) who drink begin to do so before age twenty-one. Therefore, those who avoid alcohol until they
reach the legal drinking age are nearly certain to continue to do so.
If the industry doesn't get them young, it's liable not to get them
at all.

In America today young people under twenty-one drink roughly

11 percent of all alcohol consumed. They have little objective information about drinking; advertising fills in the gap. It creates overwhelmingly positive images and expectations that can pave the way for children to drink. Advertising and promotions attract new drinkers, invite heavier drinking, and make it hard for those who should to stop. By the time young men and women reach their freshman year of college, they have been primed to binge drink, and 44 percent do so. How does alcohol advertising whet this thirst?

SPENDING MONEY
TO MAKE MONEY

Airplanes fly beer-logo banners behind them as they pass over packed sports arenas; heat-sensitive liquor ads light up from the bottom of bar urinals; huge plasma screens seduce young people already drunk at the bar with solicitous sounds, shapes, and colors; brand-name alcoholic beverages appear in blockbuster movies thanks to lucrative product-placement deals; and NASCAR racers sport enough corporate logos to rival the Tattooed Lady. Sports heroes, celebrities, and supermodels further hype alcohol products on the small screen. The alcohol industry has devised numerous, sometimes humorous, and often insidious ways to promote its products.

Although many students have a hard time recognizing the impact of these promotions on their own drinking, others see right through the smoke and mirrors. "Obviously the advertising affects people," said one student. "I see much, much more out there for Bud and Labatts, and those are the two more popular beers. Maybe that's why people are drinking them."

FROSH MEAT

For a college freshman new to campus with few friends, excited and lonely, free and apprehensive, alcohol is everywhere to greet him. Thanks to the magic medium of advertising, drinking appears to be fun, sexy, social, exciting, and, yes, normal—all at the same time. To polish this image, the alcohol industry pours about $5 billion a year into advertising and promotions. And, as you might expect, the biggest players pay out the most. For instance, in 1999 alone Anheuser-Busch bought television, radio, and billboard ads—known as the measured media—amounting to $320 million, which doesn't include its investment in sports sponsorships and other big-money promotions. The distilled spirits industry, for its part, spent $365 million on advertising in 2000 (with the lion's share in magazines). That's a lot of polish—but then the returns are encouraging: The U.S. alcohol industry grosses about $110 billion a year.

The industry claims that its advertising merely identifies brands and promotes choice of product. It claims that its advertising neither induces nondrinkers to drink nor encourages heavy drinking nor leads to harms. It claims not to target those under twenty-one.

Whether the industry *intentionally* targets those under twenty-one is not the point. Although it is methodologically difficult to measure the direct effect of alcohol advertising on consumption, at least a dozen studies have shown that alcohol advertising indirectly increases consumption among young people and increases their tendency to drink in the future. Conservatively, a 1999 Federal Trade Commission (FTC) study concluded that it "could not rule out the existence of a clinically important effect of advertising on youth drinking decisions."

Alcohol companies benefit from cutting-edge advertising techniques coupled with themes and storylines that appeal to teens. The frogs, lizards, and dogs that embody Anheuser-Busch products are transparent in their appeal to the young. Official company Internet sites use sex, music, chat rooms, and interactive games in an obvious effort to attract youth to their products. It's hard to accept as coincidence, then, the fact that today in America young people begin drinking, on average, at 13.1 years of age. In our latest study we found that underage students drink almost half (48 percent) of all the alcohol consumed by college students.

Alcohol advertising so permeates students' sense of themselves that they often integrate it in to their home décor. Jeremy, a student at a private Eastern university, said, "People have posters that say LIFE IS FULL OF TOUGH CHOICES, and the graphic is of all of these drinks. Everyone has these on their dorm walls."

THE KING *of* BEERS

The crowd delights when an eight-hitch team of Clydesdale horses pulls an old-fashioned Anheuser-Busch beer wagon down Main Street or in front of a sports arena crammed with fans. But when the parade is over it's plain to see that the gentle giants prancing by on white feet have left behind a mess. Such is the beer business—the economic core of an industry that is all about appearance.

According to alcohol industry data, 57 percent of the total alcohol consumed in this country is beer (29 percent is distilled spirits such as vodka, rum, and whiskey, and 14 percent is wine). Some eighty-eight million American men and women drink beer. It stands to reason, then, that beer companies spend the most alcohol-advertising dollars.

Among the big brewers, Anheuser-Busch is king. The $13 billion-company commands nearly half of the domestic market share in beer sales. Its two closest competitors combined, Miller and Coors, control just another 31 percent.

In 2001, A-B hit an all-time sales record when it shipped 99.5 million barrels to its wholesalers—the equivalent of about 115 bottles of beer for every man, woman, and child in the country. Today, A-B's Bud Light brand is the number-one selling beer in the country. Second is Budweiser—which is also the largest selling brand in the world.

GLOBAL GOLIATH

Alcohol is a global affair. American brewers export their beers to approximately one hundred nations around the world. Anheuser-Busch conducts business in eighty countries, including in eight of the world's ten most profitable beer markets. A-B reports that it is positioned to expand exponentially in China, which soon is expected be the largest beer-drinking country in the world, overtaking the United States. Canada's two largest beer companies, Molson and Labatt, spend about $200 million a year to promote their products. (Although Canadians aged eighteen to twenty-four make up only 2 percent of the adult population, they consume about 11 percent of all beer sold in that country.) Diageo, the world's largest wines and spirits group—its brands include Smirnoff, J&B, Captain Morgan, Johnnie Walker, and Guinness—focuses its promotional efforts on four major markets: the United States, the United Kingdom, Ireland, and Spain.

Further, alcohol companies who do international business can take strategic advantage of their experience in overseas markets. Because many countries around the world have lower legal drinking ages and even less government oversight than the United States, these companies can refine brands designed to hold special appeal to the young. These products, such as sweet-tasting alcopops, can later be marketed in the United States.

BRANDING

The industry knows that youth culture covets brand-name labels and their trendy associations. It exploits this appetite, investing huge sums of money to stimulate demand for alcohol, with various brands aggressively promoted in stylish packaging, with popular music and "cool" characters, and via a variety of creative media. Stamping an individual product with its own identity is called branding. It is simply the process of making your product stand out from the rest of the pack. Extensive market research directs these efforts, and they work.

Said one student, "People talk about whether they drink Absolut or Smirnoff vodka. It's so dumb. They think the drink gives them respect, makes them sound more sophisticated, or less—whatever they want that night."

Alcohol companies go to great expense to imbue their brands with meaning. The Budweiser brand is widely associated with male bonding and athletic success. Coors is linked to unspoiled wilderness. Rick's Spiked Lemonade—"One part innocent. One part wild"—appeals to young people stepping out of their childhoods and into the dangers and joys of independence. At one East Coast school the sailing club is named after Captain Morgan rum. As alcohol researcher Henry Saffer has pointed out, a brand's images and symbols connect to young people's fantasies and create the impression that it is possible to be transported to the place, lifestyle, and personalities portrayed in the advertising.

Students embody these connections in the clothes they wear, the drinks they choose, and their styles of drinking. "A lot of kids wear T-shirts with [alcohol] logos," said Lydia, a student at a religious school in New York State. "They're given out at bars, for knowing the name of a song, for showing a body piercing . . . T-shirts with LABATT BLUE, SMIRNOFF ORANGE TWIST, BUDWEISER, written across the front."

"WHASSUP?"

Anheuser-Busch products are a classic case of branding success. Beginning in the 1990s, the company began a makeover designed to shed its staid image of being "your dad's beer." The rise of the Budweiser and Bud Light brands since then attests to the power of branding in advertising.

Bud Light's fortunes began to shift in 1993, with its ladies'-night commercial. In a binge drinker's fantasy scenario, three working-class guys scam an unlimited supply of free beer from a bar by dressing up in drag on ladies' night. The ad proved so popular that college students still enact the scene at bars across the country. "Ladies' night is probably our busiest night, and if guys come dressed as ladies they get free drinks," said a bartender in Tallahassee. And who could forget Spuds MacKenzie? Battling frogs and lizards came later, and the Clydesdale horses went from being a conservative corporate symbol to playing football. The company's sports connection was solidified during halftime of the Super Bowl with the annual Bud Bowl contests between helmeted bottles of Bud and Bud Light.

Then in 2000, three cool, African-American, average guys scored a touchdown with their instantly classic "Whassup" repartee. August Busch IV, A-B group vice president of marketing and wholesale operations, told *USA Today*, "In our lifetimes, we'll never see so much value created from a single idea. . . . It makes Budweiser a younger, hipper, more contemporary brand."

Another example of A-B branding is Tequiza, a tequila-laced beer flavored with lime launched in spring 2001, in time for the annual *Cinco de Mayo* celebrations. The tagline—"Speak your mind. Drink your beer"—aims to suggest the free spirit and lack of inhibition associated with tequila as well as "the sociability of beer." Ads urge consumers to "Give it a shot."

A-B is advertising Tequiza on English- and Spanish-language radio and print media. The brand does a lot of work for A-B: It counteracts competing Mexican imports, appeals to Generation Next, and makes a play for young Latinos. Latino college students are an important demographic because they historically drink less than their white student counterparts. (The same is true of African-American and Asian-American college students.) In our 2001 study, 34 percent of Latinos were binge drinkers, compared to 50 percent of white students. And where there's a gap to be filled, there's a potential for the industry to grow its sales.

"A DRINK *to* MESS YOU UP"

The industry's obsession with creating new products with youth appeal has led to a whole new class of drinks called malternatives, or alcopops. Teens have described alcopops variously as "a way to get drunk without the bad taste" and "a drink to mess you up without you knowing it." The descriptions come from a focus group run by the Alcohol Policy Program of the public advocacy group Center for Science in the Public Interest (CSPI). The Center challenged the industry intentions for the new sweet drinks that debuted in the United Kingdom in the mid-1990s and soon after hit the United States. Hard. Hard lemonade, that is. In 1997 Bass's Hooper's Hooch introduced malternatives to the U.S. market. By 2000 Anheuser-Busch and the world liquor giant Diageo had caught the fever and were respectively marketing "Doc" Otis' Hard Lemon Flavored Malt Beverage and Rick's Spiked Lemonade.

In the first six months of 2001 the Bureau of Alcohol, Tobacco and Firearms approved 217 new labels for these specialty drinks. By 2002 41 percent of teens ages fourteen to eighteen had tried them, and teens were three times more likely than adults to be familiar with them. Teens like alcopops for the same reason children like cotton candy: because they are sweet. A range of fruity flavors such as apple and berry masks the taste of alcohol, which is unpleasant to many younger drinkers. Alcopops usually have a 2 percent to 5 percent alcohol content, and critics therefore considered them "bridge" drinks that pave the way to more concentrated products.

The companies that market alcopops use gimmicks that appeal to young people. For instance, behind the "Doc" Otis' brand of hard lemonade is a mystery fictional character; radio spots invite consumers to "Unlock the Doc" and offer prizes for spinning "Doc" Otis stories. Mike's Hard Lemonade uses yellow CAUTION police tape to attract consumers. Twisted Ice Tea features "a party in every bottle." In early 2001 Diageo introduced Smirnoff Ice to the U.S. market, promoting the carbonated, citrus-flavored malt beverage with a six-month, $50 million-campaign blitz.

CSPI challenged the industry's new alcopop campaigns, calling the drinks "gateway drugs that ease young people into drinking and pave the way to more traditional alcoholic beverages." CSPI asked the FTC to investigate the marketing of alcopops to teens and order labeling changes and reforms at the retail level. It also asked the Bureau of Alcohol, Tobacco and Firearms to revoke already-approved labels for several alcopop drinks, demand revisions in the design of some labeling and packaging, and require alcopop producers to disclose their marketing plans and submit "alcoholism and underage-drinking impact assessments" to the agency prior to label approval.

The industry predictably denied CSPI's charges. The Beer Institute, the major trade association of beer producers, issued a press release that stated, "Underage drinking is a societal and family issue—not an advertising issue."

Teens know differently. As one teen told CSPI, "It's what you drink every day, like lemonade or fruit punch. It's like everyday drinks."

A year after filing its petitions, the CSPI was still waiting for a response. In the meantime, the promotions keep coming.

THAT'S ENTERTAINMENT!

Television, radio, and print ads are only a small part of Big Alcohol's effort to court youth. How else does the industry spend $5 billion to sell its products? They entertain. And what better entertainment than the movies?

Many alcohol companies hire an agent or use internal staff to drum up placement of their products as props on television shows or in films, where alcohol is commonly associated with wealth, luxury, and sex. In 1997 and 1998 eight key companies—Anheuser-Busch, Bacardi-Martini USA, Brown-Forman Beverages Worldwide, Coors Brewing Company, Diageo, Miller Brewing Company, Stroh Brewery Company, and Joseph E. Seagram & Sons—placed products in 233 motion pictures and in one or more episodes of 181 different television series. Some placements were targeted to teens and children, appearing in PG- and PG-13-rated films and on eight of the fifteen television shows most popular with teens.

Establishing associations with sports teams and athletes is another critical marketing ploy. Young people look to role models, and athletes are highly visible and respected in America. The industry takes advantage of this to pursue groups such as women and Hispanic youth that have traditionally drunk less alcohol than young white males. For instance, Bud Light signed up Lisa Leslie, an Olympian and professional basketball player and 2001 Sportswoman of the Year, to appear in its ads. "They really make a point of picking up folks with a lot of cachet," said Bill Gallegos, director of the California Alcohol Policy Reform Initiative. "Oscar de la

Hoya, a boxing champion, is extremely popular among Latino youth. Anheuser-Busch got him out as a spokesperson. He's twenty-nine now and has been doing this since his early twenties." De la Hoya does Spanish-language ads for A-B, as does musician Gloria Estefan, Gallegos told us.

And what goes better with alcohol than sex and rock 'n' roll? The Bud Summer 2000 campaign jumped on Czech supermodel Daniela Pestova, of *Sports Illustrated* swimsuit-cover and Victoria's Secret fame, featuring her in a promotional calendar and point-of-sale items such as life-size Pestova stand-ups. A-B gave away $3 million in prizes and suggestively invited consumers to "Grab a Taste of Paradise." That same year Rolling Rock beer reinvented itself with a tie-in to progressive music. It threw a giant party, dubbed the Rolling Rock Town Fair, held in August in the western Pennsylvania town of Latrobe. Major music acts—the Red Hot Chili Peppers and Moby among them—anchored the event. Tickets sold out, and a bidding frenzy on eBay drove them from $33 to $170. "The promo instantly dispelled reservations many wholesalers had about the brand's ability to reconnect with entry-level drinkers," commented *Brandweek*. Following the Town Fair, Rolling Rock replaced its crank small-town philosopher ads with so-called party reports such as "Stroked teat of lactating cow" and "Forfeited pants in mosh pit." Town Fair was so successful that the company has made it an annual concert event.

Indeed, about three-fourths of the nation's major concert facilities are involved in deals with beer company sponsors, who pay between one hundred thousand and five hundred thousand dollars annually to attach their names to concert venues and tickets. Brewers sponsor concert tours of individual music acts, mostly rock and country music. A Budweiser concert series can be heard across the country. Similarly, to attract students to its Vodka Source liquor, Interbrew has sponsored a dance-music show on the Student Broadcasting network.

On a mega-scale, Anheuser-Busch equates family fun with beer through its nine entertainment theme parks that "promote our corporate image and responsible consumption messages." According to A-B's annual report, nearly twenty-one million visitors spent time

What Makes Teens Drink?

To reach their target audience, companies conduct consumer research, including the use of focus groups. A September 1999 Federal Trade Commission (FTC) report titled "Self-Regulation in the Alcohol Industry: A Review of Industry Efforts to Avoid Promoting Alcohol to Underage Consumers" reveals ways in which these groups could aid the industry in selling alcohol to teens.

Focus group participants, twenty-one years of age or older, answered questions about their first experimentation with alcohol. In one group, participants described when and what they first drank, why they selected that drink, and under what circumstances. Questions and answers traced drinking patterns back to high school. Participants also disclosed their major motivations for drinking—as a rite of passage, to bond with friends and get "buzzed," to consume what was "in," to socialize with the opposite sex, to be mature and suave, to get wild and crazy, or to get wasted.

One industry report included research on the testing of a particular ad campaign on twenty-one- and twenty-two-year-old consumers. The company wanted to know whether the brand came off as being for "young, hip people." In the course of answering questions, respondents noted that some versions of the campaign "could be for a younger audience." The company disseminated that ad.

If focus group participants *volunteered* the opinion that an ad is "juvenile" or would attract those under twenty-one, companies often—but not always—modified or rejected a campaign.

The FTC's findings raise the question: Are focus groups being used to avoid or to attract underage drinkers?

and money in the parks in 2000, where hospitality centers served more than four million complimentary beer samples. The parks mostly feature wildlife in exotic settings. Among those that help make A-B a family name even before children are old enough to talk are SeaWorld Adventure Parks in San Diego, Orlando, Florida, and San Antonio, Texas; Sesame Place, a children's play park near Philadelphia; and Busch Gardens in Williamsburg, Virginia, and Tampa Bay, Florida.

Billions of dollars a year in advertising and promotions clearly go a long way. Young people are saturated, day in and day out, with the message that alcohol is their passport to fun. The competition for Generation Next couldn't be stronger and extends all the way into cyberspace.

LOGGING ON
FOR ALCOHOL

Young people with a computer and an Internet connection have nearly automatic access to the entire world of alcoholic drinks. Millions of children log on to the Internet every month. The pull of the Internet on young people is so strong that television networks are scrambling over each other to reach eighteen- to thirty-four-year-old men, who are tuning in less and logging on more. The number of on-line thirteen- to eighteen-year-olds alone is estimated to be more than sixteen million—and growing.

Fully aware of this trend, alcohol companies have set up more than a hundred Web sites plugging their products. The sites draw visitors by the thousands. Anheuser-Busch has reported in *Business Week* that its site receives 180,000 visitors per month; another alcohol company reported more than twenty-one million site hits between 1995 and early 1997.

Although online advertising can be an effective and legal way to reach adults, sites are accessible to children and teens and often have content that captivates them. Sites include chat rooms, "virtual bars," drink recipes, games, cartoon characters, contests, and online stores that sell branded merchandise popular with young people, such as baseball caps and T-shirts. To cover themselves, many companies ask users to key in their birth dates and deny access to those under twenty-one. Anyone, of course, can enter false information.

To assess whether alcohol promotion Web sites were targeting youth, the Center for Media Education (CME) analyzed seventy-seven such sites. The 1998 study found that 62 percent of the beer, wine, and spirits sites had features that strongly appealed to youth: about 82 percent of beer sites, 10 percent of wine sites, and 72 percent of spirits sites. Many of these sites use two new advertising trends dominant on the Internet: relational advertising and viral marketing.

RELATIONAL ADVERTISING

Just like the phrase implies, this technique aims at building a relationship between the user and the product. By bringing visitors back to a site again and again, companies create a comfort level with brand names that make it difficult for young, less-media-savvy Web users to separate entertainment from sophisticated marketing techniques.

To nurture relationships, some sites offer chat rooms and/or virtual communities set in fantasy worlds. How about visiting Smirnoff's Pure-Thrill Hotel, Bacardi's Private Island, or any one of six virtual bars sponsored by Heineken, where visitors create a character and profile to represent them as they chat with others? Such devices can keep youngsters at a site for hours and induce repeat visits. They "create a community of brand-loyal enthusiasts, a place where lonely teens can talk, find peers, and support risky activities like binge drinking," said CME.

Of all seventy-seven sites reviewed by CME, only Budweiser offered substantive information on substance abuse. "Even then the information was so embedded within the site that accessing it required more patience than most young users are likely to have," noted the researchers.

VIRAL MARKETING

It works like a virus, transmitted from one personal e-mail list to the next. In a previous era, this advertising technique would have been known as word-of-mouth. But the cyberspace version—refer-a-friend e-mail campaigns—deliver the message much more quickly than the telephone. And much more cheaply. Viral marketing campaigns' conscript consumers do the company's work in exchange for a piddling reward, if any.

Canada's Molson Breweries provides a good example of a viral marketing campaign targeted to young consumers. The company piggybacked onto *Survivor*, the popular TV show, with an animated online quiz game that mimicked the show's themes. "Challenge a Friend" was the viral marketing component, encouraging participants to e-mail the link and compete against their friends. More than 116,000 players signed up, and each participant challenged an average of three friends. In addition, some 59 percent of the players volunteered information that went into Molson's database, offering their age group, gender, address, drinking habits, and the names of three favorite beer brands. This sweep of data collected from Internet campaigns allows companies to fine-tune their marketing messages to make them that much more effective.

INDUSTRY CODES
OF GOOD CONDUCT

The United States beer, wine, and hard liquor trade associations all have voluntary codes aimed at avoiding alcohol promotion to underage consumers. While the codes prohibit ads targeted at those under twenty-one, they also concede a possible spillover appeal to younger consumers. Alcohol companies and their advertising agencies evaluate their own ad campaigns—there is no government oversight or third-party review. Only those advertising campaigns that are clearly *more* appealing to those under twenty-one than to those above need be rejected.

A 1999 report by the FTC analyzed the effectiveness of the industry codes. The FTC based its analysis on reports and internal marketing documents submitted by eight leading beer, spirits, and wine companies. Its findings pointed up a host of contradictory practices, outright code violations, as well as best practices.

CONTENT

All of the industry codes have similar provisions about content. Each prohibits the use of certain characters or people in alcohol ads, such as actors under twenty-five (beer), children (spirits), Santa Claus (beer and spirits), and sports celebrities or "current or traditional heroes of the young" (wine). The beer code also prohibits use of "any symbol, language, music, gesture, or cartoon character" intended to appeal primarily to underage people. One company official stated, "We look at a campaign and ask, Would this 'work' to market a kid's product? If the answer is yes, we don't use that campaign."

And yet research has shown that Budweiser's use of animated frogs, lizards, and other animals with distinct personalities, such as the dog Spuds MacKenzie, have distinct appeal to children. In one 1995 study, 82 percent of children asked identified Spuds as "the original party animal" and connected him with Budweiser. Other researchers have noted that such affable brand spokes-characters can become misleading and trustworthy figures in a young person's life. These characters appear not just in the random television or magazine ads, but have taken on whole lives of their own in cyberspace and are readily available for online entertainment.

The codes also prohibit marketing that promotes irresponsible drinking, such as excessive consumption. The beer code specifically forbids ads that suggest "intoxication is acceptable conduct." And yet some marketing materials promote drinking rituals or use language designed to communicate the product's potency. One company report reviewed by the FTC showed that its brand was most favored by "party animals" who "like getting wild." In a marketing blitz for Smirnoff Ice, one ad shows a man's forearm covered with bar stamps—implying that he's out enjoying an all-night binge. "See where it takes you" is the ad's tagline. Responsible drinking?

PLACEMENT

The codes also govern ad placement, requiring that more than 50 percent of the audience be over twenty-one. This requirement does nothing to protect children since only 10 percent of the U.S. population is age eleven to seventeen, and only 30 percent is under twenty-one. A 50-percent standard, therefore, permits ads on programs where the underage population far exceeds its representation in the population. In contrast, the 1998 legal settlement between major tobacco companies and the states stipulated that cigarette advertisements should not appear in magazines if more than 15 percent of the readers are under eighteen.

The annual Super Bowl demonstrates the actual affect of the 50-percent guideline. As noted by CSPI, the big game has become a showcase for provocative, trendsetting, and youth-oriented beer ads. Up to a quarter of the television audience is under twenty-one. Those more than thirty million young people watching comprise as many as 40 percent of all the people under age twenty-one in America.

Nonetheless, the industry has trouble meeting its 50-percent standard. Of the eight alcohol companies included in the FTC report, two failed to provide reliable information on their ad audience and another two showed weeks when up to a quarter of their ads aired on programs with a majority of underage viewers. Only half the companies largely lived up to their own standards.

REVEALING REVISIONS

For forty-eight years, as part of its voluntary code, the liquor industry's abstained from placing hard liquor ads on television. Then in 1996, the industry trade group DISCUS (Distilled Spirits Council of the United States) revised its Code of Good Practice to allow members to advertise in broadcast media, placing ads on local television and cable television stations and radio programs. Only the major broadcast networks remained liquor-free. Then in December 2001, liquor scored a victory—temporarily.

Smirnoff vodka, produced by the Guinness/UDV division of liquor king Diageo, aired a spot on NBC's *Saturday Night Live*. The promotion was to be the first in a multimillion-dollar deal struck between the liquor giant and General Electric's NBC station.

Heavy industry lobbying preceded NBC's turnaround. The year before, DISCUS had attended the National Association of Broadcasters convention, pressed the Television Bureau of Advertising, and lobbied Congress.

The manner in which vodka returned to network television was telling—it sponsored a drunk-driving public service spot. NBC's new policy required that liquor companies run spots that promote responsible drinking for at least four months before they could place ads that directly promote the product. Just like on college campuses, "public service" messages are being used to increase brand recognition. In the case of the network advertising, they were meant to pave the way for a hard sell, and analysts predicted that the amount of money spent by liquor on television advertising would skyrocket from $4 million to $300 million a year.

But opposition to the plan came swiftly. Public opinion, the American Medical Association, advocacy groups including MADD and CSPI, and some members of Congress forcibly objected to NBC's plan. On March 20, 2002, citing pressure from Congress, NBC announced that it was canceling the Smirnoff ads.

CNN reported that DISCUS called the decision "unfortunate, but only a temporary setback for responsible alcohol advertising and equal treatment of distilled spirits, beer, and wine."

For its part, MADD called for limiting the advertisement of any alcoholic beverages to television programming in which 90 percent of viewers are over age twenty-one and to only feature actors age thirty or older. It also called for a requirement that all alcohol advertising be matched by comparable placement of ads containing alcohol-related safety and health messages.

Even without the entry of liquor ads on the major networks, children and teens view approximately twenty thousand commercials each year, of which nearly two thousand are for beer and wine, according to CSPI. For every "Just say no" or "Know when to say when" public service announcement, teens view some twenty-five to fifty beer and wine commercials. Such are the results of industry-voluntary "codes of conduct" and self-policing.

INDUSTRY INFLUENCE

With relative freedom, the alcohol industry targets entry-level consumers with its advertising. Relying on its economic clout and political muscle, the industry is used to getting its way. Yet the tide is beginning to turn. The more we understand about Big Alcohol's organization and strategy, the more effective we can be in changing the ground rules to protect young people from underage and binge drinking.

MADD SHOWDOWN

MADD—Mothers Against Drunk Driving—is the country's largest nonprofit grassroots organization whose stated mission is to stop drunk driving and prevent underage drinking. It has more than six hundred chapters nationwide, and in 2001 it took its campaign to college campuses.

MADD is supported in its efforts by funding from charitable foundations as well corporate contributors. One corporate sponsor is the automobile manufacturer General Motors (GM). Given GM's professional interest in promoting road safety, its support of MADD seems logical—unless you are a beer wholesaler.

In 2001 GM donated $2.5 million to MADD. The National Beer Wholesalers Association (NBWA) responded swiftly and bluntly. David Rehr, president of NBWA, sent GM president Richard Wagoner a letter. Rehr reminded Wagoner that beer wholesalers nationwide drive cars and trucks to deliver their products and said that they are "very concerned about policy positions that might adversely affect their bottom line."

It followed the letter with a top-level meeting between NBWA and GM officials, and GM's chief engineer, Bob Lange, appeared in front of the beer wholesalers board of directors. As reported in *Beer Perspectives*, the online newsletter of the NBWA, a near-unan-

Lobbying for Big Alcohol

Several major trade associations work nonstop to influence lawmakers and public opinion:

The Beer Institute represents the interests of more than two hundred brewers that produce more than 90 percent of the beer brewed in the United States and comprises a majority of the imported beer consumed here. Members include suppliers of brewing goods, services, and agricultural products. The Beer Institute operates an annual budget of about $2 million.

The National Beer Wholesalers Association (NBWA) represents more than 2,300 independent wholesalers in every Congressional District in the country. The NBWA is one of the Republican Party's chief backers and was the single largest contributor within the industry during the 2000 election cycle, donating more than $2 million, 80 percent of it to Republicans. In 2001, *Fortune* magazine voted it one of the top-ten most effective lobbying groups on Capitol Hill.

The Distilled Spirits Council of the United States (DISCUS) represents most of the major U.S. distilled spirits marketers—its members produce over 85

imous show of hands at the meeting made the point that beer wholesalers nationwide rely on GM products. One wholesaler asked rhetorically, "How are we, as GM consumers, supposed to justify using your products and equipment when you are supporting an organization, such as MADD, that wants to put the beer industry out of business?"

NBWA represents twenty-three hundred wholesalers across the country and is one of the industry's most powerful lobbying groups. GM, itself a corporate titan, stood firm. "We're still very much a proud sponsor of MADD," said Carolyn Markey, the company's assistant manager of safety and communications. A smaller company,

percent of the distilled spirits sold here. DISCUS employs forty-five people and has a budget of $7.5 million. One of its largest members, Seagram, was the top "soft money" donor to the Democratic Party in 1996, giving $1.2 million. Seagram was also one of the top-ten soft money donors to the Republican Party.

The Wine Institute represents more than three hundred California vintners; its members market over 75 percent of the wine sold in the United States, as well as most of the American wines sold abroad. Headquartered in San Francisco, the Wine Institute operates a $6.5 million budget. It has satellite offices in seven other cities and lobbyists in more than forty states.

The American Beverage Institute represents restaurant owners who serve alcohol, including both independent operators and some of America's largest restaurant chains.

National Licensed Beverage Association describes itself as America's largest trade association representing licensed beverage retailers. It represents more than sixteen thousand bar, tavern, restaurant, and package-store owners across the United States.

however, may not have found it so easy to resist the NBWA or any one of a number of major trade organizations that represent alcohol interests.

LOBBYING *the* LAWMAKERS

Industry representatives have incredible access to the pockets of power. NBWA's Rehr once elaborated on this access: "DISCUS President Dr. Peter Cressy has strong ties to members of Congress, having served as a liaison to the U.S. House of Representatives while in the Navy in the early 1980s. Wine Institute senior vice president Bobby Koch is a former high-ranking staffer to House Minority Leader Richard Gephardt and is related to President-elect George W. Bush. Wine and Spirits Wholesalers of America CEO Juanita Duggan has deep ties to leaders in the House and Senate majorities. I could literally list every association head, supplier, lobbyist, or individual in the industry and their connections." Rehr himself has worked for former representative Vin Weber and as a professional staff member of the House Small Business Committee.

Industry trade organizations and individual companies have a constant presence on Capitol Hill. For example, the Beer Institute, NBWA, DISCUS, and the Wine Institute all have offices in the Washington, D.C., area within easy reach of Congress. Companies such as Miller and Anheuser-Busch have their own Washington lobbyists. According to the Center for Responsive Politics, A-B was the number-one industry campaign contributor during the 2002 election cycle, giving a total of more than $1 million (53 percent went to Democrats, and 47 percent went to Republicans). Well-planned industry events, from the NBWA's Oktoberfest to its annual Brewers Legislative Conference, bring together congressmen, staffers, and industry leaders. During the 2001 conference more than 1,020 brewery and wholesaler executives and employees lobbied Congress, and four U.S. representatives delivered keynote speeches.

Lobbying takes place less formally as well. "The Wine Institute hosts an evening at the Library of Congress, and the beer people deliver beer to congressional offices for free," said George Hacker, director of the Alcohol Policies Project of CSPI. Social occasions, golf dates, receptions—all are opportunities to peddle influence.

Michael McKinney, executive vice president of the Wholesale Beer Distributors of Texas, met with President George W. Bush in April 2001 at a luncheon following the dedication of a state history museum. And, in June 2000 NBWA representatives traveled with the Democratic Leadership Council on its annual trip to JazzFest in New Orleans, where *Beer Perspectives* reported they spent a "lobbying-filled weekend."

THE INDUSTRY AGENDA

Alcohol companies do everything in their power to block efforts that would regulate the distribution and advertising of alcohol, all the while trying to win a reduction in the amount of taxes imposed on their products. At the same time, in dozens of local issues that could help limit underage access and binge drinking—such as keg registration and zoning regulations—the industry agitates against reforms, even as it claims to educate against alcohol abuse.

A UNITED FRONT

One reason Big Alcohol can seem so untouchable is its tie-in to other economic sectors: Dining, travel, entertainment, and gambling all rely on alcohol sales to increase their margins of profit. And key industry players are very much aware of the need for a united front.

In a 2001 article in *Beer Perspectives*, NBWA's Rehr strongly urged the major alcohol producers and retailers to stick together. "While we have different products, we share common goals. . . . [W]e should and must work together on common challenges which threaten the longevity of the industry," he wrote.

One example of that united front came in industry opposition to key recommendations put forward by the FTC to limit industry advertising that potentially targets youth. The Beer Institute led the way in opposing the FTC's proposal to transfer review of advertising promotions and citizen complaints from the industry to an independent third party. Such a move could have provided a needed level of protection against advertising that targets youth.

Rehr has also called on united efforts to help develop strategies that would rally state attorney generals against the idea of seeking broad class action lawsuits that would hold beer, wine, and spirits producers liable for alcohol abuse.

In addition, Rehr noted that "NBWA and DISCUS aggressively worked together to prevent Neo-Prohibitionists from forcing the Office of National Drug Control Policy (ONDCP) to equate beer, wine, and distilled spirits with illegal drugs. . . ." And they succeeded. The ONDCP's budget includes nearly $200 million for a comprehensive media campaign to reduce teen drug use, but by dint of the alcohol lobby and Congress, none of this money can be spent on preventing underage alcohol abuse. Congress limited the ONDCP's authority to "controlled" substances such as marijuana, excluding distilled spirits, wine, malt beverages, and tobacco.

Public health advocates are now pushing for a separately funded federal media campaign to curb underage drinking—which the industry appears to firmly oppose.

DEATH *to* TAXES

One of the industry's pet projects is taxes. Specifically, it wants to decrease state and federal excise taxes that have been levied against alcohol sales. (An excise tax is a sales tax on a particular type of product.) Beer interests are lobbying Congress to pass legislation—H.R. 1305—that would roll back the tax to its 1951 level: from thirty-three cents to fifteen cents per six-pack. They claim that the federal excise tax on beer is unfair because it stems from a luxury tax that has been repealed for other items. The Wine Institute wants a rollback of taxes from the current $1.07 per gallon to the 1990 tax level of seventeen cents per gallon. The distillers are also investigating avenues to cut taxes, according to Mark Gorman, DISCUS senior vice president of government affairs. The industry's plan to roll back alcohol excise taxes would cost the government nearly $1.8 billion a year in beer taxes, $500 million in wine taxes, and $275 million in liquor taxes.

The alcohol companies paint an excise tax cut as a tax break for the middle class, when it is actually simply a way to sell more beer. What's more, MADD notes that had the tax rate kept up with inflation since 1951, it would now be more than a dollar per six-pack. Low taxation allows beer to be sold at soft-drink prices. And we know that the lower the price, the more teens and college students drink. And the more they drink, the more alcohol-related deaths on our highways.

SPINNING OPINION

The industry knows that it is not enough to influence Congress. It wants to shape public opinion. Public relations firms pump out hundreds of press releases every year to get the industry point of view into the press, and beer wholesalers are trained in public speaking.

An article in *Beer Perspectives* outlined eight principles for beer wholesalers engaged in a public debate with a so-called Neo-Prohibitionist. Among them: Truth, Flatter, Get it Heard, and Polarize. "Truth is what the people believe it to be," wrote Bill Greener, head of the public relations firm Greener and Hook. "Your challenge, then, is to have your target audience conclude that what they believe to be true and what they want are true of you as a spokesperson for the industry. . . . Flatter. People like to be made to feel important. . . . Get it heard. Penetration. Repetition. Impact." And, finally, "Polarize on your terms." He urges NBWA's members to shape public opinion through identifying the enemy.

The alcohol industry frames the "enemy" as individuals whose out-of-control drinking causes problems for others—and, therefore, for alcohol companies. It blames parents for children's problems. But alcohol itself creates addiction, and the alcohol industry encourages consumption. Alcoholics are not the enemy; they need treatment, not contempt. Parents are not the enemy; they need resources, time, and alternatives for their children.

AVOIDING *the* MIRROR

The industry is willing to look anywhere but at itself for the source of our problems of underage and binge drinking. We all own this problem. It's time to own up.

How tragic for youth that a $110 billion-a-year industry is so adept at psychological manipulation in order to maximize profits. Tragic because those who begin drinking by age fifteen are four times as likely to become alcohol dependent than those who wait until age twenty-one. Tragic because alcohol is implicated in rape, racial harassment, dropouts, overdose deaths from alcohol poisoning, and suicides.

We have succeeded in banishing Joe Camel and other cartoon characters that once sold tobacco, and we can do the same for alcohol. It takes looking past the shiny barrels and all the rows of bottles. It takes understanding the power of the industry, from the corridors of Congress to state capitol steps. The power of Big Alcohol is the power of money, of image, of myth, and of addiction. Is it unbeatable?

Tobacco wasn't. Compared to alcohol, however, tobacco was easy.

CHAPTER 7

ALCOHOL "EDUCATION"

Some of our alumni are even major beverage distributors, and they donate
a lot of money to the university. It's kind of like an onion, and every time
you peal back a layer, you notice a whole new thing underneath, and
barriers at each layer that have to be overcome.
—Jan Talbot, health educator, Cornell University

Big Alcohol has learned from Big Tobacco's mistakes. Instead of
continuing to deny knowledge of the harmful effects of its product
in the face of overwhelming evidence to the contrary, alcohol companies are playing a proactive game by warning against the abuse of
their products. Thus, they operate on both sides of the street: On the
one hand, Big Alcohol heavily promotes and advertises its products
to young people, and on the other it sponsors alcohol "education"
programs that are implemented with the blessing of school administrators on many college campuses.

At first glance, alcohol education messages seem innocuous
enough, even helpful. They stress the personal responsibility of students and the need to "know when to say when." They focus on cur-
tailing the drinking of the most out-of-control students. They tout
moderation, even as they avoid mention of the environmental factors that encourage binge drinking: a readily available and steady
supply of cheap alcohol.

These are the messages that have dominated college alcohol education efforts for decades. They are not wrong. Every human
being needs to learn and to accept personal responsibility for his or
her actions. And certainly, drinking a little is preferable to drinking

a lot. But an exclusive focus on personal responsibility glosses over the reality that alcohol—a drug that impairs judgment—is being marketed to young people who are particularly susceptible to the industry's siren song: that drinking is fun, sexy, and brings people together.

THE INDUSTRY
AS EDUCATOR

The alcohol industry disseminates its educational messages at events such as Alcohol Awareness Week, through peer-education organizations such as BACCHUS, and in complementary brochures, CD-ROMs, and other materials designed to teach parents how to talk with their children about alcohol. Some of these materials come blatantly branded with corporate logos; for example, a "responsible drinking" television spot broadcast to millions of college basketball fans displayed the logos of Anheuser-Busch and of the National Association of State Universities and Land-Grant Colleges, as if they were in close league.

Anheuser-Busch boasts that it has spent an average of some $16 million per year on alcohol education and awareness efforts since 1982. The Century Council, an organization of the country's leading distillers, has invested approximately $10.5 million a year in educational and outreach programs since 1991. These sound like substantial sums—and to many universities hard pressed for funds, the money is hard to turn down. But compared to the $5 billion the alcohol industry spends annually on promoting its products, these are significant amounts.

Beyond the apparent conflict of interest—or, we believe, because of it—health workers on college campuses will tell you that these education programs have proven largely ineffective in changing student behavior. Sarah Mart, student health coordinator at the University of Montana in Missoula, explained, "Over the past ten to fifteen years we've done what the rest of world has done to combat alcohol abuse: held alcohol education and awareness weeks, classes on addiction, signing pledges not to drink—all those really individual things that, in my personal opinion, have created a bunch of well-educated, well-informed, very aware young adults and students who still might participate in those risky behaviors."

WHEN *the* FOX GUARDS *the* HENHOUSE

The alcohol industry has positioned itself to dictate the tone and the messages conveyed through college alcohol awareness programs. This is a good marketing strategy. It would be unrealistic to expect alcohol companies to focus on their own culpability, namely the promotion of alcohol to young people and the supply of cheap alcohol on and around our college campuses. But we should not buy in to the myth of the industry's altruism. After all, as Drew Hunter of the "alcohol awareness" organization BACCHUS pointed out, "Depending on where they are getting their funding from, people get really caught up on which approach they think is best."

We don't invite the tobacco companies to develop Smoking 101 curricula, organize peer groups of responsible student smokers, or promote smoking norms programs at colleges to convince students that some amount of smoking is normal: "The average smoker has only three cigarettes in the evening." We don't allow the fast-food industry to develop dietary guidelines for young people: "The average college student eats only five burgers a week." Big Alcohol, however, has succeeded where the tobacco industry failed and where the fast-food industry has yet to be forced to act—in distracting us from the larger picture of alcohol's disastrous consequences for young people. It is time to take off the beer goggles.

MIXED MESSAGES

Three groups who coordinate narrow public-education campaigns on college campuses are the BACCHUS and GAMMA Peer Education Network, the Century Council, and DISCUS.

According to its own Web site, BACCHUS and GAMMA— acronyms for Boosting Alcohol Consciousness Concerning the Health of University Students and Greeks Advocating Mature Management of Alcohol—is "an alcohol awareness organization, not an anti-drinking group." It produces pamphlets, posters, and other printed materials that promote responsible drinking and distributes them through on-campus chapters of the organization, which recruit "peer educators." It also offers an online course for students who violate campus alcohol policy; universities pay thirty-five dollars per offender to have them sit in front of a computer for three hours, read about alcohol, and be tested on the material. Ironically, this group that "opposes the notion that excessive use of alcohol is an acceptable social practice" is named after the Roman god of wine, Bacchus, who was honored with a wild festival—Bacchanalia—marked by drunken excess. Equally ironic is the fact that BACCHUS and GAMMA receives generous funding from Anheuser-Busch, Coors, and Miller, as well as from certain liquor companies and governmental agencies.

The Century Council is a national organization funded by America's leading distillers. It addresses the issues of responsible decision making, underage drinking, and drunk driving, focusing particularly on "hardcore" drunk drivers. But such a focus ignores the enormous damage done by drivers who get behind the wheel after drinking a "moderate" amount, one that might not raise blood alcohol concentration above the legal limit yet still impairs judgment and motor control. The Century Council helped create Alcohol 101, an interactive CD-ROM that it promotes widely as an educational tool for schools.

DISCUS (The Distilled Spirits Council of the United States), which represents most of the major distilled spirits marketers, has underwritten a series of conferences to find common ground between university and industry representatives. A student drinking conference in October 2000, billed as an "academic" endeavor, received additional financial support from the Wine and Spirits Wholesalers of America, the Wine Institute, the American Vintners Association, the National Association of Beverage Retailers, and the National Licensed Beverage Association. The *Wall Street Journal* wrote that DISCUS "brought together representatives of 34 colleges . . . by offering travel grants and funding for alcohol-abuse programs." At a Department of Education conference held the following month, DISCUS president Peter Cressy stressed that the industry needs "a seat at the table" in campus-community teams that address student alcohol issues. In the November 2001 edition of the trade newsletter *Alcohol Issues Insights* (*AII*), among the "best practices" Cressy praised were social norms programs that inform students of actual drinking habits on campus and that "get about the business of changing students' expectations."

"Social norms" is the latest hot ticket in industry-funded alcohol "education." All the big brewers, including Anheuser-Busch, Miller, and Coors, are touting social norms. In a time of tightening school budgets, Big Alcohol is offering money—sometimes large amounts—to universities to take up the social norms program. Why the industry enthusiasm?

SOCIAL NORMS PROGRAMS

Most social norms programs involve surveying students on their own drinking habits as well as their perception of what is the "normal" amount of alcohol consumed by the "average" student on their campuses, and then devising advertising campaigns to convince students that the norm is lower than they think. The campaigns typically consist of posters showing vibrant, healthy, smiling students below captions making various optimistic-sounding claims, such as: 70 PERCENT OF STUDENTS AT OUR COLLEGE DRINK FOUR OR FEWER DRINKS WHEN THEY PARTY. Follow-up surveys assess change in perception and behavior.

These programs operate on the unproven assumptions that students 1) match their drinking to what they believe to be the campus norm, and 2) believe the norm is higher than it is, causing them to drink more. Theoretically, it then follows that simply informing students of the actual, lower norm will lead them to drink less.

In addition to industry backing, the federal government is throwing millions of dollars behind the social norms idea. The Department of Education and the National Institute on Alcohol Abuse and Alcoholism are funding a $4 million study that began in October 1999 and is scheduled to end in August 2004 to evaluate the effectiveness of social norms. And the California state university system has recently begun implementing social norms programs on some of its twenty-three campuses.

SOFT-SELLING the MESSAGE

The popularity of the social norms concept among college health administrators is understandable. If it worked, social norms would be a quick, cheap, and feel-good fix to a deeply embedded problem. It does not attempt to change policy, accessibility, price, or even college drinking customs. It just tries to change perceptions. Instead of saying to students, "You drank, you hurt people, you caused trouble," it delivers the kinder, gentler message, "Hey, you're not so bad; like most students, you don't drink too much, hurt others, or get into trouble with the law." Richard Keeling, M.D., editor of the *Journal of American College Health* and former health director at both the University of Virginia and the University of Wisconsin-Madison, explained why this soft-sell approach is welcomed on college campuses: "Health educators have been beaten up for years for negative messages. Social norms avoids scare tactics and long boring statistical messages. All that makes it attractive from the point of view of people doing the work on the ground."

For their part, students have had mixed responses to the programs. Some say that it is refreshing to see messages that de-emphasize the importance of binge drinking to campus social life. Others find them laughable. Following a Dartmouth graduation rehearsal, students performed a skit for their classmates and family members. "We were mocking the norms idea," said Noah. "We would recite a statistic, like 'Most students drink less than four drinks when they go out.' Then we had a chorus, and a sign with big letters that read DO YOU FIT IN? We thought it was very funny. It was pointing out that the college is trying to make us more homogenous by making us fit in to this mold."

Shelbi, a senior at an East Coast school offered this opinion:

We have an ad in our daily newspaper. It says that 54 percent of this campus doesn't ever binge drink. Except the students in the picture—one guy spotting another guy lifting weights—are stereotypical fraternity-looking guys. You look at this picture and it is the saddest looking representation; you know these guys are drinking. Where is that 54 percent who don't drink? Not where I lived when

I was living in the dorms. People were sneaking kegs in the dorms. It's tricky, but they do it.

While college officials who allow social norms programs on their campuses may be well-intentioned, and while the programs may work for some students at some schools, industry cheerleaders are celebrating it as a panacea and using it to downplay and cover up the real problems of underage and binge drinking. Think about it: Those social norms posters that blanket college campuses depicting the so-called average student? At most schools, that student would be under the age of twenty-one.

FOLLOW *the* FUNDING

Anheuser-Busch financed the opening of the National Social Norms Research Center at Northern Illinois University in July 2000 to the tune of $105,000. A more recent A-B grant is intended to pay for social norms programs at Florida State University, Virginia Commonwealth, Georgetown University in Washington, D.C., and the University of Virginia. Miller Brewing Company and Coors Brewing Company have also funded university social norms programs at Georgetown and at the University of Wyoming, respectively.

"Of course they should be funding it, because it doesn't work," said Keeling. "From the industry's vantage point, social norms is a great blessing. It is a positive, fun, upbeat intervention that does not endanger consumption. It very much normalizes drinking."

Nevertheless, some schools have implemented social norms programs while avoiding industry money. Robert Carothers, president of the University of Rhode Island, explained his position:

We have a social norms program in the sense that we try to identify for people what the actual data is about their peers' behavior. I've just chosen not to accept industry funding because I think it muddies the water. Kids are very sensitive to hypocrisy. We don't need to engender any more cynicism. The NASULGC [National Association of State Universities and Land-Grant Colleges] took a big Anheuser-Busch grant to run a social norms program, and I just thought it was wrong. It's like allowing alcohol advertisements on your stadium scoreboard. It mixes the message too much—on the one hand talking about the dangers of alcohol abuse, on the other hand advertising the product. It undermines your moral authority to lead.

Carothers was referring to ads developed by Anheuser-Busch to publicize Alcohol Awareness Week, sponsored by BACCHUS. Wholesalers placed the social norms ad messages in student newspapers, A-B adhered its corporate logo, and the NASULGC gave its final approval. This constituted a 180-degree turnabout by NASULGC, which had previously placed ads in major newspapers attacking "binge beer"—an apparent case of, If you can't beat 'em, join 'em.

DISTURBING NORMS

The worry that social norms programs may actually improve sales should be taken seriously. Leading industry executives have made clear one of their strategies: to attack "problem" drinkers (individuals who are already alcohol-dependent) while encouraging everyone else to drink "moderately" and preaching personal responsibility. In the past the industry has refused to say what it means by moderate, which the U.S.D.A.'s Dietary Guidelines for Americans defines as no more than two drinks a day for a man, one for a woman. Now, however, college social norms programs have set the number as anywhere up to five drinks in one sitting—an amount that we know regularly results in serious problems.

"The social norm that I have not seen in educational programs is the fact that alcohol is unimportant for the vast majority of the American public," said Robert Hammond, director of the Alcohol Research Information Service in Lansing, Michigan. "That's the social norm that I think would be more effective for kids to understand. If college students think the social norm is to keep it at under five drinks in a sitting, they're going to have trouble."

According to *AII*, Paul Clinton, president and CEO of the giant distiller Guinness/UDV North America, bemoaned the rejection of "moderate" drinking by a large segment of the American public. "Only about one-third of the country believes drinking can be part of a balanced life," Clinton said. He added that another third says it cannot, and the remaining third is unsure. Clinton regaled the industry, saying that in the seventy years since Prohibition, "that's the best we've been able to do." To correct this situation, he advocates increasing the availability of alcohol, including being able to sell liquor "around the clock and on Sunday." If local laws prevent that, "we'll need to work together, with our retail partners, to make sure those laws change."

This surprisingly frank exhortation to do whatever it takes to sell more alcohol, including aggressively changing local laws, was printed in a trade publication read almost exclusively by members of the alcoholic beverage industry. It reveals an aspect of industry thinking that is carefully avoided in presenting industry goals and intentions to the general public.

Further, the industry has followed its push for increased "moderate" drinking with an attack on the word *binge*. This controversial and confrontational move is no ivory-tower debate. It has prompted outrage among health professionals and has been reported on the front page of the *New York Times*. The attack on the term

(continued on page 146)

The Myth of Social Norms

The popularity of the social norms phenomenon—due to the promise of easy solutions and easy money—has obscured real problems. To understand the potential pitfalls of social norms both in theory and in practice, we interviewed Richard Keeling, M.D., editor of the *Journal of American College Health*, who has reviewed dozens of journal article submissions on social norms programs from campuses across the country. Dr. Keeling is also on the management team of Outside the Classroom, a Boston-based educational company that delivers online health and life-skills solutions to colleges and universities nationwide.

What are the assumptions underlying social norms?

First, it assumes that there is such a thing as a typical student, because the idea is that people are ignorant of what a typical student actually does and that somehow they are interested in being like a typical student. Second, it assumes that there is an underlying healthier norm in the community, and that students adapt their behavior to fit their perceptions.

What are the problems with social norms theory?

The big theoretical problem is that there is no such thing as a typical student. Every student has different peer groups and social networks and moves from crowd to crowd. Each network has its own norms of sex, drinking, etcetera. Nobody wants to be the average student, and nobody is. The idea has no relevance. Students' perceptions of norm are deeply related to their own immediate social networks, but not the broader norms in the student body.

The second problem is that for social norms to work you have to assume there *is* an underlying healthier norm. What's the point of telling people they don't know the norm unless the real norm is better? For groups in which drinking is the biggest problem, the underlying norm is not healthy at all. Among fraternities you have a binge-drinking rate of 70 percent. What good would it do to tell them that 70 percent of fraternity members drank last weekend? And, if you tell them only 34 percent drank last weekend, they would say, Yeah, but that's not me.

On the other hand, if you tell abstainers that 34 percent drank last weekend you create growth pressure on students to drink more.

Has social norms been shown to work?

Social norms folks will say there is evidence that the programs are effective. But if you ask, Is there independently verified, reproduced evidence published in peer-reviewed journals? the answer gets wobbly. There is lots of anecdotal evidence, but not valid scientific evidence.

The big flaw is that there is no controlled intervention. You have no idea what factors might have influenced drinking other than social norms, since you don't have a control group that wasn't exposed to the social norms program. For example, what if a student died from alcohol poisoning the week before a survey to determine whether the social norms program had changed people's drinking? The death would have a suppressive effect on students' drinking.

You also have the problem of the salience effect: When you ask the question over and over again, as you resurvey people, they will try to give the right answer because they are trying to be good students.

Does social norms make a difference where it matters?

It doesn't help the problem if you change the behavior of an abstainer by encouraging them to drink. Nor do you need to change the behavior of students who drink a little, or even occasionally binge drink but don't get into trouble. The point is to change the behavior of binge drinkers who get in trouble and of frequent binge drinkers. And those are groups where an underlying healthy norm does not exist.

When social norms has been used with Greeks or athletes, it has not worked. It has not been shown to change the behavior or perceptions of high-risk drinkers. The intervention is not effective with the people who have the problem. And it's not needed where the problem isn't. So it's meddlesome.

If you go in to a population trying to manipulate their norms and perceptions, you have to have a justification for doing that, otherwise it raises ethical problems. What justifies the manipulation?

Does social norms further the mission of higher education?

Higher education is intended to be liberal in the sense of thought, to encourage individual thinking, to encourage questions, to free the mind. If you

(continued)

The Myth of Social Norms—cont.

hold all that up against the social norms approach—which says adapt yourself, be like everybody else is—this causes interesting conflicts on the mission level. Colleges don't play the role of telling people what to think. So, on the academic side, on the level of people who teach, there is a lot of concern about social norms. Telling people how they should think and what they should be like is contrary to the mission of higher education.

Why is the alcohol industry funding social norms?

The industry likes social norms because it's no threat, it won't interfere with high-traffic consumption, it may improve sales, and it looks positive. They like it because they can put their name and money behind what appears to be a responsible alcohol intervention. They can claim to be supporting efforts to improve the drinking climate on campus, while it has very little risk of influencing consumption and therefore profit.

binge drinking is yet another attempt by Big Alcohol to divert attention from the problem of drinking on campus and to minimize its culpability while maximizing profits.

WHAT'S IN A WORD?

In 1995 ten of the world's largest alcohol companies formed a not-for-profit organization that they named, benignly, the International Center for Alcohol Policies, or ICAP. (ICAP's current sponsors are Allied Domecq, Bacardi-Martini, Brown-Forman Beverages Worldwide, Coors Brewing Company, Diageo, Foster's Group, Heineken, Miller Brewing Company, Molson, Joseph E. Seagram & Sons, and

South African Breweries.) ICAP promotes itself as an international public health organization whose mission includes promoting cooperation between the public health community, the alcohol industry, and others interested in alcohol policy.

Public health workers have noted in *The Marin Institute Newsletter*, however, that ICAP's real job is to "promote industry-favorable alcohol ideology." In keeping with this goal, the organization launched an attack on the word *binge*.

One of ICAP's first papers, published in April 1997 and entitled "The Limits of Binge Drinking," questioned the use of the term *binge* as defined by our College Alcohol Study—five or more drinks in one sitting for a man, four or more for a woman. Several major national and international studies besides our own use the five-drink definition of binge drinking. A successful attack on the term would therefore serve to de-legitimize a body of work that has been crucial to identifying a problem in need of solutions. The paper noted binging traditions in several countries. One such is *ikki-nomi* in Japan, in which students joining college clubs down alcohol while others shout encouragement. It has led to numerous deaths from alcohol poisoning. Nonetheless, the paper concluded, "Clearly, a binge is not always a binge."

ICAP followed this paper with a second, the "Working Papers" of the Joint Working Group on Terminology, which resulted from a partnership with the beleaguered U.S. government agency the Center for Substance Abuse Prevention (CSAP). The agency had just endured an attack before Congress that threatened its funding. Doug Bandow, author of *Politics of Science*, charged that CSAP "perverted" its congressional mandate to provide national leadership in the effort to prevent alcohol, tobacco, and illicit drug problems by using "public funds to promote media and political campaigns for higher excise taxes, restrictions on advertising, and destruction of private billboards."

Apparently cowed, in 1998 CSAP joined with ICAP to publish a paper challenging basic public health terminology as well as some popular expressions. The paper, "A Guide to Some of the Words, Phrases, and Slogans Most Likely to Engender Controversy, Offense, and Misunderstanding," not only attacked the term *binge* but also objected to a roster of words, including *abuse* ("In the absence of a medical or diagnostic context, the term is tainted by an array of unsavory cultural associations"); *advertising targeted to youth* ("There is disagreement on whether advertising results in more underage drinking"); *alcohol (tobacco) and other drugs*; *beer gut*; and more.

BELIEVING *the* HYPE

The industry attacks have percolated outward, and, ironically, some higher-education organizations have joined in confusing the issue. In the fall of 2000 the Inter-Association Task Force on Alcohol and Other Substance Abuse Issues passed a resolution calling on the media, academics, and universities to drop use of the term *binge drinking*. The task force, a coalition of twenty-one organizations— almost half of them fraternity or college athletic groups—objected to the term's vagueness and for lumping a large number of college students "into what is widely promoted as problematic and even dangerous behavior." Heading the charge was a familiar group: BACCHUS. "Students themselves are getting tired of being portrayed negatively as a whole for the behavior of a few," said BACCHUS president Drew Hunter.

Allied in this effort was the Higher Education Center for Alcohol and Other Drug Prevention, funded by the Department of Education. The center is both a principal opponent of the term *binge drinking* and an outspoken supporter of social norms. Though funded to provide objective information and coordinate services, it boasts of its policy of emphasizing positive and downplaying negative news about college substance use. The center's position reflects the disjointed nature of the federal government's response to the problem of college binge drinking.

In the past decade, a period of no improvement in alcohol problems on college campuses, the Department of Education has spent $36 million on the same types of programs supported by the industry. Its current unfortunate support of the social norms concept appears to be a continuation of this narrow approach.

A BINGE *by Any* OTHER NAME . . .

Call it what you will, our research—corroborated by others—has shown that male students who drink five or more and female students who drink four or more drinks in one sitting account for most of the alcohol problems on campus. The five/four measure represents a danger sign—a warning of health, social, economic, and legal consequences ahead. Frequent binge drinkers, comprising about one-fourth of all students nationally, account for more than three-fifths of serious alcohol-related problems on campus *and drink almost three-quarters of all the alcohol consumed by college students.* For instance, frequent binge drinkers account for 62 percent of alcohol-related injuries and 65 percent of property damage.

Again, by focusing debate around the term *binge drinking*, the industry has succeeded in deflecting attention from the problem itself. George Hacker, director of the Alcohol Policies Project of the Center for Science in the Public Interest (CSPI) in Washington, D.C., noted that a focus on social norms programs and the accompanying attack on the term *binge* "is the flip side of the cover-up game that the alcohol industry plays. Its purpose is to blind the public and policy makers to the fact that alcohol is so heavily involved in massive societal harm and horrendous expense."

SEARCHING
FOR SOLUTIONS

In addition to the private and nonprofit groups that are committed to attacking the binge-drinking problem, such as Outside the Classroom and MADD, some governmental agencies and representatives are also genuinely engaged in the battle. The U.S. surgeon general has established as a national health goal a 50-percent reduction in college binge drinking by the year 2010. Likewise, the National Institute on Alcohol Abuse and Alcoholism formed a special task force to find solutions to the college drinking problem; it recently released a report attributing fourteen hundred deaths and half a million injuries a year to college binge drinking. The Centers for Disease Control and Prevention provides measures of binge drinking in their state-by-state reports. Both the Senate and the House of Representatives adopted resolutions—introduced by Senator Joseph Biden and Representative Joseph P. Kennedy II—calling for national action to address the problem of binge drinking.

All of this activity reflects a growing dissatisfaction with the status quo. Despite the industry's continued efforts, college binge drinking is now recognized as a serious societal problem, and people are beginning to demand real change. And the alcohol industry is reacting.

"In the last year or so, the alcohol beverage industry has become much more aggressive in focusing on alcohol prevention activities on college campuses," said Hacker at CSPI. "The industry is trying to counteract an emerging environmental approach that addresses alcohol problems and to refocus attention on individual responsibility and education efforts."

JUST SAY NO

But not all schools are accepting the industry line. At the University of Montana in Missoula, Sarah Mart and her colleagues on the Campus Drug and Alcohol Advisory Committee spent a year reviewing the issue of industry funding of alcohol education campaigns.

An offer of twenty thousand dollars a year from Anheuser-Busch to the school's athletic department had spurred the review. Mart said that A-B's offer came with a portfolio of promotional materials on responsible drinking—branded with the company's logo. "Distribution of the materials was expected of anyone who participated, as well as having press conferences and events," she said. She viewed the materials as a way for A-B "to sell a product, and that's not our goal and not our intent. We decided it obviously was fitting a purpose for them and it didn't fit our purpose."

Based on the advisory committee's recommendation, the university just said no. Its new policy ruled that the school would not use beer, liquor, or tobacco product names, trademarks, or logos in advertisements and promotions. At the same time, the school would not use any university logo, trademark, or name in conjunction with alcoholic beverages or tobacco products.

This action by the University of Montana administration is an encouraging step in the right direction. Denial is a trait of those afflicted with alcohol problems; it should not become a tool of those charged with finding solutions.

Part III
THE BOTTLE
AND THE DAMAGE DONE

CHAPTER 8

ALCOHOL'S EFFECT
ON BODY AND BRAIN

In the past we thought of alcohol as a more benign drug. It's not
included in the war on drugs. . . . [But] the most popular drug is also an
incredibly dangerous drug.
—Sandra Brown, researcher at the University of California, San Diego

Cindy McCue had two children, a twenty-year-old son and an eighteen-year-old daughter. Then tragedy struck. In the early morning hours of his twenty-first birthday, her son, Bradley, died of an alcohol overdose. He was "drinking his age" at a birthday celebration in an off-campus bar. Always out to push his limits, Bradley didn't stop at twenty-one drinks. He downed twenty-four shots of hard liquor—and went into respiratory arrest.

At the time of his death, Bradley was a student of parks and recreational management at Michigan State University. He was handsome, strong, self-confident. "He was always the first one to say, 'Don't worry about me, Mom; don't worry about me, Dad—I can take care of myself,'" his mother recalled.

Earlier in the day, Mrs. McCue and her husband had talked to their son. "We knew he was going to celebrate. We told him not to do anything stupid," she said. But only hours later she received a devastating phone call from her daughter, who had been informed of Bradley's death by a Lansing police officer.

In the days and months that followed, the McCues pieced together what happened that night in the bar. "There were two bartenders. One served the first ten drinks, the other the next fourteen. The bartenders knew how many drinks he had; they stamped his hand BIRTHDAY when he walked through the door. He was allowed to drink until he could no longer stand, and still he was drinking."

McCue has tried hard to understand why her son lost his life. "At that age everybody thinks they're invincible," she said. "They think they understand the risks because they have the limited information they have. The kids who were with him on his birthday were worried about him throwing up and choking—they thought they were being responsible.

"We didn't know how easily alcohol poisoning could kill someone. Many people close to us expressed the same confusion. When we found out that it was the twenty-four shots that killed him, we'd talk to other parents close to us. They inevitably said, 'My kids would never do that.' Then they would talk to their kids, who would say, 'Oh yeah, Mom, my best friend tried that; I tried that.' We found out it happens a lot."

The McCues wanted to respond in some positive way. "We wanted to talk to kids and parents and give the facts about what alcohol in large quantities can do." Still, it was not an easy decision to speak publicly of their son's death. "One of the concerns we had with opening ourselves up to the public is that everyone will remember Bradley only for the way that he died, and that's not the person he was," she said. Nonetheless, they soldiered on.

"I am one who always says, Why? I wanted to give them why, give them the information and let them make good choices. Those are my feelings as a mom. That's what pushed us."

McCue has talked to parents from many states, including Minnesota, Texas, and Michigan, who share her grief. They too have suddenly lost sons or daughters to alcohol. Unfortunately, this is not an uncommon occurrence: According to a study sponsored by the National Institute on Alcohol Abuse and Alcoholism, approximately fourteen hundred students attending two- and four-year colleges died from alcohol-related injuries in a one-year period. At the same time, more than half a million students were unintentionally injured, and about one hundred thousand became victims of sexual assault while under the influence of alcohol. All of these tragedies were avoidable.

CONSEQUENCES OF ALCOHOL ABUSE

Few young people seem to worry much about what binge drinking does to themselves or to others. They may routinely shrug off hangovers and even blackouts; laugh off violent, out-of-control behavior; and give in to the pressure—often against their better judgment—for unplanned and unprotected sex. Cirrhosis of the liver, which produces irreversible scarring, seems decades away, and heart disease as remote as retirement. But daily life in campus health centers and nearby emergency rooms shows that bodily harm is not some distant danger. For the binge drinker, it exists in the here and now in the form of alcohol poisoning, assault, and rape.

In addition, new research shows that when it comes to brain function alcohol gives young people plenty to worry about. Teenagers who drink heavily may lose as much as 10 percent of their mental capacity, affecting tasks as varied as learning new information and thinking through complex problems. Because the human brain continues to develop into a person's twenties, excessive drinking even in college has the potential to destroy a significant amount of mental capacity. While research into these effects is new, initial results point to a potentially serious risk in both the short and long term.

ANATOMY *of a* HANGOVER

Following a night of binge drinking, you will feel the physical after-effects, even though your body may have already eliminated the alcohol you consumed. (It may not have, too, depending on how much you drank.) You are out of whack. Your internal chemical balance, your digestive organs, the nerves surrounding the lining of your brain, your blood vessels—all are out of balance. You are suffering from a hangover.

A hangover is what happens after prolonged or heavy drinking. It indicates alcohol withdrawal, as the body and brain cells that had adjusted to the presence of alcohol try to adapt to its absence. Just four or five drinks can trigger withdrawal symptoms, which typically kick in between six and forty-eight hours after the last drink. These commonly include headache, nausea, diarrhea, fatigue, muscle pain, jittery hands, and mild anxiety. A more serious form of withdrawal is delirium tremens, or DTs. The DTs typically begin more than forty-eight hours after the last drink and elicit profound confusion, hallucinations, and severe nervous system hyperactivity.

Even a mild hangover can be a ready excuse to skip class or pass up going to the library. It's no wonder then that increased alcohol consumption results in less time spent studying, lower grade point averages, and a greater likelihood of falling behind at school. Our data show that consuming a little more than five drinks per occasion is associated with a half a grade lower GPA. For upperclassmen, adding one more drink increases the probability of getting behind in school by about 5 percent. These results, however, probably underestimate the problem because they are based on students who were enrolled in colleges at the time of the survey and do not include students who dropped out of college. According to the Core Institute, a nonprofit organization that assists colleges and universities in drug and alcohol prevention efforts, about 159,000 first-year college students will drop out of school for alcohol- or drug-related reasons.

One student told us, "The weekends start on Thursday here, so a big portion of the class is missing on Friday, from hangovers and such things. Drinking and partying take more priority around here than school work does." Another student who drank heavily throughout his first semester as a freshman said, "Fall semester, basically, you just kiss it away."

BLACKOUTS

Thousands of students experience regular warning signals of the damage they are doing to their brains. That warning comes in the form of a blackout.

During an alcohol-induced blackout, the drinker is conscious but forms no memory of events; she may wake up the next morning in a stranger's bed with no clue as to how she got there. This dangerous condition is likely due to alcohol completely shutting down the hippocampus, a deep structure in the brain that is key to learning and memory, said Aaron M. White, Ph.D., a biological psychologist at Duke University Medical Center. Following a blackout, students must rely on the reports of friends or others to know what they did the night before. White surveyed students at one college to learn what kinds of activities they had been involved in during their blackouts. He found that students did everything from spending large amounts of money to engaging in sexual activity to getting in arguments, vandalizing property, and driving a car—all without a memory of what had happened.

Chuck, a junior applying to medical school, described a recent blackout:

> It was a week after my twenty-first birthday, and we had been snowed in all week. I hadn't had a chance to go to a bar yet. When we finally went out to celebrate, I had four drinks in my dorm room before we left. At the bar there was some kind of sorority event. I

had fifteen or sixteen drinks in a three-hour period. The last thing I remember—the drinks were really strong—I finished my drink and asked for another. I apparently continued to dance. I danced in a cage and spun on the floor. I was dancing with all these girls. A friend jumped on my back in the parking lot and we went running around piggyback. Apparently my friends tried to drive me home. But I had to get out of the car. Apparently I got sick and I was face-down in the snow throwing up. I was so sick that I wouldn't get back in the car. My best friend half-carried, half-walked me home. I went to visit a friend in my dorm; I climbed into bed with him. I don't remember any of this. There are pictures of me hovering over the toilet. I woke up the next morning with a garbage pail full of vomit next to my bed. I don't remember any of this. I was hungover for a day and a half. It's funny—we laugh about it. But really I could have been very close to being dead there. It's not a funny situation.

In the past researchers assumed that blackouts were an indicator of alcoholism. Now, however, they are realizing just how common blackouts are among nonalcoholics. In our College Alcohol Study, one out of every four students who drank reported having forgotten where they were or what they did while drinking during the school year. The incidence of blackout more than doubled, to 54 percent, among frequent binge drinkers. The White study also found that female students experience blackouts at far lower doses of alcohol than males. The average alcohol intake of females who blacked out was five drinks per occasion, while that of males was nine drinks per occasion.

A LOSS *of* CONTROL

Chuck's friends told him about what happened during another one of his blackouts:

I was sitting on the porch; I threw a beer on my friend and he threw a beer on me. The last thing I remember was a beer hitting me in my face. The next think I knew I was in the shower. They told me that they had locked me on the porch and thrown a barrel of beer on me. I was trying to get in, they opened the door, and they doused me in a bucket of ice-cold water. I sat back down, said something to the effect that I don't want all this beer to go to waste. I was dumping it on me. I put the keg hose in my pants. I don't re-member that five- to ten-minute period. It's like it never happened.

Some students realize that blackouts are a danger sign, if for no other reason than that they signal a total loss of control. As Leslie, a junior at a Jesuit college said, "I don't know why you'd get to the point where you can't remember what happened the night before. If you have to ask, Did I hook up with so and so, How did I get home, Who drove with whom? . . . Are you kidding me? I ask my friends, Why would you get to that point?"

Whether one's experiences and behavior during blackouts are "harmless" or extreme, a blackout is a warning that fundamental changes are taking place in the brain. Some of those changes are transient, others may last a lifetime, yet few students have an accu-rate understanding of either set of effects.

ALCOHOL AND THE TEENAGE BRAIN

Scientists know that long-term excessive alcohol consumption by adults can cause brain damage ranging from a mild loss of motor skills to psychosis and even the inability to form memories. Until re-

(continued on page 166)

Watch Your BAC

Blood Alcohol Concentration, or BAC, measures the amount of alcohol in the bloodstream. A BAC of .10 means that a person has one part of alcohol per one thousand parts of blood in the body. A person's BAC level is affected by many factors, including how much they drink and how quickly; their sex, weight, physical condition, drugs and medications being used; and the amount of food in their stomach. Although federal law now requires states to pass .08 as the legal limit for drunk driving or lose a percent of their fed-

BAC Level	*Quantity Consumed in about 1 Hour*
.02–.04	Intoxication begins at about one drink for a 160-pound man; about one-half drink for a 120-pound woman.
.05–.06	About two drinks for a 160-pound man; a little over one drink for a 120-pound woman.
.07–.09	About three drinks for a 160-pound man; less than two drinks for a 120-pound woman.

eral highway construction funds, .08 is no magic number. Relatively little alcohol can cause problems, especially when you get behind the wheel.

Knowing your BAC can give you an indication of the immediate general effects of alcohol on your body, brain, and behavior. Here is a rough guide to alcohol's impact. One drink equals a 12-once beer, a 4-ounce glass of wine, a 12-ounce wine cooler, or a shot of 80 proof liquor (1.5 ounces) taken straight or in a mixed drink.

Effects

Slight intensification of existing moods; some impairment of judgment or memory. A driver's ability to divide attention between two or more sources of visual information can be impaired by BACs of .02 and lower. The pleasure produced by alcohol, which begins at very low doses, is related to increased dopamine levels in the nucleus accumbens area of the brain.

Feelings of warmth, relaxation, mild sedation, exaggeration of emotion and behavior; slight increase in reaction time, impaired judgment about continued drinking; visual and hearing acuity reduced; slight speech impairment. Loss of motor coordination begins at BACs as low as .05 and is probably due to disrupted activity in the brain's cerebellum. Mild memory impairments such as forgetting someone's name after they've been introduced to you can begin around .06 or so, probably due to altered activity in the brain's frontal lobes.

More noticeable speech impairment and disturbance of balance; impaired coordination; feeling of elation or depression; definite impairment of judgment and memory; major increase in reaction time; may not recognize impairment. The increased urination that begins after a few drinks is due to suppressed ADH (antidiuretic hormone) released from the brain's hypothalamus. This effect is largely responsible for the dehydration that contributes to hangovers. In a growing number of states .08 is the drunk-driving limit.

(continued)

Watch Your BAC—cont.

BAC Level	Quantity Consumed in about 1 Hour
.10–.13	A little more than four drinks for a 160-pound man; less than three drinks for a 120-pound woman.
.14–.17	About six to seven drinks for a 160-pound man; less than four drinks for a 120-pound woman.
.20–.25	Less than nine drinks for a 160-pound man; a little over five drinks for a 120-pound woman.
.30–.35	More than ten drinks for a 160-pound man; about eight drinks for a 120-pound woman.
.40	About 15.5 drinks for a 160-pound man; a little less than 10 drinks for a 120-pound woman. (If consumption is spread over six hours, about 18.5 drinks for a man and 12 drinks for a woman.)
.41+	About sixteen drinks for a 160-pound man; more than ten drinks for a 120-pound woman. (If consumption is spread over six hours, about 19 drinks for a man, and about 12.25 for a woman.)

Effects

Noticeable disturbance of balance; uncoordinated behavior; major increase in reaction time; increased impairment of judgment and memory.

Major impairment of all physical and mental functions; difficulty in standing and talking; distorted perception and judgment; cannot recognize impairment. Blackouts are usually observed at BAC levels above .15; they can also occur at much lower BACs, however, depending on many factors.

Confused or dazed; major body movements cannot be made without assistance.

Minimal perception and comprehension; general suspension of cognitive abilities. At very high doses alcohol can suppress the activity of nuclei in the brainstem that control vital reflexes, like gagging and breathing. A common way for someone to die from the direct effects of alcohol is to drink enough to suppress the gag reflex. They then pass out on their backs, vomit, and choke on their own vomit. Enough alcohol can shut down breathing all together. The exact level at which humans die from the direct effects of alcohol on the brain is not known for sure, but the evidence suggests that the LD1—the level at which 1 out of 100 people would die—is a BAC of about .35.

Unconscious/coma.

Deep coma/death.

cently we have had no clue as to the effects of alcohol on the brain during adolescence—that period of transition from childhood to adulthood that spans the second decade of life.

Because the brain reaches 95 percent of its final size by age five, scientists had for a long time assumed that most development was also complete by that age. Now we know that while the total size changes little after age five, the parts that make up the brain go through some major remodeling during the teenage years.

THE CEMENT *Is* STILL SETTING

It has been hard to study the teenage brain. Teen mortality is low, and autopsies are rarely performed. A major source of information on brain development is the Yakovlev-Haleem Brain Collection housed at the Walter Reed Army Medical Center in Washington, D.C. Begun in 1930, the collection includes hundreds of adult brains but just eleven brains of children who died between the ages of three and eighteen. "A lot of what has been known about teen brains has been based on these eleven brains," said Jay Giedd at the National Institute of Mental Health in Bethesda, Maryland.

Beginning in the 1990s, Giedd used a noninvasive technique called magnetic resonance imaging to study the living brains of more than eight hundred people between the ages of three and eighteen. Every two years he scanned their developing brains, and he now has more than twenty-five hundred images showing developmental patterns.

"Adolescence is a very busy, tumultuous time in the brain; its wiring is laid down much later than we used to think," Giedd said. "Since the cement of the brain is still setting, if teenagers do use alcohol or drugs they may not just be affecting their brain for that night or weekend, but for the next eighty years of their life."

TUMULTUOUS TIMES

Two of the most noticeable changes occur in the brain's prefrontal cortex and in its limbic system. The prefrontal cortex, located behind the forehead, is the brain's chief decision-maker and voice of reason. The limbic system includes the brain's hippocampus, a wishbone-shaped structure that is responsible for many types of learning and memory, and the amygdala, which responds to matters of life and death. It is mobilized when a person is hungry or frightened or angry and helps the brain process such survival impulses. Both the prefrontal cortex and the limbic system must be able to work in concert for a person to make sound decisions.

During adolescence, the prefrontal cortex changes more than any other part of the brain. At around age eleven or twelve its nerve cells, or neurons, branch out like crazy, only to be seriously pruned back in the years that follow. All this tumult is to good purpose. In the adult brain the prefrontal cortex executes the thought processes younger people struggle to master: the ability to plan ahead, think abstractly, and integrate information to make sound decisions. It transforms from functioning in a more global to a more specialized way.

In teenagers the hippocampus is loaded with estrogen receptors and grows larger in girls than in boys during these years. On the other hand, the amygdala is loaded with testosterone receptors and grows more rapidly in boys. These changes continue up until age twenty in some young people, Giedd said.

Now, researchers are seeing some of the worst alcohol-related brain damage occurring in these parts of the brain during the teenage years. One disturbing finding is that alcohol-induced cell death and damage shrinks the hippocampus. Michael De Bellis at the University of Pittsburgh Medical Center used magnetic resonance imaging to compare the hippocampi of youth from fourteen to twenty-one years of age who abused alcohol to those who did not. The longer and the more a young person had been drinking, the smaller his hippocampus. The average size difference between healthy teenagers and alcohol abusers was roughly 10 percent. That's a lot of lost brain cells.

SHORT- *and* LONG-TERM EFFECTS

Pharmacologist Fulton Crews, director of the Center for Alcohol Studies at the University of North Carolina in Chapel Hill, has investigated the different patterns of brain cell death in adolescents and adults by studying rats. While juvenile and adult rats both showed severe damage in the back areas of the brain and the frontally located olfactory bulb after four-day drinking bouts, only the adolescents suffered brain damage in other frontal areas, and that damage was severe. The regions of cell death in the rat experiment correspond to the human prefrontal cortex and to parts of the limbic system, which is especially worrisome because they play an important role in the formation of an adult personality. "Binge drinking could be making permanent long-term changes in the final neural physiology, which is expressed as personality and behavior in the individual," Crews said.

Another set of experiments by neuropsychologist Scott Swartzwelder at Duke University has shown that alcohol disrupts a brain process called long-term potentiation, or LTP, more severely in adolescent than in adult rats. Scientists think that an LTP-type process is necessary for the brain to form memories. Swartzwelder found that exposure to the equivalent of just two beers inhibits this process in adolescent rats while it takes more than twice as much beer to similarly inhibit adult rats. These findings led him to suspect that alcohol consumption might retard learning in adolescents.

To see whether this was true for humans, Swartzwelder recruited a group of volunteers aged twenty-one to twenty-nine years old. (He could not use younger volunteers because drinking is illegal for those under age twenty-one.) He split the volunteers into two groups: twenty-one to twenty-four years old, and twenty-five to twenty-nine years old. After just three drinks, with a blood-alcohol level slightly below .08 percent, the younger group's learning was impaired 25 percent more than the older group's. "The adolescent brain is a developing nervous system," summarized Swartzwelder, "and the things you do to it can change it."

To find out if heavy alcohol consumption could cause long-term cognitive damage in bingeing adolescents, Swartzwelder's colleague, Aaron White, devised another experiment. He gave adolescent and adult rats very large doses of alcohol every other day for twenty days—the rough equivalent of a 150-pound human chugging twenty-four drinks in a row. Twenty days after the last binge, when the adolescent rats had reached adulthood, White trained them in a maze memory task. Both the younger and older rats performed equally well when sober. But when intoxicated, those who had binged as adolescents performed much worse. "Binge exposure to alcohol during adolescence appears to produce long-lasting changes in brain function," White said. He suspects that the early damage caused by alcohol could surface *whenever* the brain is taxed or stressed, not just when it is again challenged by alcohol.

The collective damage caused by having so many American adolescents reach for one drink after another may be incalculable. "People in their late teens have been drinking heavily for generations. We're not a society of idiots, but we're not a society of Einsteins either," said Swartzwelder. "What if you've compromised your function by 7 percent or 10 percent and never known the difference?"

MEMORY PROBLEMS

Taking another approach, Sandra Brown, Susan Tapert, and Gregory Brown at the University of California, San Diego, and the VA San Diego Health Care System have been following a group of thirty-three teenagers—all heavy drinkers—for eight years. Repeated testing shows that these problem drinkers perform more poorly on tests of cognition and learning than do nondrinkers.

On average, each teen had used alcohol more than seven hundred fifty times—the equivalent of drinking every day for two and a half years. Bingeing was common: The teens downed an average of eight drinks at each sitting. The researchers matched drinkers with nondrinkers of the same gender and similar age, IQ, socioeconomic background, and family history of alcohol. Then, three weeks after the drinkers had their last drink, all the teens took a two-hour battery of tests.

The teens with alcohol problems had a harder time recalling information, both verbal and nonverbal, that they had learned just twenty minutes earlier. Words such as *apple* and *football* escaped them. The performance difference was about 10 percent. "It's not serious brain damage, but it's the difference of a grade, a pass or a fail," Tapert said. Other tests evaluated skills needed for map learning, geometry, and science. Again, there was a 10 percent difference in performance.

Furthermore, Tapert and Sandra Brown found the single best predictor of neuropsychological deficits for the adolescents was withdrawal symptoms, and that just several years of heavy alcohol altered their brain functions in ways that hamper learning. In other words, those young people that experience regular hangovers—a result of the brain's withdrawal from alcohol—are at higher risk of learning deficits. This is especially true of those youth who experience the most extreme withdrawal, DTs.

Sandra Brown is following the teens until they reach age thirty, and some have already passed twenty-one. "Those who continue to use alcohol heavily are developing attentional deficits in addition to the memory and problem-solving deficits that showed up early on," she said. "In the past we thought of alcohol as a more benign drug. It's not included in the war on drugs. This clearly demonstrates that the most popular drug is also an incredibly dangerous drug."

PREMATURE PLEASURE

Sandra Brown's research team is also using a brain imaging technique called functional magnetic resonance imaging to compare the brain function of alcohol abusers and nondrinkers. Initial results show that the brains of young adults with a history of alcohol dependence are less active than those of nondrinkers during tasks that require spatial working memory, such as being able to remember the location of your car in a large parking garage. In addition, the adolescent drinkers seem to exhibit greater levels of brain activity when they are exposed to alcohol-related stimuli. For instance, when the drinkers read words such as *wasted* or *tequila* on a screen, the nucleus accumbens—a small section of the brain associated with craving—lights up.

The nucleus accumbens is integral to the brain's so-called pleasure circuit, which scientists now believe also undergoes major remodeling during adolescence. Underlying the pleasure circuit is the neurotransmitter dopamine, a natural chemical in the brain. Sex, food, and many drugs, including alcohol, can all induce the release of dopamine, which creates feelings of pleasure and in turn encourages repetition of the original behavior.

During adolescence, the balance of dopamine activity temporarily shifts away from the nucleus accumbens, the brain's key pleasure and reward center, to the prefrontal cortex. Linda Spear, a developmental psychobiologist at Binghamton University in New York, speculates that as a result of this shift in balance, adolescents may find drugs less rewarding than they would earlier or later in life. And if the drugs produce less of a kick, more would be needed to get the same effect. "In the case of alcohol, this may lead to binge drinking," she said.

CAN *the* BRAIN BOUNCE BACK?

In adult alcoholics, some alcohol-related brain damage will reverse with abstinence and time. For example, at least some lost brain volume will be restored. Also, one study found that cognitively impaired alcoholic patients use different brain pathways than unimpaired patients to complete the same mental tasks. In essence, the brain rerouted its mental traffic from damaged routes to routes that had previously been reserved for other tasks. This resilience offers hope, but no one knows whether damage done by alcohol to the adolescent brain can be overcome in the same way. Damage from alcohol could arrest the teenage brain's development and lock in adolescent patterns of brain functioning.

To test this possibility, Swartzwelder and White recently conducted another test with rats. Adolescents—rats *and* humans—suffer less immediate motor impairment during a drinking session than do adults. In other words, adolescents must drink more than adults to lose their balance and fall over. As both people and rats age, however, they become more susceptible to alcohol-induced motor impairment. The experiment found that repeated bingeing by young rats locked in the adolescent pattern of motor-control response to alcohol. Even after reaching adulthood, the rats that binged in their youth remained less affected by alcohol in their motor responses.

This suggests that other neural circuitry may also become frozen in time as a result of heavy alcohol use while young.

YOUNG AND ADDICTED

As we have seen, alcohol changes the brain in many ways. It can even cause changes that discourage one from stopping drinking. For example, repeated alcohol use makes it harder for an individual to learn new ways of doing things, rather than repeating the same actions over and over again. In short, it becomes increasingly difficult to stop reaching for beer after beer after beer.

Alcohol works these changes through altering our brain chemistry. Alcoholism, or alcohol dependence, is not a result of moral weakness; it is a physiological addiction and a disease that if left unchecked will get progressively worse. Individuals may be genetically predisposed to alcoholism, but if anyone puts enough alcohol into his or her brain over a long enough time, he or she will become physically dependent on the drug.

The essence of addiction is an inability to stop taking a drug regardless of its consequences. A student could be flunking out of school, ruining friendships, spending money needed for books and food on alcohol instead, and still continue drinking. The alcoholic knows he is hurting himself and others but cannot stop, even when he tries. The condition generally includes four symptoms:

• *Craving:* a strong need, or compulsion, to drink.

• *Impaired control:* the inability to limit one's drinking on any given occasion.

• *Physical dependence:* withdrawal symptoms, such as nausea, sweating, shakiness, and anxiety, when alcohol use is stopped after a period of heavy drinking.

• *Tolerance:* the need for increasing amounts of alcohol in order to feel its effects.

About 6 percent of the students in our survey—and one in every five frequent binge drinkers—can be diagnosed as alcohol dependent. Alcohol dependence is a chronic and often progressive disease that runs a generally predictable course with recognizable symptoms. About 31 percent of students can be diagnosed as alcohol abusers. Alcohol abuse is a harmful drinking pattern that continues despite having persistent social or interpersonal problems caused or exacerbated by the effects of alcohol use. Students who were frequent binge drinkers were eighteen times more likely to be impaired than drinkers who didn't binge.

Some students know they have a problem but don't know where to go for help or what to do. Many more students are aware of friends with alcohol problems. One Cornell student described alcohol this way: "It's insidious and it sneaks up on people. My understanding is colored by the fact that my father drinks too much, and he started doing so in college." A student from Dartmouth reflected, "It's very sad to think that you became an alcoholic because you went to college."

We know that the younger a person is when he starts to drink, the more likely he is to experience a range of problems, including alcohol dependence, later in life. A study by the National Epidemiologic Survey found that approximately 40 percent of the drinkers who got started before age fifteen were classified later in life as alcohol dependent, compared to only 10 percent of those who began drinking at age twenty-one or twenty-two. Overall, beginning at age fifteen, the risk of future alcohol dependence decreased by 14 percent with each passing year of abstention.

When college administrations, parents, or students accept underage drinking as a fact of life, they are paving the road to futures of ongoing alcohol problems and possibly compromised intellectual ability. When the alcohol industry argues that alcohol is not a drug and fights for its right to advertise on campus and promote cheap drink specials, it is ensuring a steady supply of future customers—the most loyal of whom will be addicts.

While recovery from alcoholism is possible—and treatment must be made available to young people who have already developed alcohol problems—only changing the college drinking environment will prevent large numbers of students from sacrificing their potential to the beer or liquor bottle.

CHAPTER 9

BAD BEHAVIOR
UNDER THE INFLUENCE

We know that decent, bright, young people do dumb
and even dangerous things when they drink to excess.
—Gregory C. Farrington, president of Lehigh University, in a letter to parents

As a resident advisor at her Ivy League school, Whitney commonly heard students complain of other students wandering into their rooms drunk in the middle of the night. Then, in an act of drunken vandalism, a men's bathroom in her dorm was turned into a disgusting mess. "There was feces involved, paper towels, just about every liquid you can imagine, and it was just torn up," she recalled. "People couldn't go in there. I was extremely disturbed."

This kind of behavior—a secondhand effect of binge drinking—is just as bad as secondhand smoke. Considering the injuries and deaths caused by heavy drinking, its economic costs, and the profound effect on the quality of campus life, the losses caused by binge drinking on our college campuses are staggering.

Over the years, our College Alcohol Study has documented the fact that the more students drink, the more problems they themselves will experience and the more problems they are likely to cause. Binge drinkers are more prone to fall behind in their schoolwork, get hurt, and damage property than non-binge drinkers. They are also far more likely to drive drunk, threatening both themselves and the general population. (About 57 percent of frequent binge drinkers, 40 percent of occasional binge drinkers, and 19 percent of non-binge drinkers reported that they drove after drinking.) Further, about 159,000 freshmen drop out of college every year for alcohol- or drug-related reasons, according to the Core Institute, a nonprofit group that gathers information on college drinking and drug practices. Clearly, alcohol abuse is costly to students as well as to the communities surrounding colleges.

One estimate of the economic cost of alcohol abuse in the United

PROBLEMS FOR STUDENTS WHO DRINK

Alcohol-Related Problem	% Drink, but Don't Binge	% Occasional Binger	% Frequent Binger
Miss a class	9	30	60
Get behind in school work	9	21	42
Do something you regret	17	37	62
Forget where you were or what you did	10	26	54
Argue with friends	10	22	43
Engage in unplanned sexual activities	9	22	41
Not use protection when you have sex	4	10	21
Damage property	3	10	24
Get into trouble with campus or local police	2	6	14
Get hurt or injured	4	12	28
Require medical treatment for overdose	1	0	2
Drive after drinking	18	40	58
Experience 5 or more of the alcohol-related problems above	4	16	48

States puts the figure at $167 billion in 1995, which was higher than the cost of smoking ($138 billion) or of drug abuse ($110 billion). The estimated cost of all underage drinking is about $53 billion a year. This includes costs associated with serious social and health problems such as crime, traumatic injury, suicide, fetal alcohol syndrome, alcohol poisoning, and treatment for alcohol dependence and abuse. The largest cost, some $19 billion, is associated with traffic crashes.

While it might be possible, if inexact, to assign a dollar amount to the physical damage caused by those who abuse alcohol on today's college campuses, there is no way to measure the emotional suffering. One need only to talk to the parent of a child who has died or been seriously injured due to alcohol to realize this. And while death, rape, and assault may be the most violent outcomes of binge drinking, they are only the tip of the iceberg. Many lesser insults and injuries, ubiquitous as they are, tend to fade into the background hubbub of life, often failing to elicit more than a shrug. Yet these secondhand effects of college binge drinking extend into every aspect of life, affecting drinkers and nondrinkers alike.

COLLATERAL DAMAGE

Like the suffering caused by secondhand smoke from cigarettes, the secondhand effects of binge drinking range from annoying to severe. Nationally, about 61 percent of students who reside on campus and don't binge drink say they have had study or sleep time interrupted, 50 percent say they have had to take care of a drunken student, and 29 percent say they have been insulted or humiliated by a drunken student. Alcohol has also been determined to be involved in more

SECONDHAND EFFECTS OF BINGE DRINKING ON CAMPUS

Percentages of non-binge drinkers living on campus who experience these secondhand effects at low-binge campuses (less than 37 percent of students binge drink) and high-binge campuses (more than 50 percent binge drink).

Problem	% Low-Binge	% High-Binge
Been insulted or humiliated	21	36
Had a serious argument	14	23
Been pushed, hit, or assaulted	6	11
Had property damaged	7	16
Had to take care of a drunk student	37	57
Had studying/sleeping interrupted	43	71
Experienced an unwanted sexual advance	15	23
Been a victim of sexual assault or date rape	.6	1
Experienced at least one of the above problems	64	86

than half of all campus crime. It's a simple equation: The lower the price of beer, the more students get in trouble with the police, damage property, argue, and fight. The price of alcohol affects violence because it affects the amount of alcohol that students consume. The cheaper the beer, the more students drink, and the more violence occurs.

AGGRESSION *and* VIOLENCE

In our survey, a large proportion of college students have reported being victimized by intoxicated individuals. Heavy drinkers were themselves more likely to be victimized by a fellow intoxicated student. Similarly, at high-binge schools—which we define as a school where more than 50 percent of the student body binge drinks—86 percent of college administrators said that sexual assault was a problem on their campuses; 61 percent said that physical assaults were a problem, and 53 percent noted a problem with damage to campus property.

"So far this year I've had my bike broken because of a drunken brawl between my roommates. My door was kicked in, and the bar in my closet broke because one of them fell on it. The funny thing is that this doesn't seem to bother them," wrote one college student answering our survey.

Although student violence is often accompanied by alcohol, no one is certain exactly how the two are linked. A common theory holds that alcohol drowns inhibitions, increases excitability, and boosts courage. That was certainly Alex's feeling after he had downed a few:

> There were a lot of fights in the fraternities, serious arguments where people were holding me back, or they were holding the other person back. Alcohol enhances your sense of strength; you think you can beat anyone up. It makes you feel okay to say things that you probably haven't thought through.

Alcohol may also affect the brain in such a way that it reduces a person's ability to reason abstractly or to psychologically cope with different situations. In narrowing a person's perceptions, it paves the way to misinterpretation of other people's words and actions, sometimes prompting violent reactions. Evidence also exists for alcohol-induced chemical changes in the brain that encourage violence, particularly in men. These changes can increase the amount of testosterone, which increases aggression, and reduce the amount of serotonin, which lowers inhibitions.

Expectation may also play a role. That is, if a student believes that alcohol leads to aggression and then consumes alcohol, he might be more likely to act aggressively. Regardless of the precise underlying psychological and physiological changes that occur, it is clear that increased aggression is often alcohol's companion. A study sponsored by the National Institute on Alcohol Abuse and Alcoholism determined that more than six hundred thousand students were hit or assaulted by another student who was drinking.

Testing Aggression

One way that researchers have investigated the relationship between alcohol and aggression in college students is through an experiment known as TAP: the Taylor Aggression Paradigm.

In these experiments students compete against a fictitious opponent on a mock reaction-time (RT) task. Prior to each RT trial, student participants select one of ten shock intensities that they wish to inflict on their opponent. An RT trial then follows. If the subject wins the trial, his/her opponent ostensibly receives the selected shock. If the subject loses the trial, s/he receives a shock. Although in reality no opponent exists, subjects can receive both high- and low-intensity shocks.

To measure aggressive behavior, TAP averages the shock intensity and duration that subjects select during the trials. To assess the effects of alcohol on this behavior, researchers compare the shock intensities selected by both intoxicated and sober persons.

Intoxicated students typically administer shocks of higher intensity and duration than do sober students. The studies support the contention that acute alcohol intoxication facilitates aggressive behavior in college students.

HATE CRIMES

The combination of alcohol and aggression can inflame underlying tensions, including racial hostility, on college campuses. One African-American graduate of an elite Eastern university recalled that when alcohol was involved,

> A lot of racial stuff would come up. As an amateur anthropologist, I would find that fascinating. Sometimes I wouldn't drink at parties, because I wanted to be sober so I could hear what people were saying to me. People who were drunk would state long-held stereotypes or ask pent-up questions that clearly demonstrated a lack of any cultural sensitivity. That points more toward some national problems that have nothing to do with alcohol, but alcohol certainly brings them to the surface.

Anecdotal evidence demonstrates some of the links between alcohol and racial hostility. For instance, in September 2000 several white fraternity students beat up African-American student Atuanya Priester, a freshman at Washington State University who had recently pledged a rival fraternity. The night of the attack he was celebrating his eighteenth birthday. Witness reports by the Associated Press and in the *Seattle Times* stated that many of the people involved, including Priester, had been drinking. The first blow knocked a tooth out of his jaw and splintered two others.

Several days later the group Black Men Making a Difference staged a peaceful demonstration in front of Priester's fraternity, alleging racism. The fraternities involved later issued a news release denying that there were racial overtones to the attack. The university, however, felt compelled to sponsor a forum on campus safety and cultural diversity. President V. Lane Rawlins formed the Council on Campus Climate to study racism, violence, and intolerance at the university, where 496 members of the 18,000-member student population are African American.

Similarly, alcohol played a role in a hate crime at Georgetown University in 1999. A student who vandalized an outdoor display of a Jewish menorah said later that he was drunk at the time. Currently we do not know what proportion of hate crimes, on and off campus, are fueled by alcohol, but it is clear that alcohol has facilitated many destructive actions that sobriety might have discouraged.

BAD NEIGHBORHOODS

Students are not the only ones subjected to the secondhand effects of binge drinking. From the East Coast to the West, neighborhoods with large student populations often live daily with the noise, garbage, and human waste generated by drunken students.

In our survey of twenty-three hundred household residents we found that neighbors living near college campuses were more likely to report a lowered quality of neighborhood life through such secondhand effects of heavy alcohol use as noise and disturbances, vandalism, drunkenness, vomiting, and urination. Neighbors of high-binge colleges were much more likely to experience these secondhand effects.

Robert lives in a once-stately neighborhood next to a university in Nevada. "The street parties become wilder each year," he said. "Neighbors who complain to police find their car windows broken, trucks driven into their front yards, beer bottles thrown at houses, people—both men and women—urinating in their yards." Today about a half-dozen fraternities and sororities own homes in the neighborhood, and many others have been converted into student rentals. Street parties of six hundred-plus students are common. When Robert organized a community meeting to discuss the problems, about seventy neighbors showed up. One older woman brought a box of underwear—panties, bras, and men's shorts—she had picked up in her yard after all-night parties. "The university ignores the problem and ignores the people who live around the school whose lives are so disrupted by this negative behavior," Robert said. "Between the local neighborhood bars and city casinos, alcohol is available twenty-four/seven, no questions asked."

RIOTS *and* ARSON

Such situations are not uncommon in the communities surrounding colleges, and the mischief and violence take on many variations. From impromptu acts of vandalism and arson to spontaneous student riots, the bad behavior of students immersed in a culture of binge drinking has taken on a more aggressive and destructive edge recently, as college street parties across the nation have spun out of control:

• **Washington State University, May 1998.** In a five-hour rampage in College Hill, the neighborhood that houses Greek Row, students, angry at a new policy banning alcohol at fraternity social functions, threw beer cans and rocks at police officers. Police used tear gas in response; at least twenty-four officers were injured, and three people were arrested. In the first month of the 2000 school year, police reports of alcohol-related violence jumped more than 100 percent from the same period the previous year in the College Hill and Campus Commons neighborhoods.

• **Pennsylvania State University, July 1998.** Students caused fifty thousand dollars in damage to cars, storefronts, and street lamps during an alcohol-induced riot. The two-and-a-half-hour disturbance grew to a crowd of fifteen hundred shortly after bars announced last call. The crowd moved along a main avenue near campus and near high-rise apartments that house students; fourteen police officers were injured.

• **Kent State University, May 2001.** Block parties on two successive nights led to seventy-seven arrests. On the second evening, some two thousand revelers at a parking lot barbecue set a couch and car ablaze.

• **University of Utah, December 2001.** Neighbors living alongside fraternity and sorority houses met with the mayor of Salt Lake City in December 2001 to search for ways to contain the lewdness and raucous behavior associated with alcohol abuse.

The unpredictable consequences of such events ended with the suicide of one student at the University of Northern Colorado. One night in April 2000, police estimate that a thousand people attended various street parties. The drunken energy coalesced into a riot, as students and others hurled rocks and bottles at police and set fires in the streets. Police responded with rubber bullets and teargas.

In the aftermath, videotapes shot by neighbors helped police identify thirty people for arrest. One was college sophomore Kurt Pydyszewski, charged with second-degree arson for tossing a couch into a bonfire and inciting a riot. He had been arrested several days earlier for suspicion of drunk driving. The new felony charge meant the twenty-year-old possibly faced four years in jail. Several weeks after his arrest, Pydyszewski returned to his parent's home in Denver. There, he killed himself with a single shot to his head.

Said one senior at another school:

I think people don't realize the importance of the problem of extreme drinking unless they've witnessed something that's significant—knowing someone who died, a car accident, or having a friend who is date-raped. Once you do experience it, that changes you forever. So often, things do happen and nobody talks about them. If people get out there and talk about it more, maybe things would change.

TAKING BACK *the* NEIGHBORHOOD

People living near high-binge student housing and some university administrators *are* talking more. And they are acting. The University of Washington is buying up problem properties in the Capitol Hill neighborhood and creating low-interest loans to encourage families to recolonize the neighborhood, which had been taken over by Greek houses in recent years.

In neighborhoods near the University of Delaware, community members, local government leaders, students, and university administrators formed a neighborhood campaign to curb excessive drinking. When the campaign was launched in September 2001, students were in their second week of the semester, and one had already hurled an empty quarter-keg through the front door of an apartment building. The previous year, the same apartment complex had replaced about a dozen glass front doors and moved mailboxes indoors after students had ripped up outdoor mailboxes bolted into the cement. As part of the campaign, the Delaware Undergraduate Student Congress is encouraging off-campus students to have safe and responsible parties, and the police chief has announced a zero-tolerance policy for noise violations. Campaign members say they are not against partying but against the kind of irresponsible drinking that disturbs the peace and damages property.

ALCOHOL
AND OTHER DRUGS

Besides the antisocial behavior that it alone promotes, binge drinking is also associated with an increased likelihood that students will use other controlled substances. College binge drinkers are far more likely to smoke cigarettes, smoke marijuana, and do other illegal drugs.

In our study about 53 percent of frequent binge drinkers reported smoking cigarettes in the past thirty days, compared to 15 percent of non-binge drinkers. A recent study in *Alcoholism: Clinical and Experimental Research* sheds light on the relationship between heavy drinking and smoking, which often go hand in hand. The study, conducted on rats, found that nicotine appears to blunt the effects of alcohol, which may lead people to drink more in order to feel alcohol's intoxicating effects. The study found that when rats were given nicotine and alcohol together, their blood-alcohol levels remained lower than when they took alcohol alone.

Less is known about why binge drinkers are more likely to do other drugs. Nonetheless, our surveys show that 62 percent of frequent bingers used marijuana in the past year, compared to 20 percent of non-binge drinkers; and 10 percent used cocaine, compared to 1 percent of non-binge drinkers. A similar pattern is true for ecstasy (18 percent of frequent binge drinkers used it in the past year, compared to 3 percent of non-binge drinkers) and other illegal drugs.

People who drink and use drugs both are likely to have and cause more serious problems. Sometimes the combination proves lethal. For example, in September 2001 Soraya Ali-Omar, a member of the California State University, Chico, sorority Kappa Sigma Delta, died of a probable overdose of GHB and alcohol, according to the Associated Press. Experts describe GHB, gamma hydroxy butyrate, as a form of degreasing solvent mixed with drain cleaner. It produces a euphoric high and has become a so-called club drug of choice for some teens and college students. Also known as the date-rape drug, slipped into a drink it can quickly incapacitate the drinker, leaving her vulnerable to sexual assault. Alcohol exacerbates the effects of GHB, which in a large enough dose can shut down the respiratory system.

SECOND *to* NONE

Alcohol, and beer in particular, is clearly the college student's drug of choice, the substance most often abused on campus and in the community. Yet many parents are more concerned about illegal drugs *other than alcohol*—which *is* illegal for the vast majority of college students to consume because of their age. Although using any illegal drug can be dangerous, the dangers of drinking alcohol tend to be minimized when viewed in the shadow of such infamous substances as cocaine or heroin. In fact, a study by researchers at the University of California, Riverside, showed that in general alcohol is far more likely to be linked to violent behaviors than heroin, cocaine, or PCP.

In our 1999 survey less than 1 percent of students reported having used crack cocaine, heroin, or LSD in the previous thirty days. Less than 2 percent reported using barbiturates, amphetamines, tranquilizers, PCP, or cocaine other than crack. Roughly 5 percent reported having used any of these illicit drugs ever. About 27 percent reported smoking marijuana, and 29 percent had smoked cigarettes. In contrast, 68 percent of students consumed any alcohol, and 44 percent binge drank in the previous two weeks.

Although alcohol use dwarfs the use of other drugs on college campuses and causes far more harm to students and their neighbors, the federal government excludes alcohol from its well-publicized war against drugs. The alcohol industry lobbied for this exclusion, and it has the effect of legitimizing alcohol abuse, even among underage students. Furthermore, it reinforces the idea that alcohol is a benign substance.

But alcoholic beverages are not benign. They are mind-altering, addictive drugs that have the ready potential to do violence to body, brain, spirit, and community. Hence the status of alcohol misuse as the number-one public health problem on America's college campuses.

HOW SAFE IS YOUR CAMPUS?

One way to get a sense of how safe students are at specific schools from the secondhand effects of college binge drinking is through the U.S. Department of Education's national collection of campus crime statistics. First published in 1999, these statistics are now gathered annually as a result of the Clery Act.

The Clery Act, originally called the Campus Security Act, resulted from the crusade of Howard Clery and his wife, Connie, after their nineteen-year-old daughter, Jeanne, was raped and murdered by a fellow student at Lehigh University in Bethlehem, Pennsylvania, in 1986. The Clerys founded an organization that ultimately convinced Congress to take action. The Clery Act requires colleges and universities to report crimes on and around campus and allows colleges to be fined $25,000 for each misreport. The 2000 report documented 42,455 arrests for liquor-law violations and 124,673 disciplinary referrals.

To find statistics on a specific school, go to the U.S. Department of Education Office of Postsecondary Education (OPE) Web site on campus security at http://ope.ed.gov/security. On the site you can search campus security statistics for more than six thousand U.S. colleges and universities. You can search by geographic region, state, city, type of institution, instructional program, student enrollment, and/or by the name of the institution. If more information is desired for a particular institution, the Web site provides contact information for security officers and personnel.

As you peruse the site, keep in mind that even under threat of fines, not all campus crime gets reported. The Department of Education Web site itself notes, "The statistics represent *alleged* criminal offenses *reported* to campus security authorities or local police agencies." In fact, *USA Today* reported that when the government's general accounting office audited twenty-five colleges in 1997, it found that twenty-three of them had failed to properly report their crime statistics, particularly incidents involving assaults and rapes.

Crimes of rape are frequently underreported by campus administrations. An in-depth study by journalists at the *Sacramento Bee* found that nearly two-thirds of the University of California's nine campuses omit sexual assaults reported to university sources other than police when they compile their annual crime statistics. Some campuses miscategorize sexual assault cases under the broad heading of "physical abuse." In 1998, the nine UC campuses reported 60 forcible sex offenses, including rapes. The *Bee* found at least 190 cases of rape and forcible sex offenses reported to officials other than campus police.

This last figure alone is a strong reason to take seriously the problem of binge drinking on our college campuses. Alcohol consumption facilitates violence against women, and the youngest college women—seventeen- and eighteen-year-old freshmen—face the highest risk. Knowing that even nondrinkers are likely to be affected by the drinking scene, we urge parents to talk to their sons or daughters before they arrive at school to prepare them for what they might find.

CHAPTER 10

COLLEGE WOMEN, SEX, AND ALCOHOL

*At the beginning of the school year, I drank way too much at a sorority/
fraternity football tailgate. I blacked out on my way home (by myself).
I don't remember my walk home or anything occurring afterwards. I have
dysthymia, and alcohol is a depressant. I tried to kill myself by overdosing
on Tylenol and Wellbutrin, apparently without any real cause. This is a
decision I know I never would have made had I been sober. I ended up in
the hospital for three days. I am an A/B student, so to speak, but because
of the basically inherent complexity regarding the aforementioned event,
I began failing most of my classes and withdrew my semester.*
—Terri, a student from the CAS survey

In November 1999 two freshman athletes at a Midwestern college
were expelled from school after being charged with rape. The two
had videotaped themselves sexually assaulting an unconscious
woman. The victim, an eighteen-year-old student from a neighboring university, was visiting friends in an off-campus apartment
and had been drinking heavily before she passed out and was assaulted. Other students reported the videotape to college officials; it
was seized and charges were filed. In her affidavit the young woman
said that she had been unaware of what happened until another student told her that he had seen the videotape.

Nearly every college woman has either experienced, or knows
somebody who has experienced, unwanted sex associated with alcohol consumption. The American Medical Association reports that
one out of every four college-age women is a victim of rape. Other

experts say that as few as 10 percent of rape victims report the crime. A study by Mary Koss at the University of Arizona found that 74 percent of perpetrators and 55 percent of victims of sexual assaults on college campuses had been drinking.

Clearly, binge drinking is a women's health issue. It can affect a woman's physical, sexual, and emotional health more immediately and profoundly than a man's. Female students not only face all the common alcohol-related problems that plague males but also the more a woman drinks, the higher her risk for sexual abuse and assault. Our surveys show that about 10 percent of female students who are frequent binge drinkers reported being raped or subjected to nonconsensual sex during the school year. Younger women, who are likely to be less experienced with heavy drinking and with sex, are at particular risk.

Acknowledging this connection is not blaming the victim. There is never an excuse for sexual assault. But it is essential to educate women about how to look out for their own interests. Young women need to be aware of themselves and their environment; they need to respect the integrity of their sexual desire and understand the ways in which alcohol can disempower, even while it appears to be a normal, harmless, and fun part of college life. Said one female student, "If you're a woman and you're drinking, you're putting yourself out there."

COED SEXUALITY

College students, women and men both, may experiment with alcohol as well as with sexuality. Such experimentation can be seen as part of the process of personal development that often begins before college. One study reports that 75 percent of boys and 60 percent of girls have had sex by the time they graduate from high school, and the majority of those who have not already will have their first sexual experience while in college. What makes the college atmosphere particularly risky to women is the pervasive practice of binge drinking. The regular and excessive use of alcohol to facilitate sociability and sex among both women and men leads to a broad range of problems. The more alcohol available, the higher the risk and the graver the dangers.

Giselle, now a graduate student at Cornell University, recalled her undergraduate experience:

> There are so many incidences of women giving in to things that they wouldn't normally have. From personal experience, after drinking I often decided that I wouldn't mind if he touched me here, that that would be okay. I know that afterward I would feel like I had given in. This is not something women even say very much to each other. Personally, it was not good for my self-esteem.

Women who drink to loosen up socially or to facilitate sex often learn too late that one drink can lead to another, and they may end up consuming much more than they need just to loosen up. "It's happened to me and my friends," said Joy. "When you take just a few shots, it takes twenty minutes to hit you. You don't realize it; you take a few more. When you go out, you keep drinking, and when you're really drunk, you don't realize it." At some point in this continuum, often sooner rather than later, alcohol will seriously affect the student's judgment—and her ability to defend herself.

Lillian recalled the experience of a friend:

> When Jill was a freshman, she met this guy at a party. He was a senior on a football team. He had a girlfriend that he had been with for a couple of years, but it didn't matter. My friend ended up

going home with him, and they had sex. She has this really big chest. He thought this was awesome. He was drunk so he didn't realize what he was doing. Her chest was literally black and blue. She ended up showing us. She was black and blue for days and telling everyone about it. They were both drunk. It became this big saga. She always talked about it. She did the walk of shame home, and he didn't talk to her again.

The "walk of shame" takes place on nearly every campus. Said Lillian: "It's everywhere. After you've gotten totally drunk and go back to some guy's house and the next morning you wear his shirt over your pants. It's the walk of shame, you have to walk across campus hungover." Although men—and women—may boast about their exploits, what they feel inside might be quite different; they may feel hurt, angry, or confused, wondering if they'll ever see their partner again. Intoxication may enable all parties involved to rationalize the events as consensual, but in fact an intoxicated person is not able to give consent. The situation may be complicated if a female appears to initiate sex. Rapes committed under the influence of alcohol typically turn into he-said she-said cases in court.

When a woman "gives in" while under the influence of alcohol, it can lead to a vicious cycle: Alcohol can temporarily reduce the physical and emotional pain caused by such experiences, but a woman who gets into a pattern of self-medicating her feelings is a woman at risk for revictimization.

LOOSENING INHIBITIONS

Women do a lot of things to try to feel better about themselves, and the message implicit in much alcohol advertising is that drinking will not only make you feel better, but it will make sex better, said

Sharon Wilsnack, a psychologist at the University of North Dakota School of Medicine and Health Sciences. Wilsnack launched a national study of women's drinking in 1981. Every five years she interviews the original group included in the study, and every ten years she adds another several hundred women, many of them college students.

Many of the women in the study say that they drink because alcohol reduces sexual inhibitions. Wilsnack recalled one sorority member who told her, "We're in college, we're high-achieving young women, and we're supposed to be liberated, modern, and comfortable with ourselves sexually. But many of us have inhibitions. If I'm in a situation where I want to be sexual, I drink intentionally to loosen up."

If women—or men—get into the habit of only feeling good sexually when they drink alcohol, they risk becoming alcohol dependent. And, further, if drinking to facilitate sex becomes a pattern, it will be that much harder to cut back on or give up drinking. Wilsnack witnessed this tendency in her previous clinical work with older alcoholic women. A large number of women, especially those with sexual difficulties, equated stopping drinking with stopping being sexual. "The more young women come to rely on alcohol for sex, the greater the risk of becoming an alcoholic," Wilsnack said.

BLIND DRUNK *to* BODY IMAGE

Much of the advertising aimed at seducing Generation Next invokes an idealized sexual partner whose body type is invariably thin, tall, and big breasted. This stereotype has particular implications for college women, whose drinking habits often are tied to body image. Richard Keeling, M.D., editor of the *Journal of American College Health* and former director of health services at the University of Virginia and the University of Wisconsin-Madison, said that there are important relationships between binge drinking and certain patterns of abnormal eating and food preoccupation for female college students. Both binge drinking and certain eating disorders have impulsive characteristics and seem to be related behaviorally.

"For women very worried about body image, being drunk is one of the few times they're not looking in the mirror," Keeling said. And many college women are desperately concerned with body image. At any given time, 25 percent to 30 percent of female students meet the diagnostic criteria for "eating disorder not otherwise specified," in which they obsess about the details of calories and fat and monitor their appearance. Another 3 percent to 6 percent have a true eating disorder such as anorexia or bulimia. "When college women have abnormal patterns of eating, they often also have problems with alcohol," Keeling said. Not all groups of women have the same level of problems, and race is an important factor. African-American women, for example, have lower rates of binge drinking and of body dissatisfaction and eating disorders than do white women.

Joy, a freshman at a large public university, said, "Everyone's concerned they're going to gain weight. My girlfriends and I watch how many times we order in food late, because you're not going to be doing anything after you eat, and nothing is going to be burned." This is a reasonable practice; but women who are overly concerned about their body image might choose to skip eating when they know they are going to drink—for fear that the calories in the food will make them gain weight—and that will only increase the effects of the alcohol.

Many college freshmen do gain weight, and although the gain itself poses no health risks, it may cause depression, which in turn can lead to increased drinking as a form of self-medication. Lily, a freshman at a college in Ohio, observed that

Some freshmen gain weight from all the drinking they do that they're not used to. I know someone from high school who has gained twenty pounds already—now her self-esteem is down. People start eating and drinking more because they're sad and depressed about changing location. Alcohol is supposed to kill your brain cells or something, I don't know what. The people at my school who like to drink a lot, do drink a lot.

Some mothers who are concerned about the drinking of their college daughters mistakenly urge them to think about the calories. In light of the strong connection between binge drinking and eating disorders, this is probably not the best way to try to dissuade young women from drinking, as it may inadvertently fuel problems with body image.

SELF-MEDICATION *and* ADDED RISK

"Alcohol for almost everybody is a form of self-medication," Keeling said. "The college guy who gets drunk so he won't feel funny about approaching a woman is self-medicating." Gay and lesbian students may also self-medicate with alcohol. "Gay men have more significant drinking problems than do straight students, in direct proportion to their comfort with their sexuality," said Keeling. So, while gay men who are comfortable with their sexuality have no more problems with alcohol than non-gay students, those who are struggling with their sexuality are more likely to problem drink. "Gay men who are just coming out or confronting homophobia may drink to reduce their own discomfort and relieve anxiety," Keeling said.

Ironically, those who drink to feel better about themselves are often putting themselves at greater risk. Our surveys show that alcohol consumption increases the incidence of risky sexual practices such as using no reliable form of protection; having multiple partners; having risky, casual, or unknown partners; and engaging in risky sex acts such as unprotected anal intercourse. For instance, in our 2001 survey we found that 41 percent of frequent binge drinkers had unplanned sex, and 21 percent had unsafe sex as a result of their drinking in the past year.

Despite all this risk the majority of students failed to protect against both sexually transmitted diseases (STDs) and pregnancy: 12 percent of sexually experienced college students reported having been diagnosed by a doctor at least once with an STD; one in five female students reported having been pregnant; and one in ten male college students reported having gotten a partner pregnant.

Similarly, a survey of thirteen- to nineteen-year-olds found that 36 percent had consumed alcohol prior to intercourse at least once in the past six months, and a study of British college students found that the percentage who had unprotected sex with a stranger rose from 4 percent among nondrinkers to 27 percent among heavy drinkers. Obviously, such practices increase the risk of contracting AIDS. In nearly all studies of STDs, rates are higher, in some cases nearly twice as high, among women than men.

Another serious risk to college women involving sex and alcohol are the so-called date-rape drugs, including Rohypnol (commonly called roofies) and GHB (gamma hydroxy butyrate). A mere two milligrams-worth of roofies that dissolves in a drink can quickly sedate the drinker; combined with alcohol it can cause a serious overdose. GHB is most often available as an odorless and colorless liquid. Such date-rape drugs can be used to incapacitate women prior to sexual assault. Although there is widespread fear of their use, no data exists that accurately documents the extent of their predatory use. Many college women have grown wary of consuming drinks that have been out of their sight or drinking from an open punch bowl. Although such precautions may be wise, it is all too easy to forget that alcohol itself is the main date-rape drug, implicated in more rapes than all the specialized rape drugs combined.

THE FRATERNITY FACTOR

One factor that greatly influences student drinking habits and that has a measurable impact on campus safety, especially for women, is the presence or absence of fraternities. While we have already looked at the ways in which the Greek system promotes alcohol abuse on campus in general, fraternities and sororities are also notorious for promoting a "hook up" culture in which the combination of alcohol and sex often leads to various levels of sexual abuse.

For one thing, in the raucous world of frat parties the playing field is rarely equal. Alcohol allows the exercise of power differences, both physical and social, especially between young female students and the older "brothers" who may try to take advantage of their status in the party-culture pecking order. In fact, our survey found that while most fraternity men have been binge drinking since their high school days, most sorority women are less experienced, only beginning to drink this way in college. Alcohol becomes part of a rite of passage in which he is older and wiser—and wilder—and she is less-old, less-wise, and available for either seduction or assault.

Frat brother Clay gave us a glimpse behind closed doors:

> One time, when I was a junior, we had a party at my [fraternity] house. It was prospective-student weekend, so high school seniors were coming in to look at school—fresh meat. My roommate was dating a woman who was attracted to me. She was hosting a

prospective student and they both came over. I drank a little, then went upstairs. They kept drinking downstairs, and a little later the two girls came up just plowed and started dancing in my room, taking their clothes off, and jumped in bed for a threesome. It wasn't your every weekend occurrence, but certainly not that far-fetched either.

Another scenario involved a seventeen-year-old who attended a soccer camp at a university in Maine prior to the start of her freshman classes in the summer of 1997. One night during the camp she partied at a fraternity where she met a young man who walked her back to her dormitory room. After she thought he had gone, she propped open her door for fresh air. He returned, entered her room, and sexually assaulted her. Later court depositions described the young woman as "devastated."

Further evidence of the negative influence of frat life on college women can be found at women's colleges—where there are no fraternities. Here there is less alcohol abuse than at coeducational institutions: Only about one in nine women at women's colleges are frequent binge drinkers, compared to one in five at coed colleges. Students at women's colleges have fewer alcohol-related problems, experience fewer negative effects from other students' drinking, and are less likely to combine drinking and driving than are women at coed colleges.

This difference can be explained partly by the simple fact that a higher percentage of students who choose to go to women's colleges do not binge drink in high school. But other factors also play a role. Women's colleges tend to have more female faculty and administrators, providing a larger pool of role models and mentors. They offer more opportunities for women to assume leadership roles, as women don't have to compete with men for participation in the classroom and in social organizations. All of these factors can build women's self-esteem and encourage healthy choices when it comes to alcohol. None of these factors apply to the party atmosphere fostered by most fraternities.

Unfortunately, changes may be occurring in these relatively protected environments. Our most recent College Alcohol Study revealed that while the difference between women's and coeducational colleges in binge drinking rates remains, it has diminished: Rates of drinking at women's colleges have increased sharply in just the last several years.

THE DARTMOUTH AFFAIR

A graphic example of the sexist and abusive attitudes that characterize much of male frat culture came to light at Dartmouth College in spring 2001, when the school newspaper, *The Dartmouth*, published a story about sexual muckraking in the *Zetemouth*, a newsletter published by the Zeta Psi fraternity.

But the story really began the previous summer, when sorority member Melissa Heaton was hanging out in the fraternity with a group of friends, drinking and joking around. "A brother who was very intoxicated showed me the *Zetemouth*. That was his first public mistake," Melissa told us. The brothers were supposed to destroy the newsletters, but Melissa's friend had saved them. He fished through a big pile to bring out the issue that mocked and libeled Melissa.

The *Zetemouth* chronicled the fraternity brothers' sex lives. Various issues included the names of Dartmouth women who would purportedly sleep with any man in the house. They included provocative photos of women the brothers claimed were their sex partners. The women were described as "loose," "dirty," "guaranteed hookups," and "sure things." There were lewd references to sexual acts between brothers and named female students. A "special" edition called the "Manwhore Edition" reported that a female student "strikes again": "She's dirtier than ever. . . . If young [name deleted] hooks up with one more Zete, I'm going to need a flow chart just to keep up." Another edition promised to deliver date-rape techniques in the future.

Melissa and her friends were hurt and outraged. She later told the *New York Post*, "It was the worst thing I ever read. I couldn't believe that these guys, who I thought were my friends, would stand around and talk about how fat—and what sluts—we all are."

Seeming to realize their mistake, the brothers promised Melissa and her friends that they would no longer print the newsletter. "But the following winter, halfway through the term, someone told me they were still making it," she recalled. While Melissa's friends urged her to approach the administration, she wanted proof before taking such a drastic step. "They share a dumpster with our sorority," she said. "And one night they threw their trash away." Melissa found a copy of the *Zetemouth*, and although she had to scrape vomit off to see the print underneath, what she read inside was enough to send her directly to the administration and the school newspaper with her story.

THE *MOUTH Is* SHUT

The day the story broke, about 250 students protested on the fraternity's lawn. Dartmouth president James Wright, meanwhile, responded in an open letter to the campus community: "Zeta Psi undermined fundamental values we hold dear. . . . When such conduct violates our standards, the college must take action."

On May 11, the college permanently "derecognized" Zeta Psi on campus.

Zeta Psi president Gene Boyle said that the college's action "was not justified on the merits. The penalty imposed was overly harsh and grossly disproportionate to the offenses charged." A later Zeta Psi statement said that the fraternity "did not threaten or harass any women" and insisted that the content of the *Zetemouth* was merely satire and humor.

Student responses, reported by both *The Dartmouth* and the *New York Post*, were mixed. While most female students were outraged, one student told the *Post*, "Personally, as a female, I wasn't offended. I know they didn't mean to hurt anyone." On the other hand, Tasha Francis, the president of the campus-wide sorority organization, the Panhellenic Council, said the college's sanctions against the fraternity were fair.

Male opinion was also divided, although the majority seemed to side with the fraternity. Some felt that the brothers had violated an unspoken pledge to keep offensive frat activities underground. "If it was just within their own house, I don't see any problem with that," said one fraternity member. "I guess I would do a little better job of keeping it out of peoples' hands." Some men, mostly non-Greek members, were critical of the fraternity. One told *The Dartmouth* that he was appalled. "I don't want to morally and financially support an institution that supports this kind of behavior." Another fraternity member said, "I don't think this is a problem only within the Greek system or at Dartmouth, but a societal problem as far as disrespect for women."

THE ROLE *of* ALCOHOL

Curiously lacking from the school paper coverage of these events was comment on the role of alcohol. Melissa Heaton, however, pointed out its subversive role: "In a social culture that values how much you can drink and how many women you can score with as the two things your masculinity can be judged upon, alcohol definitely plays a role. I'm not sure that this kind of thing wouldn't happen if there weren't alcohol present, but I'm not sure that the fraternity organization would be what it is if it wasn't based upon a drinking culture," she told us.

Yet, as seen in the varied student responses to the incident, the connection between alcohol and sexual behavior, including abuse, can be a confused one. The confusion arises from the intersection of an extremely effective and insidious drug and one of the most complex aspects of human development and life—sexuality. Add to that an industry that uses sex to sell alcohol and a population of young people eager to experiment, and the confusion is understandable. Nonetheless, on a day-to-day level, when bad things happen to female students they often involve alcohol—and shame and denial, by women as well as by men.

Dartmouth itself recognizes the role of alcohol in sexual abuse on the campus, where in 1998 roughly 48 percent of students surveyed said that they binge drank. According to the college's Sexual Abuse Awareness Program, in roughly 90 percent of incidents reported to Dartmouth officials, one or both parties to the assault said they were intoxicated. The vomit that Melissa scraped off the *Zetemouth* bears its own testimony to the role of alcohol in the Zeta Psi sex scandal.

THE DRINKING HABITS OF COLLEGE WOMEN

This message about the unhealthy and dangerous link between sex and alcohol needs to be heard now more than ever. Our surveys show that the heaviest forms of drinking are increasing, even among female college students. A national study in 1948 found that only 6 percent of college women reported drinking more than once a week. In 2001 41 percent of college women were binge drinking, and 21 percent were frequent binge drinkers (which we define as binging more than three times in two weeks). The percent of women who drink to get drunk has also increased dramatically. And although men are still more likely to drink to extremes—49 percent of men in the 2001 study identified themselves as binge drinkers—women unfortunately are not too far behind.

Adam, who recently graduated from Dartmouth, recalled his first impressions as a freshman: "I wasn't expecting the drinking scene to be as hard as it was. I didn't expect to find so many drinking as much, as frequently, and in the quantities that they did. For girls too—that always surprised me. In certain sororities girls were trying to be just as hard as the guys."

DRINKING *like a* MAN

It is dangerous for a woman to try to "drink like a man." Women tend to get intoxicated more quickly than men, making them more vulnerable to alcohol-related harms. The reason is simple: Women absorb and metabolize alcohol differently than men. Since, on average, women are smaller than men and composed of less water, women achieve higher blood alcohol concentrations after drinking the same amount as a man. They feel alcohol's effects more readily and become impaired more quickly.

If a woman tries to match a man drink-for-drink, she faces greater health and behavioral risks. Our College Alcohol Study has shown that women who typically consume four drinks in a row have a similar likelihood of experiencing many common alcohol-related problems as do men who usually have five drinks. Therefore, we define binge drinking differently for women (four drinks in a row) than for men (five drinks in a row). Using the same standard for both sexes would underestimate both the problem of binge drinking among women and its negative health risks.

Why are college women drinking so much? Part of the answer is to be found in the environment that influences them. For instance, it stands to reason that at high-binge schools female students will binge more. Also, most high-binge schools typically have an entrenched fraternity scene, which encourages irresponsible drinking. For women, as for men, alcohol is usually plentiful in a college setting and often available at cut-rate prices.

The chief factor in the college drinking environment, however, is the alcohol industry. Wherever the industry sees an undertapped market, it seeks to maximize its influence and its sales. Young women represent one such market and are therefore a sector worth targeting by industry advertising. Certain kinds of drinks are pitched directly to women—in particular, lite beers, vodka, and sweet drink mixtures. The University of North Dakota's Wilsnack pointed out that some ads cultivate young female customers by depicting drinking as a symbol of gender equality and power. "A Ron Rico rum ad shows a woman in a hockey goalie uniform. The message is 'Break tradition—buy this rum.'" Similarly, a beer ad features a woman marathoner. Miller Lite pursues women with a reversal of sex roles in a spot in which two babes in a bar spy two gorgeous guys. Their delight melts away, however, when the men tenderly join hands. In ads such as these, women are subtly told that to be equal with a man they need to drink like a man and take on other "manly" attributes.

These ads, however, are the exception, not the rule. The majority of industry advertising continues to exploit sexual stereotypes and offers the promise of a never-ending party—an idea that is enticing to young women as well as to young men.

A WOMAN'S ROLE
in the PARTY SCENE

Advertising that targets young people, both men and women, often relies on sex to sell alcohol. This has particular implications for college women. The young people depicted drinking in ads are uniformly slim and attractive—the so-called beautiful people. Women are usually cast in the role of sex object. Alcohol ads promote sexual stereotypes of masculinity and femininity and implicitly portray sexual relationships as casual encounters void of commitment or emotional attachment. There is nothing subtle in the messages of most of these advertisements.

In many ads, then, women are offered up mainly as bait to the binge drinking crowd, an image that many young women are themselves susceptible to.

Bars also seek to attract women, not only for the money they'll spend but even more so for the heavy-drinking men who will follow them in. This is why some bars regularly offer women free alcohol and charge them a lower or no cover charge. Further, women are billed as the featured attraction in such promotional events as wet T-shirt and bikini contests. The window of a college bar in Louisiana displays a picture of a T-shirt with the slogan HELPING UGLY PEOPLE GET LAID.

In spring 2001 Smirnoff Ice launched a $50 million marketing blitz with the tagline "See where it takes you." Aimed squarely at young male partygoers, a print ad shows scraps of paper scrawled with women's names and phone numbers. Also, the Smirnoff Ice Web page is animated with small photographs and video clips, one showing a young couple dancing. In the first shot the couple is seen from the waist up: The young man holds his scantily clad partner close with one arm; the other arm is raised and holds a bottle of Smirnoff Ice. The second shot focuses on their closely pressed torsos; his arm comes down, pounding the bottle of Smirnoff Ice on her derriere. As the two shots alternate, his arm pumps up and down, rhythmically thumping the bottle on her butt.

Over on the Captain Morgan rum Web site, visitors are invited to use a "pickup line generator" that offers such suggestions as, "Excuse me, mind if I *carouse* your *kitty*?" Click the button marked PICK UP and the highlighted words change: " . . . Mind if I *wheedle* your *nookery*?" The accompanying graphic is of a tall, nearly empty glass placed on a piece of paper scribbled with the word "Alice" and a phone number. A "blow-off line generator" works the same way, with the standard line some variation of "Sorry, I can't that night. I have to *buff* my *sea otter*." Elsewhere on the site, this challenge appears: "Do you have what it takes to join The Captain's merry band of Morganettes? Tell us a little about yourself, and attach a recent photo(s). Click here to send The Captain your contact information and photos." Visitors can ogle the current stable of "Morganettes" (one for each month), who are invariably thin, well-endowed young women who show a lot of cleavage and leg.

At the same time, Anheuser-Busch advertises its Tequiza brand with taglines such as "Actually, size does matter" and "They're not real, so what"; Miller Genuine Draft urges drinkers to "Never Miss a Genuine Opportunity"; and international fashion retailer French Connection has begun to market a sweet-flavored vodka beverage with the brand name of fcuk.

Gimmicks such as these exploit young women's and men's natural interest in exploring sex and developing their own sexual identities. Advertising is a powerful way that young people learn to associate alcohol with sex, an association that can last a lifetime.

SUPPORT SISTERS

The bars that surround college campuses frequently host ladies' night and other specials; females and males respond readily, keeping many bars packed five or six nights a week. And where there's alcohol, there's likely to be overtures to sex. One advertisement printed in the student weekly at Central Connecticut State University read: "How does having Sex on the Beach or an Orgasm sound? . . . Get your head out of the gutter . . . we mean shots!!" The university president, Richard Judd, called the ad "tasteless, uncivil, and offensive." He had it pulled from the paper and threatened to cease university business with the bar, arguing that, as it is, "College campuses have considerable problems with the use of alcohol as it relates to sexual activities."

While young women are drinking at higher rates than ever, their drinking is less visible than that of their male counterparts. In part, this is a credit to the friendships of young women, who vow to look out for one another as they enter the challenging environment of college. Sarah recalled the time a best friend got sick on New Year's Eve:

> We brought her water and made her drink it. She didn't want to. She was cold so we gave her a sweatshirt and put her in her bed on her side. We put a bucket by her side to make sure she didn't puke on herself, on her hair or whatever. Girls are better at that stuff. Sometimes guys would just be like "suck it up." Girls put friendships more importantly.

Trusted male friends can also be part of a female student's network of support. One freshman said,

> Most of my guy friends, they will take very good care of my girlfriends and I, especially if we're at a frat party. My friends and

209

I look out for each other. You don't want someone walking off with some guy they don't even know. The guys are very good with walking people home, especially people who have been drinking.

Sorority sisters—who still drink much less than their fraternity brothers—are famous for their buddy systems, in which inexperienced women are connected to more experienced women. But men—and alcohol—can be very good at breaking down those systems, and once broken, they are useless.

Part IV
A CALL TO ACTION

CHAPTER 11

WHAT STUDENTS
AND SCHOOLS CAN DO

I realized things were not what I wanted them to be, or what they could be. Instead of just accepting things as they are, I would much rather exercise my agency. I am not one to sit by and let things happen, especially when becoming that agent could have profoundly positive effects for other people besides me.
—Justin McEvily, a junior at Cornell University

Most presidents are afraid to take on the problem of alcohol abuse on their campus. They think it will hurt enrollment and offend alumni who have fond memories of the haze of alcohol. I tell them that I found just the opposite. I have very strong support in terms of enrollment patterns, support from parents and from 95 percent of the alumni. Taking a principled and intelligent stand on these issues brings good things to the president.
—Robert Carothers, president of the University of Rhode Island

When all is said and done, it's true that students are responsible for their own binge drinking and the problems it produces. After all, it is the student who lifts beverage to lips and chooses to chug. But as we have pointed out, students don't become binge drinkers without the help of others. There is plenty of credit to go around: the alcohol industry for providing the high volume of cheap alcoholic beverages that fuels binge drinking; communities for not enforcing minimum-drinking-age laws and required standards for responsible serving practices; college administrators for don't-ask don't-tell policies; and

213

parents for not checking up on how their tuition money is being used. As a consequence, campus social life is often steeped in alcohol, and many students find it nearly impossible to get through college without drinking so much that they forget why they are there in the first place: to learn.

The quality of student social life is not separate from academic life. Social life sets the tone and context for the college experience. But the reinvention of college life—to make it the vibrant, meaningful experience that students crave—will take a major effort by students and university administrators, by parents and the community.

This chapter discusses the first two parts of this equation: students and university administrators. The final two chapters discuss what parents can do, what communities can do, and what we should expect of the alcohol industry.

STUDENTS AS AGENTS OF CHANGE

Students are frequently overlooked as agents of change, yet in dozens of ways they constantly invent and reinvent their social options. Even at high-binge campuses, where more than 50 percent of students binge drink, some students envision a different reality for themselves and strive to make it happen. They take an active part in bringing meaning to their college experience. They find other groups of students with whom they share similar values and cultural interests. They volunteer—and our studies show that volunteerism helps to buffer students from binge drinking. Sometimes they demand change.

"Many changes in the campus-drinking environment cannot happen without students taking the lead," said Jan Talbot, who has been the campus health educator at Cornell University for twenty years, "because they are the ones affected by the situation, day in and day out."

SOCIAL ALTERNATIVES

Following a nationally publicized sex scandal at Dartmouth College that was fueled by alcohol, hundreds of students rallied outside the implicated frat house. They demanded changes in social life and university policy. Other students at the school—which by its own admission has a serious drinking problem—have participated in commissions to rethink residential life and alcohol policy.

Many Dartmouth students consciously take part in social activities and clubs that minimize the role of alcohol, including the Dartmouth Outing Club. Through the club, students can push their physical limits in a variety of outdoor sports or just find some respite from the binge-drinking madness that intrudes on so many aspects of college life. One member reflected on how he "escaped alcohol" and stayed sane through his first three years of college:

> It's easy to take out a canoe and go paddling. I have access to a serene part of the campus, separate from the academic, busy, stressful side of Dartmouth. It's a mental break, similar to when students go into the basement of a frat with all their brothers in a safe haven that the college can't control. That lack of university control is appealing. The Outing Club is student-run. It's not a chance to go out of control but to be self-reliant and personal. And group decision-making is really refreshing after being told what you should do in school.

Despite the initiative shown by some students to find their own alternatives to the college drinking culture, at universities nationwide too many students succumb to feelings of being alone and isolated, unable to fit in. Some students transfer to other schools or drop out of school altogether—not because they are drinking too much, but because they do *not* want to drink and as a result feel alienated from their peers. Many others adapt themselves to the binge scene and soon find themselves consuming more alcohol than they can imagine. Given the opportunity to reflect, however, many of these students say that they would both prefer other social options and also support enforcement of policies to limit the effects of binge drinking on campus.

CALLING *for* TOUGHER ENFORCEMENT

Our surveys show that a majority of students want a change in the tenor of campus life. A growing number are fed up with having to suffer the effects of others' out-of-control drinking. They want to sleep through the night and use a clean bathroom in the morning. They do not want to baby-sit roommates who pass out from excessive drinking.

As a reflection of this sentiment, many students say that they support stronger enforcement efforts and harsher punishments for underage drinkers. "If there were consequences, people might not drink out of control as much," said one senior. "It might change the freshman that comes in and says it's cool to drink. If people got arrested, got kicked out of school, it might not seem that cool. It's going to deter people."

Students can organize to clean up their dorms of alcohol's sec-

STUDENT SUPPORT FOR TOUGHER ALCOHOL POLICIES

Alcohol Policy	% Supportive Students
Crack down on underage drinking	67
Enforce rules more strictly	65
Crack down on drinking in Greek houses	60
Prohibit kegs	60
Hold hosts responsible for problems	55
Ban ads for alcohol at campus events	51

ondhand effects, which are no more a natural part of the college life than pollutants are a natural part of the environment. By *organize* we don't mean forming a bucket brigade, but passing a code of conduct and supporting the administration in reasonable measures to enforce it.

Other positive trends surfaced in our 2001 College Alcohol Study. We found that one-third of students surveyed had asked someone they knew to stop drinking. Also, more students are opting for life in substance-free dormitories—28 percent, compared to 17 percent in 1993—and fewer are joining the Greek system or attending parties in fraternities. These are signs of healthy student attitudes.

But while most students support the tougher enforcement of alcohol policies, in some schools a substantial minority resists change. The heaviest drinking students may "fight for their right to party." In the past few years riots or public disturbances have occurred at the University of Northern Colorado, the University of New Hampshire, the University of Oregon, Pennsylvania State University, Michigan State University, Kent State University, and Ohio State University, to name a few. The tightening of alcohol restrictions limiting alcohol at tailgate parties, a sports team's loss or win, or even the changeover to daylight savings time have triggered riots—students at Colorado State University at Boulder rioted because bars closed an hour earlier with the seasonal time change. The common element in these occurrences is not a social cause or a personal injustice. It is alcohol. We have come a long way from the social protests of the sixties to the beer riots of today.

But just as students in an earlier generation helped win the divestment of U.S. corporations from apartheid in South Africa, students today can insist on the divestment of alcohol money from college campuses. Students concerned with issues of equity and globalization can investigate the role of the alcohol industry in undermining the health and well-being of people in developing countries—realizing that the World Health Organization has called alcohol "a significant threat to world health."

If higher education is to fulfill its mission of truly *educating*, campus administrators must work with students to limit the misuse of alcohol. The desire of students for a clear code of conduct and its fair enforcement does not mean that they want to live and learn in an authoritarian environment in which they are told how to act. They simply want opportunities to set their own agenda and create their own alternatives, free from the constant pressure to consume alcohol and from the demoralizing secondhand effects of binge drinking.

LEADING *a* RENAISSANCE

In the past few years student groups have begun to address the need for more campus social activities that don't involve alcohol. Unfortunately, these efforts often fall flat. One campus that *has* stayed the course is Cornell University. There, a student group called Renaissance began by asking fellow students what they liked about Cornell's social scene, what bothered them about it, and what changes they would suggest. Nearly every response commented on the prevalence of alcohol and its negative secondhand effects. Others objected to the social barriers between different groups of students and the lack of a sense of community.

In response, Renaissance decided to sponsor late-night activities that don't involve alcohol; the group also started a Web site to advertise social events to the entire student body. The group is weighing its next course of action, including reviewing the issue of student hazing.

Renaissance received seed money from the Center for Science in the Public Interest and has since gained financial support of the student government. It has the backing of campus health educator Jan Talbot and a university president who launched a President's Council on alcohol abuse. "It's the first time on campus that we've had presidential leadership on this issue," Talbot said. "We need the top-down and the bottom-up approach."

Cornell is not the only school where groups like Renaissance are active. At the University of Nebraska in Lincoln, the NU Directions coalition began two events, the Back to School Bash and The End, held during the first and last weekends of the academic year. The Bash includes a midnight pancake breakfast on the student union plaza. The End includes a night at the recreation center for climbing the wall, playing volleyball, or engaging in other recreational activities. A number of schools have opened their rec centers past the midnight hour or set up midnight-movie programs.

Still, many such coalition and student-run programs remain marginal and underfunded. The college administration—from the president on down—must mobilize behind the effort to recreate college life.

"We Exist to Not Exist"

Students around the country are taking the initiative in creating alternatives to the binge drinking scene. We interviewed student leader Justin McEvily about the efforts of the student group Renaissance at Cornell University.

Why did you get involved with Renaissance?

Throughout my high school career I was more or less Straight Edge. It's a movement that extolled the virtues of substance-free living and abstinence in all areas of life: promiscuous sex, alcohol, and drugs. The Straight Edge paradigm that I most closely related to is that we are all humans, we have no great strength of muscle, we have no claws, fangs, or sharp teeth. What we have is our minds. Keeping your mind as sharp as you can will set you above the rest. Therefore, do not dull your mind with substance abuse. That struck a chord with me way back in middle school.

Over time I began partying with kids who did consume alcohol and smoke, but I could set myself apart. Part of my self-esteem was rooted in the idea of control and abstinence. So by the time I got to college I liked to get rowdy and party, but not with that element of alcohol added.

Now I'm also in a fraternity. It's one location where you see the quintessential embodiment of the negative secondary effects of alcohol consumption—whether it's from losing an average of one or two guys a year who leave school because of alcohol problems, or vomit all over the bathroom, or a girl so far gone that you have to take care of her all night, or a cigarette hole burned in your comforter—I've seen all of it happen.

I got involved. I realized things were not what I wanted them to be, or what they could be.

A TWELVE-POINT ACTION PLAN FOR SCHOOLS

Every school has its own unique history, spirit, and student body. When it comes to changing the alcohol environment, school admin-

What is the Renaissance philosophy?

We advocate for a change in the social scene, a change in the culture. Our purpose is to tackle the wider problems that create this unhealthy behavior. We're identifying unhealthy behavior as not enough outlets for stress. It's not just about getting people away from bars and frat parties, but getting the students who never leave their dorm rooms out of their rooms and promoting a greater sense of community on campus.

We exist to not exist. Somewhere along the line we're hoping we won't be needed any more. In the ideal, Cornell does not need Renaissance. But we take it one step at a time. The first push is alternative late-night programming on weekends, on the evenings when students go out drinking. We think that students wouldn't drink as much if we provided them with fun, viable alternatives, and that this would lessen the negative secondhand effects.

Alternative social programs often fail. What leads to success?

It's important to pay close attention to the underlying social currents at your school. Certain buildings are stigmatized as being uncool, and you want to avoid those. Also, we have a very big Greek scene and a good-sized bar scene. We don't program events on nights when there are three big fraternity parties. Attendance would be way back. We're conscious of who we're competing with.

One good way to break the bonds of association between fun and alcohol is to take what is enjoyable from the scene where alcohol is a pervasive element and bring it to your scene. An event we cosponsored this semester called The One-Night Stand drew about five hundred students. We brought in Steven Bard, a popular one-man band who plays at local bars. The hybridization worked.

istrators must diagnose the situation on their own campuses. One size does not fit all. For instance, banning alcohol altogether is not feasible at many colleges and even if feasible, it is not necessarily a solution. While fewer students at alcohol-ban colleges may drink, those who do drink just as heavily and have as many related problems as drinkers at non-ban colleges.

What general steps, then, can schools take? Based on our research and on visits to many campuses, we have developed a twelve-point action plan, an evolving guide to help school administrators in their efforts to confront the problem of binge drinking.

1. Colleges must first acknowledge that an alcohol problem exists, then assess its scope.

For decades, universities kept the problem of alcohol abuse hidden in the closet. Over the last several years, however, the problem has gained national attention. We are again at a critical juncture. If you are a campus administrator, you know that at many universities years of effort have produced few results. Some administrators and health workers are growing weary of fighting an uphill battle. The alcohol industry is working overtime to minimize the problem.

Rather than stuffing this problem back in the closet, you should honestly confront a problem that everyone knows exists. As Robert Carothers, president of the University of Rhode Island, has found, forthright acknowledgement of the problem and dedicated work to change it wins the respect of students, parents, staff, and alumni.

To assess the scope of the problem, top administrators should take an unannounced weekend campus tour of fraternities, dorms, the health-services office, and local bars. Then do your homework. What follows is a list of the kind of information to collect before drawing up your plan:

- How many students visit the local hospital emergency room because of alcohol-related injuries or overdose from Thursday to Sunday?

- How many campus security incidents occur during that same time?

- How many students face school disciplinary action because of violations of alcohol policy? How many are arrested?

- Where did the students charged in these incidents have their last drink?

- How many of these students were members of fraternities, sororities, or athletic teams?

- What is the annual cost of repairs for vandalized property?

- How many students cut classes on Fridays?

- How many bars and liquor stores surround the campus? How busy are they on weekends?

- How many establishments are cited for alcohol law violations?

- What special drink prices are available to students?

- How does a five-drink session compare in price to a movie?

- How much money does the school accept from the alcohol industry?

The answers to such questions will help you determine what actions to take.

2. A systematic effort to curtail the binge drinking problem begins with the president, includes all segments of the campus and surrounding community, and organizes for the long-term.

Presidential leadership is essential. It sets the tone, the priorities, and the pace of change. Staff, faculty, and students need the direction and the backing of the president's office. Board of trustees and alumnae support, though often hard to get, is also very helpful. The problem is too big to assign to a single office or to approach in a piecemeal way.

Call everyone together who can help you. Student life officers and residence and security personnel have probably been fighting a losing battle for many years. Give them the help they need. Call in the athletic directors, chaplains, faculty, advisors and mentors, and student leaders. Extend the outreach to the community. Include town officials, police, licensing boards, and the chamber of commerce. Reach out to parents through orientations, letters, and other regular communication. Xavier University in Cincinnati, for example, enrolled the parents of 95 percent of its freshman class in a program to talk about alcohol and drugs with their children at least once a month.

Parents should be informed of alcohol policy and the consequences of breaking that policy. Some schools will notify parents if their son or daughter is disciplined for alcohol violations. At the University of Delaware parents also learn the financial and educational consequences of continued violations: Two more occurrences would lead to suspension and a loss of tuition and housing expenses. "Parental notification might be window dressing if it wasn't tied to an accounting of the consequences," said Steve Martin, a researcher at that university's Center for Drug and Alcohol Studies.

3. Provide a rich academic and extracurricular environment for students by encouraging community service and the pursuit of special interests.

To an educator there is no more damning view of a college than the oft-voiced student complaint, "I drink because there is nothing else to do here." Universities need to provide a rich and varied palette of campus activities to combat the on-your-own quality that permeates much of the college experience, particularly at large universities. Students involved in volunteerism, community service, or special interests such as art or music are less likely to binge drink. One school's dramatic arts department offers a program called Putting Theater to Work in the Community, which promotes connections between students and locals and has students create theater that addresses the problem of binge drinking. A student at one low-binge school said, "There's a lot to do here that drinking wouldn't necessarily make more fun. Student-run theater and installation art are good and worth going to. Alcohol doesn't play a very large role in campus culture or social life."

Many schools have begun offering leadership classes, and these, too, could tackle alcohol issues. "The real key is finding ways to connect inside- to outside-the-classroom experience," said Jenny Michael, executive director of the CIRCLe Network, a national organization whose mission is to reinvent campus life. "As it is now, in these classes students learn about how to be a leader, but not that there are social issues on campus that need to be addressed."

Colleges should hold classes and exams on Fridays. A college should not enable students to binge from Thursday to Sunday. Universities should provide full-time education for a full-time tuition. Show students that you expect them to act responsibly, to fulfill their academic requirements, and to behave as adults.

Start freshman orientation before students arrive on campus. Use the admissions office, high school counselors, and alumni to get the message out that underage drinking is not tolerated. Students need to know that they can expect to enjoy school, develop lasting friendships, and become prepared for the future, all without binge drinking.

Finally, don't underestimate the value of having a diverse student body. Student diversity discourages the kind of conformity that's at work in mass binge drinking. A wide array of cultural, religious, and economic differences in the student population allows nondrinkers to bond over activities they can relate to. Interestingly, an increase in the number of older students and minority group members will help a school drop its binge-drinking rate.

4. Avoid simple solutions for complex, longstanding problems: If it looks too good to be true, it probably is.

Our studies have shown that the problem of heavy drinking at college stems from many causes. Some students bring the habit with them from their high school days, from what they have learned at home, or from their genetic makeup. Others have developed expectations about college life that include heavy drinking. Some colleges introduce students to binge drinking through their highly valued traditions, their Greek system, or their drinking customs around school sports. Some students are drawn to drink more than they planned to because of cheap prices and promotions by local alcohol outlets. Some don't know the potential consequences of large volumes of alcohol. Whatever the reason, no single approach, no matter how well-conceived, would work to stop binge drinking among all students.

Just as alcohol advertisers segment their market, so too should prevention planners segment the student body. Steps that may keep light social drinkers from joining the heavy drinking lifestyle may not work with experienced heavier drinkers.

Yet some programs have been offered for all students. The current panacea is social norms. While this method may indeed work on some students at some colleges, it is being offered as a cure-all for all campuses. Social norms as practiced in this way is a snake oil medicine based on flimsy evidence of success. The fact that the brewers tout it is reason enough to suspect it. How convincing, for example, is the claim made in an Anheuser-Busch booklet says, "67% of college student's don't drink and drive." Are we satisfied with that? Should we feel good about the implied assertion that *only* 33 percent of students drink and drive?

5. Support student efforts to create alternatives to an alcohol-powered social life.

Respect and support students' efforts to create their own social activities. Rely on students for these initiatives; they know what they would enjoy. Brainstorm with them. What feelings do they associate with heavy drinking? We need to find ways to evoke those feelings that are not self-destructive or dangerous.

Make funds available for social and recreational activities that are alcohol-free. Alternatives are especially needed during traditional times of heavy drinking, such as during Homecoming and at the beginning and the end of the school year.

Administrators and faculty may need to question their own assumptions about when and where alcohol is appropriate. Faculty who host an after-class party for their students and offer alcohol have probably not thought about the responsibility they are assuming or the awkward situation they may be creating for students who are underage, in recovery, or who just don't want to drink. Schools should have programs that raise teachers' awareness of alcohol issues.

6. Work with students to develop and implement a code of conduct and alcohol policy.

Students are key contributors to the success of any prevention efforts. Work with non-bingeing students to establish their rights and develop a code of conduct for all students. Most students support

(continued on page 230)

Building a New Culture for Learning

Universities have already gained valuable experience, as a growing number of college administrations take steps to change the binge-drinking culture and environment on their campuses. We interviewed Robert Carothers, president of the University of Rhode Island, a school of fourteen thousand students in southern New England. Carothers launched a major overhaul of campus alcohol policy and practice in 1993, after *The Princeton Review* named URI the nation's number-one party school.

Why did you begin taking student alcohol abuse seriously?

When we were named the number-one party school. We were also a high-binge school on the College Alcohol Study list; approximately 70 percent of the student body was engaged in binge drinking. At that time we were in a big reengineering project to focus on quality in the university, to upgrade the preparation level of students entering the university, and to change the way we did instruction and research. It was clear that we were not going to be able to change educational quality or the perception of it as long as we had the mantle of "party school" hanging over us.

What steps did you take?

We put together a comprehensive set of policies and programs to change the culture of the university. Our vision was called "Building a New Culture for Learning." And doing that required us to deal with a lot of fuzzy minds and bad behavior that were a function of a high level of alcohol abuse.

The most dramatic thing that we did was to prohibit the serving of alcohol at any social function sponsored by the university, including our fraternities and sororities. Then we developed a policy for the residence halls that had the "three strikes and you're out" deal. It started with fines and training and community service, but get a third violation and you're suspended from school.

We developed a more aggressive education program and developed our treatment relationships so we had a better system to deal with problems of acknowledged abuse. We did all of this in a very public way.

Was there a turning point?

A serendipitous thing occurred. It was very unfortunate, but it gave us a chance to say we meant business. A group of football players attacked a fraternity house and beat people up. It was a pretty ugly scene. We suspended the whole football team in 1995. To make a public statement, I decided we should forfeit a game. It was the first time in the history of the National Collegiate Athletic Association that anyone forfeited for disciplinary reasons. We kicked several football players out of school permanently.

By that year we were locked in a battle with the fraternities. They had made the decision that they were not going to change. Now, six or seven years later, we've kicked eight fraternities off the campus. There are a bunch of empty frat houses being converted one by one to other functions.

What lessons have you learned?

One thing I've learned is that it's pretty hard to change this alcohol culture without changing the fraternity culture, as well, because they are deeply wed to that notion of themselves. Sometimes they would try to be different, but they couldn't stay with it. We went through a tough period there in 1995.

Also, the system is very complex and interwoven. For instance, our police officers were highly dependent on these parties at fraternities. To make extra money, they worked there on overtime, providing security. To change these parties meant they lost that money. So they were not our allies.

How have you worked with the community?

In the last three years we've taken the issue of community relations seriously. A university-community coalition works on these issues. They are changing the nature of house leases and the way politicians do their work. They are trying to get a keg registration law passed. They are undertaking a whole array of initiatives.

We've had some progress. But every year it's a new effort. We're right down on the shore, in a resort community region. In the summertime the community is full of people who come to party, and during the school year

(continued)

229

Building a New Culture for Learning—cont.

our students live there. The area has a lot of bars and clubs in addition to house parties. We have an agreement with bar owners not to do specials, but you always see pamphlets around campus. We have to keep on it all the time.

Does the school's alcohol policy have much support?

Every year I speak to the students coming in to be recruited at the Meet the University days. I talk about values and how I expect them to have some clarity about what they stand for and believe in when they leave. And I say that we've become much clearer about what we stand for—so if your idea is to abuse alcohol and other substances, don't come here, we don't want you, we don't need you.

I often get an outburst of applause. I think it's from the parents. It makes a difference. They feel more comfortable, safer, about their kids coming here.

Before, the student body was made up of a significant body of abusers, and people who knew them followed them in here. When we broke that cycle, said we're not going to be tolerant of your behavior, slowly, over time, a different kind of student came here—and they began to replicate themselves.

At the same time, we're in the middle of the student government election now. Each candidate is trying to promise that they'll bring alcohol back to homecoming, because I eliminated it. So there is a continual desire to go back to another time around. But they're not going back.

policies that curtail excessive drinking and the behavior that accompanies it. Enforce the code strictly. Bingeing students, not their sober classmates, should pay the consequences of their own disruptive behavior.

A code of conduct should protect the rights of everyone to live in a civil environment conducive to learning and personal growth. Involve students in policy development, review, and implementation.

What impact have the new policies had?

We have the payback. Our enrollment is wonderful, the quality of the student body is up dramatically, and alumni support is up. The embarrassing and tragic incidents that marred the life of the university and tarred its reputation have by and large stopped. Still, some folks are unhappy about the loss of fraternities.

We are up almost two hundred SAT points on average in freshmen compared to a decade ago. We are getting a lot more scholarship dollars. The number of hours spent in the library is up. We have a much higher number of students involved in music groups—and there is a high correlation between academic performance and students involved in music.

I can't say that the changed alcohol policy is the sole cause of these changes, but certainly it is a contributing cause. People used to call this place "U-R High." They really don't do that anymore. I wouldn't pretend that we've eliminated all of that, but we've certainly suppressed it significantly.

Do you have any advice for other presidents?

Most presidents are afraid to take on the problem of alcohol abuse on their campuses. They think it will hurt enrollment and offend alumni who have fond memories of the haze of alcohol. I tell them that I've found just the opposite. I have very strong support in terms of enrollment patterns, support from parents, and from 95 percent of the alumni.

Taking a principled and intelligent stand on these issues brings good things to the president, not bad things. People don't want to believe it. But it's true.

Encourage their participation in campus alcohol task forces and in campus-community coalitions. Include students on judicial review boards that cover the full range of alcohol infractions that arise in student life, from honor code violations to sexual offenses. What an education for the students involved.

When developing penalties for code infractions, make the punishment fit the crime. Fines do not affect everyone in the same way.

Some students merely have dad pay the assessment, much as they get money from home to cover their bar bills. Community service is an important tool. Make the violator who polluted the dormitory environment part of a cleanup detail the following week, or have him assist EMTs on runs to the hospital on a "wet" weekend. Punishment can serve an educational function if it makes the student view the weekend revelry from another perspective. Do not make penalties too severe. Students will feel it is unfair, and resident assistants and security officers will become reluctant to cite violators.

7. Realistically evaluate the influence of Big Alcohol on your campus.

Alcohol industry sponsorships and gifts send mixed messages to students and may appear to endorse underage drinking. In addition, they can create conflicts of interest for the university. End these. End direct on-campus alcohol advertising, whether in student newspapers, distributed as flyers or posters, or aired on student radio stations. And let's get the alcohol industry out of the student alcohol education business. Why should we leave the education of students about drinking to the people who make money when students drink?

If industry members are truly civic minded and trying to do good, they should agree to advertising restrictions and stop appealing to underage youth in their promotions. They should reform sales practices that push high volumes on young drinkers. If the industry wants to educate, let them educate bar owners and liquor store owners about what constitutes responsible sales and marketing practices.

Get rid of Alcohol Awareness Week—students are plenty aware of alcohol—and turn it into Drunkenness Avoidance Year.

8. Work with the local community to limit underage drinking and the availability of cheap, high-volume alcohol.

Colleges should work to limit the supply and marketing of alcohol in the surrounding community. This means allying with other community forces and using your own political and economic powers to enforce and enact laws aimed at reducing this problem.

We discuss many strategies for campus-community coalitions in the final chapter. Here, suffice it to say that college drinking is a community as well as a college problem. The university president and the city mayor, the campus chief of security and the town sheriff, college revelers and high school students all drive down the same streets and pass the same billboards, bars, and stop signs. The more that campus and community leaders work together, the more likely progress will be made.

9. Provide alcohol-free living arrangements.

Students are lining up for alcohol-free living arrangements. In 1993, one in six students chose an alcohol-free environment on campus; by 2001, two in seven students lived in such accommodations. Nonetheless, there were not enough spaces available to meet student demand. One administrator told us, "Our substance-free housing program has grown tremendously over the past few years. The program has expanded from 40 students the first year to 185 this year. We will be expanding into a second building next year."

Our studies have shown that students who live in these "dry" houses are less likely to take up binge drinking, especially if they did not already binge in high school. Students who enter a heavy drinking college are more likely to take up bingeing even if they didn't do it before. The substance-free dorm offers a safe haven from

233

the wet college environment. Colleges should offer such housing to all students who seek it.

Make these residences especially attractive to go along with the more pleasant atmosphere due to the lower level of secondhand effects. One parent told us her daughter selected substance-free housing because it was the only housing with air conditioning. All those who choose to live in alcohol- or substance-free housing—whatever their reasons—should sign an agreement not to bring alcohol or other drugs into the hall and not to be in the hall while under the influence.

10. Address problem drinking at fraternities and sororities.

The Greek system is one of the most intractable on-campus contributors to heavy drinking. Yet every campus situation is different, and schools must assess what steps are appropriate, from banning Greek houses to working to improve the system.

One administrator told us that security officers now patrol residence halls and Greek houses. "This has been the single greatest contributor to reducing alcohol consumption on the campus, particularly in the fraternities," he said. Alcohol can be served on campus only with prior approval for a specific event. In addition, only the chancellor or one of five vice chancellors can grant such approval.

At a minimum, fraternities should be expected to uphold the law. Underage students commonly drink—and drink to excess—in these settings. Colleges need to stop the illegal sale of alcohol without a license, hold national organizations accountable for serving underage students, and gain alumni support to change fraternity and sorority practices.

11. Address problem drinking with athletes and fans.

Both athletes and fans binge drink at higher levels than the overall student population, and the alcohol industry targets them in its marketing. These are reasons enough to ban advertising in stadiums and in printed programs and to prohibit alcohol sales at athletic events.

Just as addicts must be detoxed from drugs, athletic departments must be freed from their dependence on alcohol-industry money. Make yours go cold turkey. The withdrawal pains may be acute at first, but gradually other sponsors will fill the void.

The University of Colorado at Boulder illustrates what can be achieved by eliminating alcohol from a stadium. The first season after the ban, ejections of football fans decreased 50 percent, arrests decreased 45 percent, and student referrals to the judicial affairs office fell 89 percent. These decreases have been maintained since the ban was enacted. Although some fans and season ticket holders objected to the ban, they still renewed their tickets. The ban faces a further challenge, however, as the stadium expands its skyboxes and club seats. Alcohol is allowed in these expensive seats, raising issues of fairness and hypocrisy.

Prohibit heavy drinking at tailgating—which often begins in the morning and lasts well into the night. Some campuses have implemented dry tailgates, and others prohibit students from bringing their own alcohol, allowing alcohol to be purchased only in very controlled circumstances.

To address problem drinking with athletes, review team policies and their enforcement. Some schools, like the Catholic University of America in Washington, D.C., prohibit the use of alcohol by athletes during the playing season. Alcohol can also be eliminated from victory celebrations and end-of-year banquets.

12. Encourage problem drinkers to seek the help they need, and provide treatment on demand.

We estimate that one in every ten male college students under the age of twenty-four is alcohol dependent. Furthermore, close to one in three college students report at least one symptom of alcohol abuse. Alcohol dependent students are also more likely to suffer from various forms of emotional distress, including anxiety, stress, and depression.

Alcohol dependence and alcohol abuse are diagnostic categories detailed in the Diagnostic and Statistical Manual of the American Psychiatric Association. These conditions may recur in individuals throughout their lifetime. Yet few students report that they have sought out treatment. At a high-binge college they are simply part of the alcohol haze, often indistinguishable from others with a heavy drinking lifestyle.

Schools need new strategies for educating students about alcohol abuse and helping students understand when they or their friends need help. Schools should develop early recognition and intervention programs. Working with John Knight, a physician at the Harvard Medical School, we have identified basic steps schools can take in this regard:

- Colleges can provide diagnostic assessments for students who violate alcohol regulations.

- Campus health services can screen students for alcohol disorders when they present with drug-related problems, sexually transmitted diseases, or for pregnancy tests.

- Health education departments should train resident assistants in the warning signs and symptoms of alcohol disorders.

Medical professionals have developed a variety of treatment strategies. Students and parents should be informed of the options and the evidence of their success. The sooner students with problems receive the appropriate screening and intervention services—whether provided on campus or through referral to specialized community-based services—the better off they will be.

DON'T GIVE UP

If school administrators were to total up the costs associated with binge drinking—from vandalism to dorm clean up, from emergency health services to security details—they would surely be surprised to see how high these direct costs are. If one were then to add the indirect costs associated with students who miss classes, fail to benefit from their education, and drop out of school, the picture becomes yet starker. Schools would be better off spending that money on prevention programs, on cooperating with the community, and on funding treatment and social alternatives to heavy drinking.

The problem of college binge drinking took decades to develop. You won't get rid of it overnight. If you need inspiration, look at smoke-free air in classrooms, lecture halls, and sports arenas. Fifty years ago, before the surgeon general's report on tobacco, and before the recognition that secondhand smoke hurts nonsmokers, the air was thick with smoke. Cigarette companies advertised that "More doctors smoke brand X." Today that is no longer the case.

We can change the norms about binge drinking in college in the same way if we are determined to succeed. Ultimately, this change must come from both the top down and the bottom up.

CHAPTER 12

WHAT PARENTS CAN DO

I found empty beer bottles in my son's bedroom. He's told me that his stress was so high at school that he couldn't deal with it, and this was his way. I look at myself. I ask myself is that the example I'm setting for him. I stopped drinking in the evenings during the week. The change in my behavior is primarily for him. But now I'm finding that I also have more energy at night.
—Linda, mother of a high school junior

The important thing for parents to realize is that the process of policy change is not just the province of lawyers and lobbyists. If communities are organized they can effect fantastic changes. It is an arena in which parents can become very expert, very effective.
—Bill Gallegos, parent of two sons in college and
director of the California Alcohol Policy Reform Initiative

We are citizens of a nation that prides itself on solutions. Yet we have been largely stumped by the problem of young people's alcohol abuse. Millions of parents struggle daily with issues of alcohol and substance abuse by their children. These parents are puzzled, angry, scared. They may blame themselves or their children. But while some parents grapple with moral and legal predicaments that might seem impossible to solve, others casually dismiss underage or binge drinking as a rite of passage.

Problem drinking is not just an individual problem. Parents need to engage in discussion and agree on a code of acceptable conduct. In a world where fake IDs can be ordered off the Internet, we need to all agree—or a helpful majority of us, at least—that we will not make it any easier for our children or their friends to consume alcohol. We will not be enablers, hosting parties that serve alcohol to underage students, whether they are in middle school, high school, or the first years of college. We need to pledge to do the hard work of communicating with our children and with our spouses about issues we wish did not exist. We need to understand that we can't wish the problem away.

Given the industry's aggressive marketing of alcohol, we need to broaden our understanding of what good parenting means. While talking with and listening to our children is a good start, it is not enough. We need to band together to make sure that our children have social alternatives to getting drunk or getting high. We need to create healthier learning and living environments. We need to *apply* the values we teach our children about right and wrong—to the local bar that sells all-you-can-drink specials; to the beer brewers and liquor distillers who use talking animals and sports stars to sell their products to young people; and to an industry that dispenses advice to parents about how to discuss alcohol with their children even as they paste up beer and liquor billboards across from middle schools and spend some $5 billion a year in advertising and promotions. When will we react to the terrible irony that Anheuser-Busch delivers its pamphlets to middle schools in conjunction with guest appearances by its Clydesdale horses or that the Beer Institute prints and distributes a parent-discussion guide entitled "Let's Talk Over a Beer"?

Subtly but insistently, the alcohol industry blames parents when their children develop drinking problems. Obviously good parenting *is* crucial to children's healthy development. But parents cannot expect to solve the problem of binge drinking by youth alone. Law enforcement agencies, the government, local businesses, high schools, and the universities themselves must play their parts. You can be a great parent and your child can still end up cited for public drunkenness, charged with driving under the influence, or worse.

A TEN-POINT ACTION PLAN FOR PARENTS

It is hard to overlook the extent of underage and binge drinking that takes place on campuses and in communities across the country and the scope of the suffering and damage that results. The peer pressure and easy accessibility of alcohol to middle and high school students is only the beginning of the problem. Just when you thought that your college-bound child had made it through the most difficult and dangerous adolescent years, alcohol assumes a potentially even more destructive role in his or her life.

Of course you worry. But as a parent you do have power. There are a number of things you can do to reduce the risk that your child will have alcohol problems on the journey to adulthood:

1. Communicate with your child.

Not just about drinking and drugs but also about all manner of things. Good communication from an early age builds strong parent-child relationships that help ground a young person as he or she is confronted with difficult choices.

"In order to have self-esteem, children need experiences that teach them how to have an impact when they communicate," said Helen Kramer, a psychotherapist in New York City who has worked extensively with families. Kramer warns that children are increasingly being deprived of adult contact. "The average kid has a face-to-face conversation with an adult for four minutes a day," she said. "True communication lets kids feel powerful because they talk to you, they make an impact, and they feel there is an exchange."

Between providing good meals, helping with homework, and keeping their children healthy, most parents put a lot of time and effort into taking care of their children. "But often parents haven't been taught that the way they speak to and listen to their child can play an essential role in the child's well-being," Kramer said. "When you pay attention to your child's feelings you teach him or her to learn to focus on their own internal cues. It is these cues that will guide them to make good choices."

No matter how busy you are, don't let yourself become too busy for your children. Even at a very young age, doing things as a family such as having meals together reaffirms a child's sense of himself. When these things are lost, "children begin to lose the feeling of their own humanity," Kramer said. "They get a numbness, and to get out of it they can do things that are very dangerous—not to hurt themselves, but to feel. A lot of dangerous behavior is a person looking for a way to feel alive."

The National Center on Addiction and Substance Abuse at Columbia University (CASA) has found that teens who have an excellent relationship with either parent had risk scores for substance use that were 25 percent lower than the average teen; those with excellent relationships with both parents had risk scores 40 percent lower.

From communicating and sharing activities, you'll know what makes your child click—what gives her joy, or what he finds exciting. That way you can continue to suggest activities that will be challenging and satisfying as the pressure to drink increases.

Linda's son Nick is fanatical about BMX biking and stunt riding. "He's the kind of guy who will ride down steps, rails, do tricks in the air when jumping off bumps. It was scary when I saw my son wanting to do this. I realized that I was going to have to help him do it safely or he would do it behind my back," Linda said.

We need to be there for our children, even during the adolescent years when he or she turns to the peer culture and away from us. Iris, a college freshman, told us about the positive influence of her parents:

When I was fifteen and got in trouble for drinking at [an] afterparty, my parents talked to me, posed the problem. They said it's not safe, you're not old enough, your body can't handle that right now, that's awful for your body. My parents and I were pretty open. I didn't want to listen to them just because it was my parents. But sometimes when I would be out with friends, I would have a beer and that would be it. I wanted to be cautious so that I didn't end up in the hospital, or cited by the police.

It is easy to lull yourself into thinking that you are communicating with your adolescent children, but in fact you may have to be creative in finding ways to talk about alcohol and other sensitive topics. Look for openings, such as when your child talks about what her friends are doing or how so-and-so got into trouble. You may need to approach some conversations in a more abstract, less personal way. When the daughter of one parent was getting ready to go away for spring break, the mom brought out newspaper articles about alcohol-related problems in Cancun. "It gave us a way to talk that was less emotionally charged," she explained. In this way her daughter was less apt to feel like her mother was criticizing her or did not trust her. Husbands and wives need to talk to each other as well. Don't wait for a crisis to discover that one of you thinks it's just fine if your sixteen-year-old son gets drunk, while the other is appalled. Understand each other's feelings and their bases, and know whose views will take precedence if a situation arises that demands a response. Try to reach agreement—one day you may be thankful that you did.

2. Model good behavior.

Teach by example as well as by words. Don't show your children that it takes a drink to relax. One parent told us how she came to examine her own drinking:

My husband and I have very stressful jobs. We were drinking wine every night; as soon as we walked through the door we'd open a bottle. When my daughter visited us during college breaks, she mimicked the same thing. It made me stop and say what kind of role model am I being. It made me stop drinking like that. Now, to deal with the stress, I get a massage every Friday night that I can. I try to pay attention to myself. I don't go to work until I've exercised or at least done some stretches in the morning.

For some parents, modeling good behavior requires more than giving up a glass of wine at night. Tens of thousands of students come from families in which one or both parents are alcoholics. As difficult as it may be to acknowledge your problem and get help, failing to do so can set your children up for problems of their own. Home environment as well as genetics can influence your child's drinking behavior.

3. Delay the first drink—including beer—as long as possible.

The longer you can delay the first drink your child takes, the less likely he or she will have alcohol problems later in life. In addition, delaying that first drink will lessen the possibility of his future involvement in car accidents, exposure to physical violence, and the practice of unsafe sex. A number of studies, including our own, point to these results.

Some parents oppose their children drinking hard liquor but don't mind beer. One student told us about her father's response to alcohol: "On prom night I went to my friend's house; his parents were not home. Dad wasn't sure he was going to let me go; he was concerned about drugs, sex, and drinking. I told him that I could promise two of the things, but couldn't tell him there wasn't going to be beer. He said that was the least of his worries." In fact, beer is involved in more problems than all illicit drugs combined.

4. Don't enable your child's drinking.

Don't leave alcohol around casually, and certainly don't provide it to your children and their friends—at your home or anywhere else. Our study shows that increasing numbers of underage college students obtain alcohol from a parent or relative: 17 percent in 1993 and 23 percent in 2001. Similarly, CASA reports that one-third of sixth- and ninth-graders obtain alcohol from their own homes. Many parents do not realize the harm this is doing. Some think they are protecting their children, reasoning that they would do it anyway.

Adults need to set a positive example—for their own children and their children's friends. This does not always happen. Larissa told us about her high school graduation party, hosted by the school principal:

> He told us he'd collect our keys so no one can drive. He said that we should stay and just have fun—party. "You guys deserve it," he said. More and more kids started showing up. The principal and his wife started drinking with the kids. They lost track of their responsibility. They didn't collect everyone's keys; they didn't make sure no one was sick. The principal's wife got robbed of all of her jewelry. The next morning, they had to call the police to report the theft. The police showed up and saw the mess. The backyard was mud, they had kegs outside, the basement was gross.

This kind of irresponsibility is unacceptable. Talk with other parents and know who feels the same way you do. Don't let your children go to parties at the homes of enabling parents or to parties where no parent is present. Don't encourage or accept underage drinking as a rite of passage.

"I've been strict about calling friends' houses to make sure a parent is home, and making sure that kids are not given alcohol or have access to it. I've had to become a bit more of a spy," said one parent.

We are not talking here about a sip of wine during a particular cultural event or religious ritual. But parental tolerance or encouragement of underage drinking on other occasions may lead children to believe that drinking is acceptable, and studies have found that parents less tolerant of underage drinking have children less inclined to drink.

5. Set rules and enforce consequences.

Although parents generally are concerned about underage drinking and its adverse consequences, only 23 percent of parents explicitly prohibit their children from using alcohol before the legal drinking age. Young people need to know the rules and the consequences of breaking them.

One parent of a high school junior who discovered her son was getting drunk grounded him for two weeks and put the house of his drinking buddy permanently off limits. Then she laid down the law:

> He knows if he does it again, I'm going for his license, and he's very much into driving. He knows he will lose all privileges. I've rarely had to punish this kid, so it's hard for me. But I've said I will come down hard on him. My favorite punishment is no electronics. The only thing you can turn on is your light. And he knows I'll call all his friends' parents. I said, Rest assured, if it happens again I'll give you and your friends up in a heartbeat because I do love you. So far it's working, but I no longer have any illusions.

Once your son or daughter is in college, enforcing rules becomes far more difficult. "About the only thing left is to hold back money," one parent said. This makes good communication during the college years even more important.

In addition to knowing what you expect of them, teenagers and young adults need solid information about alcohol's effects, and plenty of it, because even college seniors can be naïve. Shelbi, a college senior who tried to "drink her age" on her twenty-first birthday, thought that she could handle it: "I thought I'm doing shots made mostly with juice and lighter hard liquor, rum and stuff. I was like, I'll be okay, I'll be okay." After fifteen shots, two friends took her home. "I threw up in my bedroom, in my bathroom, on the floor, in the toilet. I don't remember throwing up. I got up the next day and went to a doctor's appointment. I couldn't walk for being nauseous. I was sick for three days."

6. Provide your child with perspective on media messages, and engage her in efforts to reduce underage drinking.

The average child sees two thousand television commercials for beer or wine a year; by the time your child turns twenty-one she has probably viewed tens of thousands. Parents need to counteract this steady barrage.

To do so, many of us need to first take a hard look at the effects of those commercials on our own thinking. For years the alcohol industry has been working overtime to "normalize" its product: beer is associated with sports and male bonding; liquor with relaxing and letting loose; wine interests have touted their product as good for your health. If you're a father and your son comes home drunk, does a part of you think, That's my guy? If you're a mother and your college-bound daughter wants to learn what the top liquor brands are, does part of you think, She's becoming quite the sophisticate? Think again; and then again. Then help your children recognize and understand the M.O. of advertising. It may be difficult—nobody wants to acknowledge that they're being manipulated.

To counteract the media deluge on our children, we need to instill in them a sense of their own goodness and self-esteem. "Kids are always looking for affirmation that they're the right way," said Helen Kramer. She added, "Advertising gives you information on what the right way is. In beer-drinking commercials, everyone's having fun. We need to teach kids other ways not only to have fun, but also to gain experiences of mastery that feel good and build self-esteem at the same time."

Children feel affirmed when they master new tasks, whether they're academic, athletic, or artistic. Working through challenges develops their sense of mastery and creates in them an internal "knowing" of how to feel good. Children who have this "knowing" are not as vulnerable to peer pressure or advertising campaigns that create a false sense of what the right way to be is. The child that has developed a sense of self-esteem isn't easily seduced by alcohol commercials. When these children drink they are sensitive to the negative side-effects of alcohol because they have already learned how to feel good in healthy ways.

Educate your children and teens about the effects and consequences of underage drinking. One mother talked to her daughter about beer commercials: "We talked about the sexism inherent in them. A brewer had a Swedish team of blonds that would come in and be part of a commercial. They were omnipresent in these commercials. My daughter was upset that that's how women were being portrayed."

We then need to engage our children in efforts to reduce underage drinking among their peers. Not only will this raise their own awareness, but helping others gives people a sense of power, and young people need to feel powerful. Alcohol promises to make them feel powerful, but they need real power, not "liquid courage."

Your child needs options to the drinking scene. Help him take advantage of recreational and cultural activities. Work with other parents in the community to create such opportunities if they are lacking. Involve local businesses and local government. Engage your children in positive future planning.

7. Help your child pick a college, and stay in contact when he or she is there.

When you and your soon-to-be college student set out to pick a school, there will be many factors to consider. One of them, though

The Proactive Way to Pick a School

1. Ask questions and get answers before you choose a school. Questions can be directed to staff in different departments, including health services, the dean of students, the president's office, admissions, campus security, the alcohol and drug education office, Greek affairs, and judicial affairs.

2. Before choosing a school, find out whether the university president provides leadership on the issue of alcohol and other drugs. Find out the school's alcohol policies and enforcement practices. Are parents informed if a student is disciplined for alcohol infractions or hospitalized for alcohol or drug use?

3. When considering a school, visit the school with your son or daughter. Discuss your concerns with him or her beforehand. If you can, stay over on a weekend to see what the social life is like at night. Check out both the campus and community scene. Are neighboring bars catering to students with specials that encourage binge drinking?

4. Check into substance-free dorms—they are a good bet for higher quality of life. Find out how many spaces are available and how difficult it is to get one.

5. Check out the fraternities and sororities. What kind of shape are they in? How many have been shut down or are on probation? What percentage of the student body belongs to them?

6. Look at the school paper. Are there alcohol ads for parties or local bars? Does it list security incidents over a weekend?

not necessarily the major one, should be the quality of life at the school. How thick is the alcohol haze? Both of you need to know what the drinking scene is at your candidate colleges as well as the school's drinking policies and enforcement practices. If your son or daughter must attend a high-binge school, determine whether she can find a niche on campus that is protected from the heavy drinking lifestyle. Our studies have shown that students who do not binge drink in high school are more likely to take up binge drinking if they attend a high-binge college.

7. If you visit a campus during football season, look for tailgating parties before the games. Is there alcohol involved?

8. Is there a full schedule of classes on Fridays? Will you be paying full-time tuition for a part-time education?

9. Talk to residential advisors about what dorm life is like. How noisy and messy are the dorms during the week and on weekends? What training do resident assistants receive in identifying and helping students with alcohol and other drug problems?

10. Ask questions about school activities on weekends. What's available besides drinking? Are there nonalcoholic late-night events? Is the recreation center opened late on weekends? What kind of community service and volunteer opportunities exist?

11. Look at the school's crime statistics. They may not tell the full story, but if there are many arrests, ask the administrators why. What kinds of alcohol education programs are available at the school? What kind of counseling and mental health services are available?

12. Often a school is picked for reasons such as cost, a particularly strong department, or special programs. Then the key question is whether your son or daughter can find a relatively less alcohol-laden niche on a heavy drinking campus. Where your child chooses to live at college may be the most important choice he or she makes.

When your child finally does leave for college, you will face a balancing act. On the one hand you need to let go—cut those apron strings and let him be his own person. For you as a parent, this is a loss as well as a gain. In anticipation of the loss—the ache of missing the person who you have cared for and lived with and laughed and cried with for eighteen years—you may deny your own emotions. On the other hand, you may enjoy the unaccustomed level of freedom. In either case, you may unwittingly cut your child off from a needed source of support.

Maintain regular contact with your son or daughter at college, with a weekly phone call at least, and the occasional visit. The first semester and the first year are particularly important. But the need for communication does not end with freshman finals. The sophomore year has been called the "lost" year. Don't let it be lost between yourself and your child.

One parent told us how she kept up with her freshman son:

> When I sent him away to college, I realized that the parenting skills I had developed were face to face, and that I needed to develop skills over the phone. I had to know the tone of his voice, to be able to hear what he was saying and determine if it was what he was meaning. And I had to pry. I felt like it was key for me to be able to do this.
>
> I call every Sunday. Sometimes if I don't call him by Sunday night he'll say, Hey, you didn't call me. I set up that regular habit. I call before their week begins, and after their weekend ends. Depending on how early you call on Sunday, you can get a sense of what their Saturday night was like.

8. Demand that the university set limits and provide alternatives to alcohol.

Chances are you'll pay a substantial sum of money for your child's college education. It's more than within your rights, then, to demand a quality education. Chapter 11 outlined crucial steps for universities to take to lift the alcohol haze from college life. But most universities will not do it on their own. Cultural inertia and contrary economic interests keep them from confronting the problem. Until parents and students demand change—demand a safe environment largely free from binge drinking and its effects—the status quo will continue.

Schools should provide alcohol-free housing, control athletic and Greek-system drinking, set up a strict code of conduct and enforce it, and work with students to provide meaningful social alternatives to alcohol.

Parents and students should demand a rich environment providing options for activities that students can be fully engaged in, whether that entails physical fitness or intramural (not spectator) sports; special interests, such as drama or cooking; or volunteer activities, from working with homebound AIDS patients to stumping for political campaigns. While activities need not be planned for around the clock, they need to fit into the students' social schedules, not that of white-collar administrators. Student nightlife starts at 11:00 P.M. and goes on until at least 2:00 or 3:00 A.M.; activities need to be scheduled accordingly.

If your child's quality of life or education is suffering because of the university's lax attitude on alcohol, you can work with campus groups or community coalitions for change. If necessary, you can initiate your own efforts: Call up your local newspaper and television news crew and go public with the abuses. Contact university officials, members of the board of trustees, and influential alumni. Make your voice heard. If all else fails, you still have options.

Some schools are less steeped in alcohol and are committed to enforcement. Your son or daughter can transfer to such a school. In cases of truly egregious negligence that results in harm, you can sue the university, the fraternity, and whatever other entities share responsibility. Colleges will have to learn that their futures lay not in playing party host, but in delivering on the promise of quality education.

9. Be proactive in your community.

You are not just a parent but also a citizen; support laws that will reduce underage drinking and high-volume sales of alcohol. Get involved in community efforts to change the easy accessibility of alcohol. Liquor stores notorious for selling to underage people should not be allowed to carry out business as usual. Bars need to end their low-price specials. Advertisements for alcohol should not appeal to teenagers. In the next chapter, we discuss many other strategies parents and community members are pursuing to clear the alcohol haze from college campuses and their neighborhoods.

Parents may feel such involvement is beyond their experience. Don't be discouraged. "The important thing for parents to realize is that the process of policy change is not just the province of lawyers and lobbyists," said Bill Gallegos, a parent and director of the California Alcohol Policy Reform Initiative. "If communities are organized, they can effect fantastic changes. It is an arena in which parents can become very expert, very effective." Gallegos's group is working to pass a tax on alcohol that would fund alcohol education, prevention, and treatment. The group is developing a statewide youth coalition and holding public forums so that parents and youth can weigh in on how alcohol impacts their communities.

10. When your child needs help, get treatment—fast!

Don't deny obvious signs that your child is in trouble. How many times does he have to stumble in drunk before you take the situation seriously? When you take your children's problems seriously, they can too. "If parents see a kid getting drunk more than once in a rare while, their child needs some kind of help, because usually what parents see is the tip of the iceberg," Helen Kramer said. She continued:

> Most parents are overstressed and may feel overwhelmed by all the negative influences that their children encounter. Often when parents ignore the signs of their children's drinking it's because they don't know what to do and feel frightened or guilty. We need a shift in attitude about asking for help. We need to see it as a strength, not a weakness. Parents cannot afford to let their fear paralyze them, because inevitably the problem will get worse. As soon as you suspect there is a problem, get help.

Talk to other parents in your community and you will quickly discover that you are not alone. Underage drinking is rampant, and it is causing havoc in many people's families.

Whatever kind of problem your child is experiencing, remember that he and his problems are not one and the same. Stella, who discovered that her sixteen-year-old son was binge drinking, told us: "This doesn't make him not a great kid, but I do have to be more vigilant. Lord knows that as a kid I made mistakes, and he will too. I just don't want to see him making the same mistakes over and over again. I want to nip this in the bud. If he chooses to drink when he's a grown man, he can, but if I can nip it in the bud I'll do it."

THE REAL WORLD

As wonderful as it is, parenting is rarely a walk in the park. It is easy to underestimate the stress on yourself, especially when your children encounter difficulties. Said one parent:

I have trouble focusing on my job when my kids are going through things. It disrupts your life as a parent. You realize your kids' lives are enmeshed with yours. If your kid has an alcohol or drug problem, it severely impacts your own life. As a parent you have to kick into gear to make sure your kid is getting the resources he needs, but you also need to make sure you get the resources you need.

Even when you've done everything right, your children can develop serious alcohol problems. Don't blame yourself. Stella thought her son was the "perfect child" until two of his friends carried him home one night and lay him down on the bathroom floor where she found him, face pressed against the tile, throwing up. "We did everything according to the book: 'Communicate, communicate, communicate,'" she said. "My illusions are shattered. I'm living in the real world now. I understand peer pressure. And someone had a fake ID. So it appears to be very easy to get and easy to do, whether out of a car or in someone's home."

Your son or daughter is going to make his or her own choices. You hope that they'll make the proper ones, but you have to be there to support them when they don't and to educate them about their future choices. At the same time, parents today need to be proactive, advocating for their children and with their children, in the community, in grades K–12, and in college.

CHAPTER 13

WHAT COMMUNITIES CAN DO

Where citizens are activated, where local coalitions are at work, where parents are making an issue of underage and heavy drinking, where there is pressure on local police—that is where we see changes that limit these practices. Where no such pressure exists, we tend to see fewer changes.
—Alexander Wagenaar, University of Minnesota School of Public Health

Until ordinary citizens—parents and students, neighbors and friends—exercise their will to change the environment that induces binge drinking, this problem that plagues our college campuses and American society in general will not be solved. Until communities apply their collective creativity to come up with engaging alternatives, young people will continue to rely on alcohol to meet their social needs. Until local bars honor their communities by ending sales practices that encourage binge drinking, and until regional distributors and the big brewers and distillers practice good citizenship by rethinking their aggressive advertising and marketing approaches, the problem will not be solved.

Ordinary citizens need to take the lead in reshaping the alcohol environment because if we do not, the industry will continue to misdirect resources and others' good intentions down dead ends while undermining efforts that would make a real difference.

Over the years, our College Alcohol Study has found conclusively that:

- The lower the price of alcohol, the higher the level of binge drinking.

- The greater the outlet density, the higher the level of binge drinking.

- The more special price promotions, the higher the level of binge drinking.

- The less enforcement of underage drinking laws, the more alcohol underage people consume.

These findings give us a good idea of where to start to effectively change the binge-drinking environment. As an extended community we need to:

1. Raise the price of alcohol.

2. Limit the number of bars and other alcohol outlets around our college campuses.

3. End special price promotions that lower prices even further.

4. Enforce underage drinking laws.

A growing number of organizations on the local, regional, and national levels are organizing to help enact such change. For instance, the national organization Mothers Against Drunk Driving (MADD) has expanded its presence onto college campuses. Also, those involved in the A Matter of Degree (AMOD) program are making changes and gaining valuable organizing experience through campus-community coalitions at ten colleges and universities. Another group that has provided many years of national leadership is the Center for Science in the Public Interest (CSPI). Their Alcohol Policy Project hits upon many of the environmental-change measures most needed today. An overview of their action plan follows.

AN ACTION PLAN FOR COMMUNITIES AND GOVERNMENT

CSPI is a nonprofit health-advocacy organization that focuses on alcoholic-beverage and food-safety issues. It led efforts to win passage of the federal law requiring warning labels on alcoholic beverages and has funded local student groups seeking social alternatives to binge drinking. Here is its organizing agenda.

RECOMMENDATIONS *for* LOCAL COMMUNITIES

- Form a coalition to promote responsible alcohol marketing and service practices.

- Enforce laws against sales to minors and intoxicated individuals by instituting routine compliance checks among other measures.

- Use zoning ordinances and license moratoria to reduce the density of alcohol outlets around campus.

- Study local laws and regulations regarding conditional-use permits, processes to challenge license renewals, and nuisance-abatement suits, and use legal and regulatory channels to promote changes at problem bars.

- Require server training for establishments that sell alcohol. Servers and managers must be able to demonstrate that they understand the terms of their licenses and local laws pertaining to the sale of alcohol and that they are operating in compliance with both. Some topics covered by server training include:

How to recognize the problem drinker

An overview of your state's alcohol laws

How to deal with problem customers

Alcohol as a drug and its effects on the body and behavior

- Promote alcohol-free community social activities, events, and festivals.

- Publicize coalition efforts to reform bar practices that encourage excessive drinking, such as deeply discounted drink specials, and recognize bars that cooperate in those efforts.

- Support state and federal efforts listed below.

RECOMMENDATIONS
for STATE GOVERNMENTS

- Prohibit alcohol marketing on college campuses, in college media, and at college sporting events.

- Restrict happy hours, ladies' nights, and other drink promotions, and require server training. Organize to ban the most egregious practices, such as "all-you-can-drink" and "two-for-one" drink specials.

- Enact or reinstate "dram shop laws" that hold alcohol vendors responsible for underage sales and sales to intoxicated persons who cause others harm. Reform local liquor laws to tighten penalties for such violations, including stiffer fines up to and including license revocation for repeat offenders.

• Raise excise taxes on alcohol products and equalize taxes for liquor, beer, and wine. The tax rates on beer and wine are significantly lower than that on liquor. Raising beer and wine taxes to the liquor level would reduce underage beer consumption and provide new revenues to treat and prevent alcohol problems as well as to reduce state budget deficits.

RECOMMENDATIONS *for the* FEDERAL GOVERNMENT

• Prohibit alcohol marketing on college campuses, in college media, and at college sporting events.

• Require campuses to report on the involvement of alcohol in campus crimes.

• Establish a national media campaign to prevent underage drinking, akin to federal efforts to prevent and reduce illicit drug use among teens.

• Require all alcohol advertising to carry health warnings on the diverse risks of alcohol use, as the surgeon general's warning appears on cigarette packs.

• Enact tougher time, place, and manner restrictions on broadcast advertising for all alcoholic-beverage products to reduce youth exposure to such ads. Such responsible advertising guidelines should include the following provisions:

- Setting a cap on the absolute number and percent of potential underage viewers exposed to alcohol advertising. Alcohol industry voluntary guidelines now allow half the audience to be underage. MADD standards call for a 90 percent-adult audience. (CSPI is currently investigating appropriate targets based on various programming and times of broadcast.) Consider imposing limits on the number of alcohol ads or the time allotted for alcohol advertising within each broadcast hour.

- Requiring equal time for public health and safety messages for young people and adults about the diverse risks of alcohol consumption. Government or independent agencies or public health experts not affiliated with the alcoholic beverage industry should produce those messages.

- Mandating that all alcohol commercials carry visible and audible health warning messages about the risks of alcohol consumption. Those messages should vary, rotate in ads, and address the numerous documented risks of alcohol consumption.

COMMUNITY SUCCESSES

Binge drinking is acknowledged as the number-one health problem at American colleges. We have seen throughout this book how student alcohol abuse can impact communities—not only those neighborhoods immediately surrounding college campuses but also the towns and cities that the students come from and those where they eventually settle.

The problem has reached a tipping point, leading to an increase in community awareness and action. This can be seen in the more than six hundred MADD chapters around the country; in the ten campus-community coalitions of A Matter of Degree that are changing local laws and culture; in grassroot campaigns in a dozen cities in California and the Southwest that are challenging the alcohol industry's co-optation of ethnic holidays and cultural symbols to sell their products; in regional coalitions forming in Texas, the greater Washington, D.C., area and other states; and in the national outrage that greeted the attempted return of liquor ads to network television.

Following are just a few of the inspiring stories of activism and pride relating to alcohol-policy reform on colleges and in communities.

IOWA CITY, IOWA: ENDING DRINK SPECIALS

The Stepping Up Coalition in Iowa City, Iowa, part of the A Matter of Degree program, tackles college binge drinking on many fronts. About twenty thousand students attend the University of Iowa in a community of about one hundred thousand citizens. Within a mile of campus students can find more than a hundred licensed alcohol establishments. In addition, the city has no legal age restriction for entering a bar.

Stepping Up was instrumental in passing a law that restricts price specials on alcohol. It prohibits all liquor-license holders in Iowa City from selling two drinks for the price of one, selling an unlimited number of servings for a fixed price, or serving more than two drinks at any one time to any one person. It also prohibits games or contests that involve drinking alcohol or awarding alcohol as a prize, and it prohibits license holders from pouring alcohol directly into a person's mouth. The law, which took effect August 1, 2001, expands the city council's authority to revoke liquor licenses—especially for serving alcohol to underage persons.

Six months after the council passed the ordinance, the police department's monthly bar check reports showed that citations for underage possession in bars had dropped about 17 percent. In that regard, it seemed like the law was working. On the other hand, some bar owners were finding ways around the limits on specials simply by slashing prices—beers for a quarter are now standard fare in some bars. "The bar owners that tend to be more receptive and supportive tend to have a clientele that is older," said Cathy Solow, an Iowa City parent active in Stepping Up.

As a result, the city's drinking environment is changing. "We used to have beer trucks rumbling down the middle of the street at the homecoming parade. That no longer happens," Solow said.

LINCOLN, NEBRASKA: LIMITING LICENSES

Every year as football season nears, the city council in Lincoln, Nebraska, meets to review and approve applications for special permits to sell beer, liquor, and wine outside of licensed bars and hotels. Businesses use these licenses to expand into their parking lots for home football games, officially moving alcohol into the streets and multiplying many times over the number of patrons and volume of drinks sold. Processing the applications is usually a routine, if mundane, task.

In the 2001 season, business as usual ceased. "[That] season we had an unusually large number of applications," said Lincoln Police Chief Tom Casady. The increase came in anticipation of the big games planned ahead, Notre Dame and Oklahoma among them. But the biggest reason for the increase was the opening of the Champions Club, a facility owned by the Nebraska Alumni Association, Casady said. "The club sits directly across from Memorial Stadium. It has four-and-a-half acres of parking lot and a beautiful pavilion, all surrounded by a wrought iron fence. It has four hundred parking stalls that lease for ten thousand dollars each. Members are high rollers, heavy hitters, corporate donors, high-profile alums that can afford that."

The Champions Club wanted to get a special alcohol license; to Casady's surprise, the city council said no. "It said we don't need it, we don't need more tailgating," Casady recalled. "You could have knocked me over with a feather."

During the following weeks, industry representatives and supporters heavily lobbied the council to change its vote. "Ultimately no council member was willing to make a motion to reconsider, out of a concern that they would look bad. That is a dramatic change in the political climate in Lincoln regarding high-risk drinking and alcohol service. We've had a major turnaround," Casady said.

Chief Casady also cochairs NU Directions, a campus-community coalition that is part of the A Matter of Degree program. Formed in 1998, NU Directions is contending with a heavily saturated drinking environment—more than one hundred licensed alcohol establishments within one mile of the main campus. "The sheer number of licenses has increased the competitive environment," Casady said.

The coalition has tried to thin outlet density by limiting the number of licenses and by revoking the licenses of establishments that break the law. It's been an uphill fight. "One major impediment is legal," Casady said. A series of Nebraska Supreme Court cases have established a legal precedent that affords local units of government very little control in the granting of liquor licenses or in revoking licenses. As a result, the coalition is beginning to focus on zoning codes. "We have spent a great deal of time casting about for other ways to control density without running afoul of the State Supreme Court," Casady said. "Zoning is our current best effort."

SALINAS, CALIFORNIA: GOING PUBLIC *with* ZONING ISSUES

Local governments can determine what activities may occur on the land within their jurisdiction. To do so, they establish land-use zoning ordinances that identify the type of development permitted within a given area, whether that is single-family residences, commercial businesses, schools, parks, or halfway houses. Local communities can often rely on land-use zoning to determine where alcohol may be sold or consumed and how it is distributed and marketed.

The U.S. Department of Justice reports one way this tool has been used: The city of Salinas, California, enacted a zoning ordinance that requires public review of proposals to open alcohol retail outlets. As a result, the city has limited the number of new outlets and imposed strict conditions on those they have approved. In one case, neighbors protested a proposal to open a liquor store in a new development that already had too many. The city council rejected the liquor store application. Neighborhood residents wanted a daycare center instead of a liquor store. They convinced the developer of the feasibility of the daycare center and assisted him in financing it.

ANNAPOLIS, MARYLAND: REGISTERING BEER KEGS

To limit heavy drinking by teens at large parties, communities have organized to enact laws that require the registration of beer kegs sold to private citizens. Consumers must fill out a registration card, and their kegs are marked accordingly. Then, if the kegs end up being served to underage drinkers—and especially if any of those drinkers is harmed or harms others—police can trace the kegs back to the retailer and the purchaser and thus hold adults responsible for the illegal sale.

Maryland citizens managed to pass keg registration over the stiff opposition of the alcohol industry. In the year leading up to the vote, the industry spent more than a hundred thousand dollars to influence Maryland legislators, according to *Washington Post* staff writer Charles Babington. "The Maryland Licensed Beverage Association, for example, had paid lobbyist Jay Schwartz $23,502. . . . The beer wholesalers had paid lobbyist George Manis $18,500, and had spent $2,507 on meals and a reception," Babington wrote in a summary of the struggle that pitted parents and citizens against the industry. Citizens triumphed by being organized. Galvanized by several tragedies, they formed the Maryland Underage Drinking Prevention Coalition. Their lobbying took them to the State House in Annapolis, where at one point, parents and children staged a demonstration with a keg and casket and signs that read TOO MANY KEGS = TOO MANY CASKETS.

Maryland passed its law in 1994. The trend has continued, and last year Georgia joined the one-quarter of all states that have enacted such laws.

LOS ANGELES: ELIMINATING BILLBOARDS

The citizens of Los Angeles took a different tack. Los Angeles County, the largest consumer market in the country, is a jungle of billboards for beer, liquor, and cigarettes. For two years alcohol and tobacco policy advocates joined together with parents, students, and ordinary citizens—with overwhelming support from the Latino community—to campaign for an ordinance restricting alcohol and tobacco billboards and storefront advertising. Passed in September 1998, the ordinance restricted such signage to at least one thousand feet from all residential zones and uses and other sites frequented by teenagers such as schools, parks, and churches.

"We won one of the best ordinances in the country—and then it got overturned by the courts," said Bill Gallegos, director of the multicultural California Alcohol Policy Reform Initiative. The industry succeeded in shelving the ordinance based on claims that it had singled them out, denying their constitutional right to free speech.

Not to be outdone, a rejuvenated coalition is now campaigning to have the city eliminate all new advertising, including alcohol and tobacco. "We're coming at it from another angle. Alcohol can't say they're being singled out. We are removing blight," Gallegos said. "We don't give up."

WORKING WITH BIG ALCOHOL

One issue that comes up repeatedly in alcohol prevention work is how to relate to the industry. This varies depending on a community's particular situation.

In Los Angeles the alcohol industry and Anheuser-Busch in particular were the strongest opponents of the billboard legislation, outdoing even the billboard companies in their resistance, Gallegos said.

Police Chief Casady in Lincoln, Nebraska, said, "The alcohol industry will fight tooth and nail on any legislative measure, like increasing excise taxes. They try mightily to co-opt people with their money. But we also have retailers and wholesalers serving on our coalition. On balance, having them at the table has been valuable to us. But I'm real watchful for letting the camel get entirely into the tent." Casady said that retailers and wholesalers have helped the coalition get mandatory server education, new state driver's licenses that are harder to fake, and more workable hearing procedures at the state liquor commission.

Other communities have met more resistance from the industry. Iowa City's Cathy Solow said that discussions with retailers about the new law limiting drink specials were typically adversarial rather than cooperative efforts to solve the problem. Nonetheless, the coalition is considering having a bar owner sit on its executive board.

The bottom line is that citizens involved in trying to change the alcohol landscape need to state upfront what they want from the industry. Said Dan Skiles, the project director for the Partnership for Alcohol Responsibility coalition at Florida State University: "We ought to be more proactive and say, Here's how you can help."

An ACTION PLAN for BIG ALCOHOL

If the industry truly wants to end underage drinking and decrease the damage caused by excessive alcohol use, it should:

- Fight the urge to make alcohol dirt cheap.

- Pay its fair share of society's costs of policing, treating, and cleaning up from binge drinkers.

- Stop trying to lower excise taxes, and support the use of higher excise taxes to develop prevention and treatment programs.

- Develop advertising programs that clearly appeal only to those over twenty-one. If there is a "spillover" effect to those under the legal drinking age, don't use the ad. Drop advertising that encourages binge drinking. If advertising is a means of obtaining brand loyalty, display the brand and not the false promises of heightened sexuality, male bonding, social popularity, and carefree adventure.

- Educate retailers about responsible marketing and serving practices. Help remove price specials, freebies, and other methods of providing cheap alcohol. Make sure bartenders and servers go through server training programs.

- Help communities limit the number of outlets near college campuses. Too many outlets heighten competition and stimulate price wars, which makes alcohol cheap.

- Help communities control high-volume drinking by restricting keg purchases and alcohol sold by the pitcher or in other large containers.

- Educate bartenders about acute alcohol poisoning and the deadly game of Drinking Your Age.

FINALLY, COMMON SENSE

We hold our institutions of higher learning in esteem for the opportunities they offer, the knowledge they impart, and the values of intellectual openness and academic freedom they foster. Entry into college represents a major milestone for a young person. Graduation as a young adult represents another. Between entry and exit, students refine and define their goals and values, skills, and commitments. The people they are, and the people they become, say a lot about where we, as a nation, may go. So does the guidance we give them and the standards to which we hold ourselves and hold the alcohol industry.

The binge drinking culture undermines the quality of education at our colleges and universities and directs precious resources to damage control. Those resources represent not only the individual investment of families, in terms of tuition, but also the resources provided by taxpayers for financial aid and the benefit universities receive based on their tax-exempt status. Both private and public universities have a responsibility to the broader community, which is often seriously disrupted by student drinking.

The solutions to college binge drinking are complex. Good communication between parents and their sons and daughters is essential, but it is not enough. Personal responsibility on the part of students is essential, but it too is not enough. Words alone will not change the drinking environment encountered by young people at our universities and in our communities.

In the end, opposing binge drinking means supporting students' individuality and creativity. It means respecting, not exploiting, cultural heritage. It requires raising social awareness and encouraging academic, artistic, and athletic excellence. Practically, it requires changing the drinking environment—limiting the accessibility and underpricing of alcohol and ending the industry's predatory advertising and promotions.

Change will come when universities divest themselves of alcohol industry money and get rid of antiquated and unhealthy drinking traditions. It will come when fraternities face the facts of their alcohol problems and seek radical treatment—today, not next year—and when college sports fans from coaches to the NCAA sever their ties with Big Alcohol. People who know better need to tell the binge drinkers that their drinking is putting themselves and others at risk and stop treating dangerous drinking like a numbers game.

Change will come when social alternatives are given a real chance. It will come through student- and citizen-led efforts that require responsibility on the part of retailers, wholesalers, and producers of alcoholic beverages. Students and parents, communities and government agencies, college administrations and faculty all have important roles. By working together, we can overcome the problem of binge drinking on our college campuses.

RESOURCES

AlcoholScreening.org
Take a self-test to assess your drinking patterns and receive personalized feedback, read frequently asked questions about alcohol and health, find links to support resources, and search a database of twelve thousand treatment centers.

A Matter of Degree (AMOD)
www.amodstrat.net
An advocacy group that seeks to make long-lasting changes in the college environment to reduce alcohol abuse among students and improve the quality of life for all community residents. It is administered by the American Medical Association and funded by The Robert Wood Johnson Foundation.

Be Responsible About Drinking (BRAD)
www.brad21.org
BRAD was founded by the family and friends of Bradley McCue, a Michigan State University junior who died of alcohol poisoning after celebrating his twenty-first birthday. The site presents educational information about alcohol.

Break Away
www.alternativebreaks.org
Their mission is to promote alcohol-free spring break programs.

Center for Science in the Public Interest
www.cspinet.org
A nonprofit education and advocacy organization that focuses on improving the safety and nutritional quality of our food supply and on reducing the carnage caused by alcoholic beverages.

Center for Substance Abuse Prevention
www.samhsa.gov/centers/csap/csap.html
Provides national leadership in the federal effort to prevent alcohol, tobacco, and illicit drug problems.

CIRCLe Network
www.circlenetwork.org
A nonprofit organization that works to improve the quality of campus life.

The CORE Institute
www.coreinstitute.com
A federally funded program assisting institutions of higher education in drug and alcohol prevention efforts via a survey to assess the effectiveness of campus-based prevention programs.

Daily Dose
www.dailydose.net
This site consists of substance misuse articles gathered from the World Wide Web.

Harvard School of Public Health College Alcohol Study (CAS)
www.hsph.harvard.edu/cas
The Web site for the study upon which this book is based.

Higher Education Center for Alcohol and Other Drug Information (HEC)

www.edc.org/hec

The HEC's purpose is to help colleges develop, implement, and evaluate programs and policies to reduce student problems related to alcohol and other drug use and interpersonal violence.

Join Together

www.jointogether.org

This group runs a news service, hosts active online discussion groups, and provides lists of resources and funding sources, including a national directory of contact information, for people working to prevent substance abuse.

Leadership to Keep Children Alcohol Free

www.alcoholfreechildren.org

A coalition of federal agencies and public and private organizations seeking to prevent the use of alcohol by children ages nine to fifteen.

The Marin Institute for the Prevention of Alcohol and Other Drug Problems

www.marininstitute.org

This site concentrates on the environments that support and glamorize alcohol use. Includes a large database about the alcohol beverage industry, alcohol policy resources, and more.

Mothers Against Drunk Driving (MADD)

www.madd.org

Provides information on the group's activities as well as counseling for victims.

The National Center on Addiction and Substance Abuse at Columbia University (CASA)

www.casacolumbia.org

A unique think/action-tank that engages all disciplines to study every form of substance abuse as it affects society.

The National Clearinghouse for Alcohol and Drug Information (NCADI)

www.health.org/aboutn.htm

Links to almost everything on the topic that is available from the federal government and claims to be the world's largest resource for current information concerning substance abuse. The site is a source of grant announcements for prevention, treatment, and research funding opportunities.

National Commission Against Drunk Driving (NCADD)

www.ncadd.com

The mission of this group is to continue the efforts of the Presidential Commission on Drunk Driving to reduce impaired driving by uniting a broad-based coalition of public and private sector organizations and other concerned individuals.

National Crime Prevention Council

www.ncpc.org

The NCPC is the nation's focal point and voice for crime prevention. A source of help for individuals, neighborhoods, communities, and governments, it is a nonprofit educational organization.

National Substance Abuse Web Index

http://nsawi.health.org

Source of relevant, authoritative information on substance abuse prevention, treatment communities, and excellent links.

Office of National Drug Control Policy (ONDCP)

www.whitehousedrugpolicy.gov

Establishes policies, priorities, and objectives for the nation's drug control program, the goals of which are to reduce illicit drug use, manufacturing, and trafficking; drug-related crime and violence; and drug-related health consequences.

Outside the Classroom

www.outsidetheclassroom.com

Many colleges and universities use this company's flagship product, AlcoholEdu, as the cornerstone of their prevention efforts. Together with its TheHealthSurvey, which provides statistically valid and actionable information online, Outside the Classroom offers institutions a cost-effective toolset for preventing the negative consequences of alcohol abuse on campus.

Pacific Institute for Research and Evaluation (PIRE)

www.pire.org

Their mission is to promote, undertake, and evaluate activities, studies, and programs that improve individual and public health, welfare, and safety. An excellent source for alcohol-related research.

Security on Campus

www.campussafety.org

A nonprofit organization devoted to fighting campus crime, established by Connie and Howard Clery in memory of their daughter, Jeanne Ann.

Students Against Destructive Decisions (SADD)

www.saddonline.com

General information on international prevention programs for college, junior, and senior high school students. SADD seeks to help students deal with the issues of underage drinking, drunk driving, drug abuse, and other destructive decisions.

Task Force on College Drinking

www.collegedrinkingprevention.gov

Sponsored by the National Institute on Alcohol Abuse and Alcoholism (NIAAA), this site gives a thorough background of the alcohol problem on college campuses and posts reports on possible solutions.

The Trauma Foundation

www.tf.org/tf/alcohol

An organization committed to preventing alcohol-related injuries and deaths, particularly among young people.

U.S. Department of Education Office of Post Secondary Education (OPE)

http://ope.ed.gov/security

Access the crime statistics for more than six thousand U.S. colleges and universities.

APPENDIX: THE 2001 HARVARD SCHOOL OF PUBLIC HEALTH COLLEGE ALCOHOL STUDY

SECTION A: STUDENT LIFE

A1. How old are you?
- ○ 17 or younger
- ○ 18
- ○ 19
- ○ 20
- ○ 21
- ○ 22
- ○ 23
- ○ 24
- ○ 25 or older

A2. Are you male or female?
- ○ Male
- ○ Female

A3. What is your current year in school?
- ○ Freshman (first year)
- ○ Sophomore (2nd year)
- ○ Junior (3rd year)
- ○ Senior (4th year)
- ○ 5th year or beyond (<u>undergraduate</u>)
- ○ Graduate student

A4. Did you transfer to this school from another college?
- ○ No, did not transfer ➡ **Go to A5**
- ○ Yes, during this current school year ➡ **Go to A4a**
- ○ Yes, before this school year ➡ **Go to A4a**

> **A4a. Was the school you transferred from . . .**
> - ○ In the same state?
> - ○ In a different state?
>   If in a different state, what state did you transfer from? _____
> - ○ Outside of U.S.A.?

A5. Are you a member of a fraternity or sorority?
- ○ Yes
- ○ No

A6. Where do you live during the current school year while you are at college? (Choose one answer.)
- ○ Single-sex residence hall or dormitory ➡ **Go to A7**
- ○ Co-ed residence hall or dormitory ➡ **Go to A7**
- ○ Other university housing ➡ **Go to A7**
- ○ Fraternity/sorority house ➡ **Go to A7**
- ○ Off-campus house or apartment ➡ **Go to A6a**
- ○ Other: _____ ➡ **Go to A6a**

> **A6a. If Off-campus, how far from school?**
> - ○ Less than 1 mile
> - ○ 1–2 miles
> - ○ 2+ to 5 miles
> - ○ More than 5 miles

A7. With whom do you currently live? (Choose all that apply.)
- ○ Alone
- ○ Roommate(s) or housemate(s)
- ○ Spouse or partner
- ○ Parent(s) or other relative(s)

A8. How important is it for you to participate in the following activities at college? (Choose one answer in each row.)

	Very Important	Important	Somewhat Important	Not At All Important
a. Athletics	○	○	○	○
b. Arts	○	○	○	○
c. Academic work	○	○	○	○
d. Fraternity or sorority life	○	○	○	○
e. Political activism	○	○	○	○
f. Parties	○	○	○	○
g. Community service	○	○	○	○
h. Religion	○	○	○	○
i. Attend sports events	○	○	○	○

SECTION B: YOUR VIEWS ABOUT POLICIES AND PROGRAMS

B1. Do you think alcohol use is a problem for students on your campus?

○ A major problem   ○ A minor problem
○ A problem   ○ Not a problem

B2. What is your school's policy about alcohol use on campus by students, staff, and faculty? (Choose one answer.)

○ Alcohol prohibited for everyone, regardless of age
○ Alcohol prohibited for all students, regardless of age
○ Alcohol prohibited for everyone under 21
○ Alcohol allowed for those over 21 but only in designated locations or at special events
○ No school policy
○ Don't know school's policy

B3. In your opinion, how strongly does your school enforce its alcohol policy?

○ The alcohol policy is strongly enforced
○ The alcohol policy is enforced
○ The alcohol policy is weakly enforced
○ The alcohol policy is not enforced at all
○ Don't know school's policy / No school policy

B4. Do you agree with the way your college is dealing with student alcohol use?

○ Agree strongly   ○ Disagree
○ Agree   ○ Disagree strongly

B5. Which of the following do you think should be your school's policy about student drinking? (Choose one answer.)

○ The current alcohol policy
○ A policy which imposes greater restrictions on alcohol use
○ A policy which imposes fewer restrictions on alcohol use
○ Don't know school's policy

B6. Since the beginning of the school year, has your school provided the following types of information to you? (Choose one answer in each row.)

	Yes	No
a. Where you can get help for alcohol-related problems	○	○
b. How to recognize when someone has a drinking problem	○	○
c. The long term health effects of heavy drinking	○	○
d. The dangers of alcohol overdose	○	○
e. College rules for drinking	○	○
f. Penalties for breaking rules	○	○
g. Students' drinking rate at your school	○	○

B7. Since the beginning of the school year, have you attended or seen the following alcohol education materials or programs? (Choose one answer in each row.)

	Yes	No
a. Attended lectures, meetings or workshops	○	○
b. Received mailings or handouts	○	○
c. Seen posters or signs	○	○
d. Read announcements or articles in student newspapers	○	○
e. Taken a special college course on alcohol and other student life issues	○	○

B8. Some universities have housing that is specially designated as "alcohol-free." Do you live in this type of housing during the current school year?
- ○ Yes → Go to B9
- ○ No → Go to B11

B9. **If you live in "alcohol-free" housing,** how were you assigned to "alcohol-free" housing? (choose one answer)
- ○ I live in "alcohol-free" housing **because I specifically requested it**
- ○ I was assigned to an "alcohol-free" housing because I am a freshman (or under 21 years old)
- ○ I live in "alcohol-free" housing because all of the housing at my school is "alcohol-free"
- ○ Other: _____

B10. **If you live in "alcohol-free" housing,** how is the alcohol policy enforced in your housing? (choose one answer)
- ○ Enforced strictly, very few students drink alcohol while in my residence hall
- ○ Somewhat enforced, some students drink alcohol while in my residence hall
- ○ Not enforced, many students drink alcohol while in my residence hall

Skip to B12

B11. If you do not live in "alcohol-free" housing, would you like to do so?
- ○ Yes
- ○ No

B12. Some universities have housing that is specially designated as "smoke-free." Do you live in this type of housing during the current school year?
- ○ Yes → Go to B13
- ○ No → Go to B14

B13. **If you live in "smoke-free" housing,** how were you assigned to "smoke-free" housing? (choose one answer)
- ○ I live in "smoke-free" housing because I **specifically requested it**
- ○ I was assigned to "smoke-free" housing because all of the housing at my school is "smoke-free"
- ○ Other: _____

Skip to B15

B14. If you do not live in "smoke-free" housing, would you like to do so?
- ○ Yes
- ○ No

B15. How likely is it that a student under 21 years of age who drinks alcohol on or near your campus in any of the following situations will be caught? (Choose one answer in each row.)

	Very Likely	Somewhat Likely	Somewhat Unlikely	Very Unlikely	Don't Know
a. In a dorm room	○	○	○	○	○
b. At a dorm party or social event	○	○	○	○	○
c. At a fraternity or sorority party	○	○	○	○	○
d. At an intercollegiate home athletic event	○	○	○	○	○
e. At an intercollegiate away athletic event	○	○	○	○	○
f. At an off-campus party	○	○	○	○	○
g. At an off-campus bar or club	○	○	○	○	○

B16. If a student is caught on your campus using a fake ID to get alcohol, what is likely to happen to the student? (Choose all that apply.)
- ○ Nothing will happen
- ○ Will be refused alcohol
- ○ ID will be confiscated
- ○ Will receive official warning
- ○ Will be fined
- ○ Will be sent to an alcohol education program
- ○ Will be required to do community service
- ○ Will be put on probation
- ○ Parents will be notified
- ○ Don't know

B17. If a student under 21 years of age attempted to purchase alcohol in the city or town where your college is located, how likely is it that he or she . . . (Choose one answer in each row.)

	Very Likely	Somewhat Likely	Somewhat Unlikely	Very Unlikely	Don't Know
a. Would be asked for an ID for proof of age?	O	O	O	O	O
b. Would be refused sale of alcohol?	O	O	O	O	O

B18. If a student is caught using a fake ID to purchase alcohol off campus in the city or town where your college is located, how likely to happen are each of the following consequences? (Choose one answer in each row.)

	Very Likely	Somewhat Likely	Somewhat Unlikely	Very Unlikely	Don't Know
a. The ID is rejected and the sale refused	O	O	O	O	O
b. The ID is confiscated	O	O	O	O	O
c. Local police are notified	O	O	O	O	O
d. School is notified	O	O	O	O	O
e. Parents are notified	O	O	O	O	O

B19. What should be the legal minimum drinking age? (Choose one answer.)

O Under 18   O 18   O 19   O 20   O 21 or over

B20. Are there places at or near your school where you or your friends usually can get alcohol without showing an ID? (Choose one answer in each row.)

	No	Yes	Don't Know
a. At a local off-campus bar or club	O	O	O
b. At an on-campus pub	O	O	O
c. At a local liquor or grocery store	O	O	O
d. At a fraternity or sorority house	O	O	O

B21. To what extent do you support or oppose the following **possible school policies or procedures**? (Choose one answer in each row.)

	Strongly Support	Support	Oppose	Strongly Oppose
a. Prohibit kegs on campus	O	O	O	O
b. Offer alcohol-free dorms	O	O	O	O
c. Ban advertisements of alcohol availability at campus events and parties	O	O	O	O
d. Provide more alcohol-free recreational and cultural opportunities such as movies, dances, sports, and lectures	O	O	O	O
e. Make the alcohol rules more clear	O	O	O	O
f. Enforce the alcohol rules more strictly	O	O	O	O
g. Crack down on drinking at sororities and fraternities	O	O	O	O
h. Hold hosts responsible for problems arising from alcohol use	O	O	O	O
i. Crack down on under-age drinking	O	O	O	O

B22. What is your school's policy about SMOKING in <u>dormitories and residence halls</u>?

- ○ Tobacco smoking is not allowed in student rooms
- ○ Tobacco smoking is allowed in student rooms only if roommates agree
- ○ Tobacco smoking is allowed in some or all dorms
- ○ No policy
- ○ Don't know school's policy

B23. To what extent do you support or oppose the following <u>possible school policies or procedures about smoking</u>? (Choose one answer in each row.)

	Strongly Support	Support	Oppose	Strongly Oppose
a. Prohibit smoking in <u>every building on campus</u>	○	○	○	○
b. Prohibit smoking in <u>all parts of residence halls</u> including student sleeping quarters	○	○	○	○
c. Prohibit smoking in on-campus <u>bars or pubs</u>	○	○	○	○
d. Prohibit smoking in on-campus <u>restaurants or dining areas</u>	○	○	○	○
e. Prohibit <u>advertisements for tobacco</u> products on-campus and in student newspapers	○	○	○	○
f. Prohibits the <u>sale of tobacco</u> products on campus	○	○	○	○
g. Enforce the tobacco policies more strictly	○	○	○	○
h. Prohibit sponsorships of school parties or events by tobacco companies	○	○	○	○

SECTION C: PERSONAL ALCOHOL USE

The following questions ask about how much you drink. A "drink" means any of the following:
A 12-ounce can or bottle of beer
A 4-ounce glass of wine
A 12-ounce bottle or can of wine cooler
A shot of liquor straight or in a mixed drink

C1. Think back over the <u>last two weeks</u>. How many times have you had <u>five or more drinks</u> in a row?

- ○ None
- ○ Once
- ○ Twice
- ○ 3 to 5 times
- ○ 6 to 9 times
- ○ 10 or more times

C2. During the <u>last two weeks</u>, how many times have you had <u>four drinks</u> in a row (but no more than that)?

- ○ None
- ○ Once
- ○ Twice
- ○ 3 to 5 times
- ○ 6 to 9 times
- ○ 10 or more times

If you answer "None" to both questions C1 and C2, then skip to question C7.
Otherwise go to questions C3 through C6.

C3. What type of alcohol did you usually have on those occasions when you have <u>four or more</u> drinks in a row?

- ○ Beer
- ○ "Low Alcohol" beer
- ○ Wine coolers
- ○ Wine
- ○ Liquor (or mixed drinks)
- ○ No "usual" drink

C4. The last time that you had <u>four or more</u> drinks in a row, how many drinks did you actually have?

- ○ 4 drinks
- ○ 5 drinks
- ○ 6 drinks
- ○ 7 drinks
- ○ 8 drinks
- ○ 9 drinks
- ○ 10–14 drinks
- ○ 15 or more drinks

C5. How long did it take you to consume the number of drinks you indicated in question C4?

- ○ 1 hour or less
- ○ 2 hours
- ○ 3 hours
- ○ 4 hours
- ○ 5 hours
- ○ 6 hours or more

C6. How much did you pay for one drink the last time you had <u>four or more drinks</u> in a row?

- ○ Nothing, it is typically free
- ○ Under $0.50
- ○ $0.51–1.00
- ○ $1.01–2.00
- ○ $2.01–3.00
- ○ $3.01 or more
- ○ I pay a set fee for all you can drink; that fee is usually _____
  (Please fill in amount.)

The following questions are for everyone.

C7. How would you best describe yourself in terms of your current use of alcohol? (Choose one answer.)
- ○ Abstainer
- ○ Abstainer—former problem drinker in recovery
- ○ Infrequent drinker
- ○ Light drinker
- ○ Moderate drinker
- ○ Heavy drinker
- ○ Problem drinker

C8. How easy is it for you to obtain alcohol? (Choose one answer.)
- ○ Very difficult
- ○ Difficult
- ○ Easy
- ○ Very easy
- ○ Don't know, I don't drink

C9. How many drinks does it take you to feel drunk?
- ○ 1 drink
- ○ 2 drinks
- ○ 3 drinks
- ○ 4 drinks
- ○ 5 drinks
- ○ 6 drinks
- ○ 7 drinks
- ○ 8 drinks
- ○ 9 drinks
- ○ 10 or more drinks
- ○ I don't know

C10. When did you last have a drink (that is more than just a few sips)?
- ○ I have never had a drink → Skip to C22 (page 10)
- ○ Not in the past year → Skip to C22 (page 10)
- ○ More than 30 days ago, but in the past year → Skip to C17
- ○ More than a week ago, but in the past 30 days → Go to C11
- ○ Within the last week → Go to C11

Answer questions C11 through C15 only if you have had a drink in the past 30 days.

C11. On how many occasions have you had a drink of alcohol in the past 30 days? (Choose one answer.)
- ○ 1 to 2 occasions
- ○ 3 to 5 occasions
- ○ 6 to 9 occasions
- ○ 10 to 19 occasions
- ○ 20 to 39 occasions
- ○ 40 or more occasions

C12. In the past 30 days, on those occasions when you drank alcohol, how many drinks did you usually have? (Choose one answer.)
- ○ 1 drink
- ○ 2 drinks
- ○ 3 drinks
- ○ 4 drinks
- ○ 5 drinks
- ○ 6 drinks
- ○ 7 drinks
- ○ 8 drinks
- ○ 9 or more drinks

C13. In the past 30 days, how often did you drink enough to get drunk? (By drunk, we mean unsteady, dizzy, or sick to your stomach.) (Choose one answer.)
- ○ Not at all
- ○ 1 to 2 occasions
- ○ 3 to 5 occasions
- ○ 6 to 9 occasions
- ○ 10 to 19 occasions
- ○ 20 to 39 occasions
- ○ 40 or more occasions

C14. In the past 30 days, how many drinks did you have the last time you attended any of the following events? (Choose one answer in each row.)

	Didn't Attend	No Drinks	1 or 2 Drinks	3 Drinks	4 Drinks	5 or More Drinks
a. Residence hall social event or party	○	○	○	○	○	○
b. Fraternity or sorority event or party	○	○	○	○	○	○
c. On-campus dance or concert	○	○	○	○	○	○
d. Intercollegiate home athletic event	○	○	○	○	○	○
e. Intercollegiate away athletic event	○	○	○	○	○	○
f. On-campus pub	○	○	○	○	○	○
g. Off-campus party	○	○	○	○	○	○
h. Off-campus bar or club	○	○	○	○	○	○

Attended and had:

C15. In the past 30 days, have you taken advantage of the following: (choose one answer in each row)

	Yes	No
a. Happy hours	○	○
b. Low priced promotions at off-campus bars (ladies nights, drink 'til-you-bust, etc.)	○	○
c. Special promotions by beer companies	○	○
d. Cover charge for unlimited drinks at an off-campus bar	○	○
e. Small admission fee for unlimited drinks at a private party	○	○
f. Small admission fee for unlimited drinks at a fraternity or sorority party	○	○
g. Free unlimited drinks at a fraternity or sorority party	○	○
h. Free unlimited drinks at a private party	○	○

Answer this question only if you are younger than 21 years of age. If you are older, go on to question C17.

C16. In the past 30 days, have you obtained alcohol in any of the following ways? (Choose one answer in each row.)

	Yes	No
a. Got it myself without being carded	○	○
b. Got it from someone who was under 21	○	○
c. Used my own fake ID	○	○
d. Got it from a student who was 21 or older	○	○
e. Got it from a stranger who was 21 or older	○	○
f. Got it from parents or relatives	○	○

Answer questions C17 through C21 if you have had a drink either within the past year or within the past 30 days.

C17. Since the beginning of the school year, how often has your drinking caused you to . . . ? (Choose one answer in each row.)

	Not At All	Once	Twice	3 Times	4 or More Times
a. Have a hangover	○	○	○	○	○
b. Miss a class	○	○	○	○	○
c. Get behind in school work	○	○	○	○	○
d. Do something you later regretted	○	○	○	○	○
e. Forget where you were or what you did	○	○	○	○	○
f. Argue with friends	○	○	○	○	○
g. Engage in unplanned sexual activity	○	○	○	○	○
h. Not use protection when you had sex	○	○	○	○	○

Continue with question C17 on next page ➡

C17. Since the beginning of the school year, how often has your drinking caused you to . . . ? (Choose one answer in each row.)

	Not At All	Once	Twice	3 Times	4 or More Times
i. Damage property	○	○	○	○	○
j. Get into trouble with the campus or local police	○	○	○	○	○
k. Get hurt or injured	○	○	○	○	○
l. Require medical treatment for an alcohol overdose	○	○	○	○	○

C18. Since the beginning of the school year, how frequently has each of the following happened to you? (Choose one answer in each row.)

	Not At All	Once	2 or 3 Times	4 or More Times
a. I was stopped or searched for alcohol when entering a dorm or residence hall	○	○	○	○
b. My own room was searched for alcohol	○	○	○	○
c. I was "carded" or asked for my ID at a campus event	○	○	○	○
d. I was "carded" or asked for my ID at a fraternity or sorority event	○	○	○	○
e. I was part of a group that was drinking and we were asked to be more quiet or less disruptive	○	○	○	○
f. I was at a campus party that was "shut down" because of alcohol	○	○	○	○

C19. Since the beginning of the school year, has your school taken any of the following actions as a consequence of your drinking? (Choose one answer in each row.)

	Not At All	Once	2 or 3 Times	4 or More Times	I Do Not Drink
a. I was cited for a violation of college rules	○	○	○	○	○
b. I received a warning	○	○	○	○	○
c. I was fined	○	○	○	○	○
d. I was required to attend an alcohol education program	○	○	○	○	○
e. I had to perform community service	○	○	○	○	○
f. I was referred to an alcohol treatment program	○	○	○	○	○
g. I received other disciplinary action	○	○	○	○	○
h. My parents were notified	○	○	○	○	○

C20. How important are each of the following reasons for you to drink alcohol? (Choose one answer in each row.)

	Very Important	Important	Somewhat Important	Not At All Important
a. To get away from my problems and troubles	○	○	○	○
b. To relax or relieve tension	○	○	○	○
c. To get drunk	○	○	○	○
d. To have a good time with my friends	○	○	○	○

Continue with question C20 on next page ➡

281

C20. How important are each of the following reasons for you to drink alcohol? (Choose one answer in each row.)

	Very Important	Important	Somewhat Important	Not At All Important
e. There is nothing else to do	○	○	○	○
f. To celebrate	○	○	○	○
g. To help me get my work done	○	○	○	○
h. I like the taste	○	○	○	○
i. As a reward for working hard	○	○	○	○
j. To fit in with my friends	○	○	○	○
k. To feel more comfortable when I'm with the opposite sex	○	○	○	○
l. Everyone else is drinking	○	○	○	○
m. Because it's cheap	○	○	○	○

C21. How much do you typically pay for one alcoholic drink? (Choose one answer.)

○ Do not drink
○ Nothing, it is typically free
○ Under $0.50

○ $0.51–1.00
○ $1.01–2.00
○ $2.01–3.00

○ $3.01 or more
○ I pay a set fee for all you can drink; that fee is usually _____
(Please fill in amount.)

The following question is for everyone.

C22. If you choose not to drink at all or to limit your drinking, how important is each of the following reasons for you? (Choose one answer in each row.)

	Very Important	Important	Somewhat Important	Not At All Important
a. Drinking is against my religion	○	○	○	○
b. Drinking is against my values	○	○	○	○
c. People in my family have had alcohol problems	○	○	○	○
d. I'm not old enough to drink legally	○	○	○	○
e. I'm going to drive	○	○	○	○
f. It costs too much money	○	○	○	○
g. I don't like the taste	○	○	○	○
h. My friends don't drink	○	○	○	○
i. I don't want to disappoint someone I care about	○	○	○	○
j. I'm going on a date	○	○	○	○
k. It is bad for my health	○	○	○	○
l. It interferes with my studying	○	○	○	○
m. It interferes with my athletic activities	○	○	○	○

Continue with question C22 on next page ➡

C22. If you choose not to drink at all or to limit your drinking, how important is each of the following reasons for you? (Choose one answer in each row.)

	Very Important	Important	Somewhat Important	Not At All Important
n. I've decided to cut down	O	O	O	O
o. I don't want to lose control	O	O	O	O
p. I recently drank too much	O	O	O	O
q. I've had problems with alcohol	O	O	O	O
r. It's fattening	O	O	O	O
s. Fear of getting caught	O	O	O	O

SECTION D: DRINKING OF OTHER STUDENTS

D1. Since the beginning of the school year, how often have you experienced any of the following because of other students' drinking? (Choose one answer in each row.)

	Not At All	Once	2–3 Times	4 or More Times
a. Been insulted or humiliated	O	O	O	O
b. Had a serious argument or quarrel	O	O	O	O
c. Been pushed, hit, or assaulted	O	O	O	O
d. Had your property damaged	O	O	O	O
e. Had to "baby-sit" or take care of another student who drank too much	O	O	O	O
f. Found vomit in the halls or bathroom of your residence	O	O	O	O
g. Had your studying or sleep interrupted	O	O	O	O
h. Experienced an unwanted sexual advance	O	O	O	O
i. Been a victum of sexual assault or "date rape"	O	O	O	O

D2. Based on what you heard or experienced approximately what proportion of the following do you think are at your school? (Choose one answer in each row.)

	0%	1–9%	10–19%	20–29%	30–39%	40–49%	50–59%	60–69%	70–79%	80–89%	90–100%	Don't Know
a. Abstainers (Students who do not drink at all)	O	O	O	O	O	O	O	O	O	O	O	O
b. Students who drink more than they should	O	O	O	O	O	O	O	O	O	O	O	O

D3. What is the maximum number of drinks in a row that is safe to consume on a single drinking occasion?

	None	1 or 2 Drinks	3 Drinks	4 Drinks	5 Drinks	6 Drinks	7 Drinks	8 Drinks	9 Drinks	10 or More Drinks
For a male student	O	O	O	O	O	O	O	O	O	O
For a female student	O	O	O	O	O	O	O	O	O	O

283

D4. How would you compare <u>your</u> alcohol use to that of <u>students at your school</u> and <u>your friends</u>? (choose one answer in each row.)

I drink...

	Much Less Than Most	Less Than Most	A Little Less Than Most	About Average	A Little More Than Most	More Than Most	Much More Than Most
Students at your school	○	○	○	○	○	○	○
Your friends	○	○	○	○	○	○	○

D5. In your opinion, to what extent do students at your school approve of the following behaviors? (Choose one answer in each row.)

	Strongly Approve	Approve	Disapprove	Strongly Disapprove	Don't Know
a. Having 6 drinks at a party	○	○	○	○	○
b. Having 3 or 4 drinks on a date	○	○	○	○	○
c. Having one or two drinks before driving	○	○	○	○	○
d. Coming back to the dorm drunk	○	○	○	○	○
e. Reporting a student who is noisy and disruptive	○	○	○	○	○
f. Reporting a roommate who often drinks too much to the health center	○	○	○	○	○
g. Playing drinking games	○	○	○	○	○
h. Refusing to drink at a party	○	○	○	○	○

D6. Since the <u>beginning of the school year</u>, how often have you asked someone who has had too much alcohol to stop drinking? (Choose one answer.)

○ Not at all   ○ 2–3 times
○ Once   ○ 4 or more times

D7. Since the <u>beginning of the school year</u>, how often have you complained to a college official or Resident Advisor about the behavior of students who were high or intoxicated? (Choose one answer.)

○ Not at all   ○ 2–3 times
○ Once   ○ 4 or more times

D8. What action was taken about your complaint? (Choose all that apply.)

○ Did not complain
○ No action
○ Student(s) were warned
○ Student(s) were disciplined
○ Don't know

Answer question D9 only if you are 21 years of age or older.

D9. In the <u>past 30 days</u>, how many times ... (Choose one answer in each row.)

	Not At All	Once	Twice	Three or More Times
a. Has someone under 21 years of age asked you to purchase alcohol for them?	○	○	○	○
b. Have you purchased alcohol for someone under 21 years of age?	○	○	○	○

SECTION E: OTHER PERSONAL BEHAVIORS

E1. How often, if ever, have you used any of the drugs listed below?
Do not include anything you used under a doctor's orders.
(Choose one answer in each row.)

	Never Used	Used, but NOT in Past 12 Months	Used, but NOT in Past 30 Days	Used in Past 30 Days
a. Marijuana (or hashish)	O	O	O	O
b. Crack cocaine	O	O	O	O
c. Other forms of cocaine	O	O	O	O
d. Barbiturates (prescription-type sleeping pills like Seconal, Nembutal, downs or Yellow Jackets)	O	O	O	O
e. Ritalin, Dexedrine, or Adderall	O	O	O	O
f. Other amphetamines (methamphetamines, crystal meth, speed, uppers, ups)	O	O	O	O
g. Tranquilizers (prescription-type drugs like Valium, Librium, Xanax, Ativan, Klonopin)	O	O	O	O
h. Heroin	O	O	O	O
i. Other opiate-type prescription drugs (codeine, morphine, Demerol, Percodan, Percocet, Vicodin, Darvon, Darvocet)	O	O	O	O
j. LSD	O	O	O	O
k. Other psychedelics or hallucinogens like mushrooms, mescaline or PCP	O	O	O	O
l. Ecstasy (MDMA)	O	O	O	O
m. Other "party drugs" (Ketamine, Special K, GHB)	O	O	O	O
n. Anabolic steroids (either injections like Depo-testosterone or Durbolin, or pills like Anadrol, Dianabol, or Winstrol)	O	O	O	O
o. Other performance-enhancing drugs (growth hormone, diuretics, fluid pills, ephedrine)	O	O	O	O
p. Chewing tobacco, dip or snuff	O	O	O	O
q. Cigarettes	O	O	O	O
r. Cigars	O	O	O	O
s. Pipe tobacco	O	O	O	O
t. Bidis (or beedies—small, hand rolled cigarettes)	O	O	O	O

E2. How old were you when you first . . .
(Choose one answer in each row.)

	Never Did This	9 or Younger	10–12	13–15	16	17	18	19 or Older
a. Smoked a cigarette	○	○	○	○	○	○	○	○
b. Started smoking regularly	○	○	○	○	○	○	○	○
c. Smoked a cigar	○	○	○	○	○	○	○	○
d. Drank alcohol regularly	○	○	○	○	○	○	○	○
e. Got drunk	○	○	○	○	○	○	○	○
f. Used marijuana	○	○	○	○	○	○	○	○
g. Started using marijuana regularly	○	○	○	○	○	○	○	○
h. Placed a bet for money	○	○	○	○	○	○	○	○
i. Started to bet or gamble regularly	○	○	○	○	○	○	○	○

E3. On how many of the last 30 days did you smoke cigarettes?
○ I never smoke ⇢ **Skip to E11**
○ I did not smoke cigarettes at all in the past 30 days
○ I smoked cigarettes on 1 to 4 of the last 30 days
○ I smoked cigarettes on 5 to 9 of the last 30 days
○ I smoked cigarettes on 10 to 19 of the last 30 days
○ I smoked cigarettes on 20 or more of the last 30 days, but not everyday
○ I smoked cigarettes every day in the past 30 days

Answer question E4–E10 only if you smoke.

E4. How many cigarettes a day do you smoke on average? (One pack equals 20 cigarettes.)
○ None
○ Less than one cigarette
○ Less than half a pack
○ About half a pack
○ More than half a pack, but less than a pack
○ A pack
○ More than a pack

E5. Compared to the beginning of your freshman year in college, how has your smoking changed?
○ I smoke more often now
○ I smoke about the same now
○ I smoke less often now

E6. Have you smoked at least 100 cigarettes in your lifetime?
○ Yes   ○ No

E7. In the past 30 days, how soon after you wake up in the morning do you usually smoke your first cigarette?
○ I did not smoke in the past 30 days
○ Within 15 minutes
○ 16–30 minutes
○ 31–60 minutes
○ More than 60 minutes

E8. In the past 30 days, do you smoke mainly when you are with people, mainly when you are alone, or do you smoke as often by yourself as with others?
○ I did not smoke in the past 30 days
○ Mainly alone
○ Mainly with others
○ As often alone as with others

E9. In the past 12 months, how many times have you tried to quit smoking and succeeded for at least 24 hours? (Choose one answer.)
○ Never   ○ 3 times
○ Once   ○ 4 times
○ Twice   ○ 5 or more times

E10. What best describes your intentions regarding quitting smoking entirely?
○ I never expect to quit entirely
○ I may quit entirely in the future but not in the next 6 months
○ I plan to quit entirely in the next 6 months
○ I plan to quit entirely within the next 30 days

The following questions are for everyone.

E11. Since the beginning of the school year, have you ever been to a bar or club when free samples of cigarettes were available?

○ Yes ○ No

E12. Since the beginning of the school year, have you ever been to an event or party on campus when free samples of cigarettes were available?

○ Yes ○ No

E13. Since the beginning of the school year, how often have you been bothered by someone else's smoking in your dormitory or residence?

○ Never
○ Rarely (once/month or less)
○ Sometimes (more than once/month up to once/week)
○ Often (more than once/week but not every day)
○ Very often (everyday)

E14. On how many of the last 30 days did you smoke cigars?

○ I did not smoke cigars at all in the past 30 days
○ I smoked cigars on 1 to 4 of the last 30 days
○ I smoked cigars on 5 to 9 of the last 30 days
○ I smoked cigars on 10 to 19 of the last 30 days
○ I smoked cigars on 20 or more of the last 30 days, but not everyday
○ I smoked cigars every day in the past 30 days

E15. During the past school year, how often did you bet or spend money on each of the following gambling activities? (choose one answer in each row.)

	Never	A Few Times a Year	Monthly, But Not Weekly	Weekly, But Not Daily	Daily
a. Betting on professional sports	○	○	○	○	○
b. Betting on college sports	○	○	○	○	○
c. Betting on horse or dog races	○	○	○	○	○
d. Casino gambling	○	○	○	○	○
e. Betting on the lottery or the "numbers"	○	○	○	○	○
f. Internet betting or gambling	○	○	○	○	○
g. Betting with a bookie	○	○	○	○	○
h. Card, dice or other games of chance while at school	○	○	○	○	○

E16. During the past school year, has your betting or gambling caused personal problems for you?

○ Yes ○ No ○ Did not gamble in the past school year

E17. If you have ever been sexually active, has it been with . . .? (Choose one answer.)

○ I have not been sexually active → **Skip to E23**
○ Opposite sex partner(s)
○ Same sex partner(s)
○ Both opposite and same sex partners

E18. How many people have you had sexual intercourse with in the past 30 days? (Choose one answer.)
- ○ 0
- ○ 1
- ○ 2
- ○ 3 or more

E19. When you have sexual intercourse, how often do you or your partner use a condom?
- ○ Never
- ○ Rarely
- ○ Sometimes
- ○ Always

E20. Since the beginning of the school year, have you had sexual intercourse against your wishes because someone used force? (Choose one answer.)
- ○ 0 times
- ○ 1 time
- ○ 2 times
- ○ 3 or more times

E21. Apart from anything you just told us in question E20, since the beginning of the school year, have you had sexual intercourse against your wishes because someone threatened to harm you? (Choose one answer.)
- ○ 0 times
- ○ 1 time
- ○ 2 times
- ○ 3 or more times

E22. Apart from anything you just told us in question E20 and E21, since the beginning of the school year, have you ever had sexual intercourse when you were so intoxicated that you were unable to consent? (Choose one answer.)
- ○ 0 times
- ○ 1 time
- ○ 2 times
- ○ 3 or more times

E23. Have you ever thought you had a drinking problem?
- ○ Yes
- ○ No

E24. Since starting college, have you ever sought help because you thought that you had a problem with alcohol? (Choose one answer.)
- ○ Yes
- ○ No

E25. Since starting college, have you ever received counseling or treatment for an alcohol-related problem? (Choose one answer.)
- ○ Yes
- ○ No

E26. In the past 30 days, how often did you drive a car, truck, or motorcycle? (Choose one answer.)
- ○ Not at all
- ○ Only a few times
- ○ Once or twice a week
- ○ Most days
- ○ Nearly every day

E27. In the past 30 days, how many times did you . . . (Choose one answer in each row.)

	Not At All	Once	Twice or More
a. Drive after drinking alcohol?	○	○	○
b. Drive after having 5 or more drinks?	○	○	○
c. Ride with a driver who was high or drunk?	○	○	○
d. Serve as a designated driver?	○	○	○
e. Ride with a designated driver?	○	○	○

E28. Since you started school this year, were you . . . (Choose one answer in each row.)

	Yes	No
a. A driver in an automobile accident in which someone was injured?	○	○
b. A driver in an automobile accident in which no one was injured?	○	○
c. Arrested for driving under the influence?	○	○

E29. Do you have a "working firearm" (defined as a gun—including pistol, revolver, rifle or shotgun) with you at college?
- ○ Yes → Go to E29a   ○ No → Go to E30

E29a. If "Yes", why do you have a working firearm with you at college? (Choose all that apply.)
- ○ Protection
- ○ Job required
- ○ Hunting
- ○ Sports shoots
- ○ Recreation
- ○ ROTC
- ○ Other: _____ (please specify)

E30. While you have been at college, has anyone used, displayed or brought out a working firearm against you in a hostile manner?
- ○ Yes
- ○ No

SECTION F: STUDENT ACTIVITIES

F1. In general, how satisfied are you <u>with the education</u> that you are receiving? (Choose one answer.)
- ○ Very satisfied
- ○ Somewhat satisfied
- ○ Somewhat dissatisfied
- ○ Very dissatisfied

F4. Do you know a member of the faculty or administration with whom you can discuss a personal problem? (Choose one answer.)
- ○ Yes
- ○ No

F2. In general, how satisfied are you <u>with your life at school</u>? (Choose one answer.)
- ○ Very satisfied
- ○ Somewhat satisfied
- ○ Somewhat dissatisfied
- ○ Very dissatisfied

F5. Which of the following best describes your grade point average this year?
- ○ A
- ○ A-
- ○ B+
- ○ B
- ○ B-
- ○ C+
- ○ C
- ○ C-
- ○ D
- ○ No grade or don't know

F3. How many close student friends do you have? (Choose one answer.)
- ○ None
- ○ One
- ○ Two
- ○ Three
- ○ Four
- ○ Five or more

F6. In the <u>past 30 days</u>, how many hours per day on average have you spent on each of the following activities? (Choose one answer in each row.)

Average number of hours per day

	0	1	2	3	4	5 or More
a. Watching TV or videos	○	○	○	○	○	○
b. Studying outside of class	○	○	○	○	○	○
c. Working for wages	○	○	○	○	○	○
d. Socializing with friends	○	○	○	○	○	○
e. Student organizations	○	○	○	○	○	○
f. Playing or practicing intercollegiate sports	○	○	○	○	○	○
g. Other physical activities (e.g., intramural athletics, jogging, biking)	○	○	○	○	○	○
h. Volunteer work	○	○	○	○	○	○
i. Non academic computer use (e.g., computer game, surfing the web)	○	○	○	○	○	○

F7. Think back over <u>the past 7 days</u>. On how many days did you exercise or participate in physical activity for at least 20 minutes that made you sweat and breathe hard, such as basketball, soccer, running, swimming laps, bicycling, or similar aerobic activities?

○ 0 days   ○ 2 days   ○ 4 days   ○ 6 days
○ 1 day   ○ 3 days   ○ 5 days   ○ 7 days

F8. Now think about your last year in high school. During a typical week, on how many days did you exercise or participate in physical activity for at least 20 minutes that made you sweat and breathe hard, such as basketball, soccer, running, swimming laps, bicycling, or similar aerobic activities?

○ 0 days   ○ 2 days   ○ 4 days   ○ 6 days
○ 1 day   ○ 3 days   ○ 5 days   ○ 7 days

SECTION G: BACKGROUND INFORMATION

G1. What is your current marital status? (Choose one answer.)
○ Never married
○ Married
○ Divorced
○ Separated
○ Widowed

G2. Are you of Spanish or Hispanic origin?
○ Yes
○ No

G3. Which of these racial or ethnic groups describes you best? (Choose one answer.)
○ White
○ Black/African American
○ Asian/Pacific Islander
○ Native American Indian/Native Alaskan
○ Other

G4. In what religion were you raised? (Choose one answer.)
○ None   ○ Islam
○ Catholicism   ○ Protestantism
○ Judaism   ○ Other: _____

G5. During an average week at college how much money do you get from . . .(Choose one answer in each row.)

	$0	$1–10	$11–20	$21–35	$36–50	$51–75	$76–125	$126+
a. A job or other work	○	○	○	○	○	○	○	○
b. Other sources (allowances, etc.)	○	○	○	○	○	○	○	○

G6. In general, how would you rate your health now?
○ Excellent
○ Very good
○ Good
○ Fair
○ Poor

G7. What is your current weight (in pounds) without clothes or shoes?
○ 117 or less   ○ 147–160
○ 118–128   ○ 161–170
○ 129–135   ○ 171–190
○ 136–146   ○ Greater than 190

G8. What is your current height (in feet and inches) without shoes?

- ○ 5'3" or less
- ○ 5'4"
- ○ 5'5"
- ○ 5'6"
- ○ 5'7"–5'9"
- ○ 5'10"
- ○ 5'11"–6'0"
- ○ Greater than 6'0"

G9. During your last year in high school, how often did you drink alcohol (beer, wine, liquor) during a typical month? (Choose one answer.)

- ○ Never
- ○ 1–2 occasions
- ○ 3–5 occasions
- ○ 6–9 occasions
- ○ 10–19 occasions
- ○ 20–39 occasions
- ○ 40 or more occasions

G10. During the last year in high school, how many drinks did you usually have when you drank alcohol? (A drink is a 12 oz. can or bottle of beer; a 4 oz. glass of wine; a 12 oz. bottle or can of wine cooler; or a shot of liquor straight or in a mixed drink.) (Choose one answer.)

- ○ Did not drink alcohol
- ○ 1 drink
- ○ 2 drinks
- ○ 3 drinks
- ○ 4 drinks
- ○ 5 drinks
- ○ 6 drinks
- ○ 7 drinks
- ○ 8 drinks
- ○ 9 or more drinks

G11. During your last year in high school, on how many occasions did you have 5 or more drinks in a row?

- ○ Never
- ○ 1–2 occasions
- ○ 3–5 occasions
- ○ 6–9 occasions
- ○ 10–19 occasions
- ○ 20–39 occasions
- ○ 40 or more occasions

G12. Where was the high school you attended during your senior year located? (Choose one answer.)

- ○ Same state as current college
- ○ Different state from current college (If different state, in which state did you attend your senior year in high school?)

○ ALAB.	○ ALASK.	○ ARIZ.	○ ARK.	○ CALIF.	○ COLO.	○ CONN.	○ DEL.	○ D.C.
○ FLOR.	○ GEOR.	○ HAWAI.	○ IDAHO	○ ILLIN.	○ INDIANA	○ IOWA	○ KAN.	○ KEN.
○ LOUIS.	○ MAINE	○ MARY.	○ MAS.	○ MICH.	○ MINN.	○ MISSI.	○ MISSO.	○ MONT.
○ NEB.	○ NEV.	○ N.H.	○ N.J.	○ N. MEX.	○ N. YORK	○ N. CAR.	○ N. DAK.	○ OHIO
○ OKLA.	○ OREG.	○ PENN.	○ R.I.	○ SO. CA.	○ S. DAK.	○ TENN.	○ TEXAS	○ UTAH
○ VERM.	○ VIRG.	○ WASH.	○ W. VIRG.	○ WISC.	○ WYOM.			

- ○ Outside of U.S.A.

G13. Did you participate in high school athletics?

- ○ No
- ○ Yes, earned a varsity letter
- ○ Yes, did not earn a varsity letter

G14. Describe your father's (or that person who served as your father in raising you) use of alcohol during most of the time that you were growing up. (Choose one answer.)

- ○ Not applicable (No father or father substitute)
- ○ Abstainer
- ○ Abstainer—former problem drinker in recovery or recovered
- ○ Infrequent or light drinker
- ○ Moderate drinker
- ○ Heavy drinker
- ○ Problem drinker
- ○ I don't know

G15. Describe your mother's (or that person who served as your mother in raising you) use of alcohol during most of the time that you were growing up. (Choose one answer.)

○ Not applicable (no mother or mother substitute)
○ Abstainer
○ Abstainer—former problem drinker in recovery or recovered
○ Infrequent or light drinker
○ Moderate drinker
○ Heavy drinker
○ Problem drinker
○ I don't know

G16. How did your family feel about drinking alcohol when you were growing up?

○ My family did not approve of drinking
○ They accepted light drinking but disapproved of heavy drinking
○ They accepted heavy drinking
○ There was disagreement about drinking in my family

G17. How far did your father (or that person who served as your father) go in school?

○ Less than a high school diploma
○ High school diploma
○ Some college or technical schooling beyond high school
○ Four year college degree or more
○ Don't know
○ Not applicable

G18. How far did your mother (or that person who served as your mother) go in school?

○ Less than a high school diploma
○ High school diploma
○ Some college or technical schooling beyond high school
○ Four year college degree or more
○ Don't know
○ Not applicable

G19. Have you ever completed a similar survey for the Harvard School of Public Health College Alcohol Study? (Choose all that apply.)

○ Yes, in 1997
○ Yes, in 1998
○ Yes, in 1999
○ Yes, in 2000
○ No, I have never completed a similar survey

G20. Is there anything else you would like to tell us concerning alcohol use at your school? If so, please write it on a separate piece of paper and include it with your returned questionnaire.

THANK YOU FOR YOUR TIME AND COOPERATION IN HELPING TO MAKE THIS A SUCCESSFUL STUDY

NOTES

INTRODUCTION

Wechsler, H., A. Davenport, G. W. Dowdall, B. Moeykens, and S. Castillo. "Health and Behavioral Consequences of Binge Drinking in College: A National Survey of Students on 140 Campuses." *Journal of the American Medical Association* 272 (1994): 1672–77.

CHAPTER 1

p. 4   *. . . fourteen hundred college students . . .*   Hingson, R., T. Heeren, R. C. Zakocs, A. Kopstein, and H. Wechsler. "Magnitude of Alcohol-Related Mortality and Morbidity Among U.S. College Students Ages 18–24." *Journal of Studies on Alcohol* 63.2 (April 12, 2002): 136–44.

    . . . $5.5 billion on alcohol . . .   Eigen, L. "U.S. Alcohol Practices, Policies, and Potentials of American Colleges and Universities: An OSAP White Paper." Department of Health and Human Services. Rockvile, MD: OSAP, 1991.

p. 5   *. . . Ithaca College . . .*   Reisberg, L. "Rites of Passage or Unwanted Traditions?" *Chronicle of Higher Education* February 11, 2000.

    . . . University of Michigan . . .   Ibid.

    . . . James Madison University . . .   White, J. "JMU President Seeks Answers to Riot." *Washington Post* August 29, 2000: page B03.

p. 6   *. . . Princeton . . . Nude Olympics . . .*   Reisberg, L. "Rites of Passage or Unwanted Traditions?" *Chronicle of Higher Education* February 11, 2000; and Herszenhorn, D. M. "Alcohol Abuse Imperils a Naked Rite at Princeton." *New York Times* January 15, 1999: page B1.

    College Student Drinking Facts   A Matter of Degree, Harvard Evaluation, Harvard School of Public Health; and Harvard School of Public Health 2001 College Alcohol Study.

p. 7   *. . . University of Dayton . . .*   Deinlein, J. "Homecoming to be Suspended Indefinitely at U. Dayton." *Flyer News* via University Wire. January 9, 2001.

    . . . Dartmouth, James Wright . . .   Wright, J. "The Dartmouth Community: Learning Together, Learning from Each Other." Speech to the Alumni Council. May 21, 1999, as found at www.dartmouth.edu.

p. 8   *. . . Cornell . . . twenty were treated . . .*   Bernard, L. "Thousands of Students Take a Bath on Slope Day—A Mud Bath." *Cornell Chronicle* May 9, 1996.

    . . . Hunter Rawlings . . .   Rawlings, H., B. Gaither, S. Rockwell, H. Hollidge, and K. Eng. "An Open Letter to the Campus on Slope Day." *Cornell Chronicle* May 1, 1997.

p. 9   *. . . Bonfire represents . . .*   Morris, D. "Memories of an Aggie Bonfire Boy." Salon.com. December 8, 1999.

p. 10   *. . . the unthinkable happened. . . .*   Brown, K. "Reports Depict Rescue." *Bryan-College Station Eagle* February 2, 2000; and "Memorializing the Fallen," as found at www.msc.tamu.edu.

p. 11   *The Commission report . . .*   "Special Commission on the 1999 Texas A&M Bonfire: Final Report." May 2, 2000, as found at www.tamu.edu.

    . . . organizational failure . . .   Ibid.

    . . . irresponsible behavior . . .   "Special Commission on the 1999 Texas A&M Bonfire: Final Report." May 2, 2000, as found at www.tamu.edu; and Ward, M. and S. Gamboa. "Bonfire Safety Warnings Spanned 40 Years." *Austin American-Statesman* March 26, 2000.

    . . . 2,300 Bonfire documents . . .   Brown, K. "Alcohol Testing Results Differ." *Bryan-College Station Eagle* December 18, 1999.

p. 12   ... *BAC of .392.*   Brown, K. "Alcohol Reports on Victims Released." *Bryan-College Station Eagle* November 10, 2000; and Brown, K. "Alcohol Testing Results Differ." *Bryan-College Station Eagle* December 18, 1999.

Laban Toscano ...   Toscano, L. Personal interview. March 2001.

... *65 percent of students* ...   "Texas A&M University Core Drug and Alcohol Survey Executive Summary," as found at http://studentlife.tamu.

... *no stranger to alcohol-related tragedy.* ...   Toscano, L. Personal interview. March 2001.

p. 13   ... *the Special Commission wrote* ...   "Special Commission on the 1999 Texas A&M Bonfire: Final Report." May 2, 2000, as found at www.tamu.edu.

p. 14   ... *quarters* ...   Stewart, A. "The Ballpark, ESPN Play Quarters in Bar Contest." *AdWeek West* 52.3 (January 14, 2002): 4; and "Quarter Bouncers," as found at http://promotions.go.com.

p. 15   *Socializing with drinking games* ...   Unpublished College Alcohol Study data.

p. 19   *Our survey revealed* ...   Williams J., L. M. Powell, and H. Wechsler. "Does Alcohol Consumption Reduce Human Capital Accumulation? Evidence from the College Alcohol Study." Submitted for publication.

p. 20   ... *Core Drug and Alcohol Survey* ...   "1995–96 Core Drug and Alcohol Survey," as found at www.med.unc.edu.

p. 21   ... *abuse or dependence.*   Knight, J. R., H. Wechsler, M. Kuo, M. Seibring, E. R. Weitzman, and M. A. Schuckit. "Alcohol Abuse and Dependence among U.S. College Students." *Journal of Studies on Alcohol* (May 2002).

... *do not binge* ...   Wechsler H., J. E. Lee, M. Kuo, M. Seibring, T. F. Nelson, and H. Lee. "Trends in College Binge Drinking During a Period of Increased Prevention Efforts: Findings from 4 Harvard School of Public Health College Alcohol Study Surveys: 1993–2001." *Journal of American College Health* 50.5 (March 25, 2002): 203–217.

... *not present on every campus.* ...   Unpublished College Alcohol Study data.

p. 23   ... *just as dangerous* ...   Zimmerman, R. "Beer Finally is Getting Some Well Deserved Recognition." *Union Tribune* November 30, 2000.

... *driving after drinking* ...   Unpublished College Alcohol Study data.

... *eleven hundred college students* ...   Hingson, R., T. Heeren, R. C. Zakocs, A. Kopstein, and H. Wechsler. "Magnitude of Alcohol-Related Mortality and Morbidity Among U.S. College Students Ages 18–24." *Journal of Studies on Alcohol* 63.2 (April 12, 2002): 136–44.

... *42,455 campus-related liquor arrests.*   Nicklin, J. L. "Drug and Alcohol Arrests Increased on Campuses in 2000." *Chronicle of Higher Education* January 24, 2002.

p. 24   ... *six hundred thousand* ...   Hingson, R., T. Heeren, R. C. Zakocs, A. Kopstein, and H. Wechsler. "Magnitude of Alcohol-Related Mortality and Morbidity Among U.S. College Students Ages 18–24." *Journal of Studies on Alcohol* 63.2 (April 12, 2002): 136–44.

... *nineteen million children* ...   Greenfield, T. K., L. T. Midanik, and J. D. Rogers. "A 10-Year National Trend Study of Alcohol Consumption, 1984–1995: Is the Period of Declining Drinking Over?" *American Journal of Public Health* 90.1 (January 2000): 47.

... *$166.5 billion.*   "Substance Abuse: the Nation's Number One Health Problem." Prepared by the Institute for Health Policy, Brandeis University, for The Robert Wood Johnson Foundation, Princeton, New Jersey, 2000.

... *$53 billion.*   Levy, D. T., T. R. Miller, and K. C. Cox. *Costs of Underage Drinking.* Pacific Institute. Prepared for the U.S. Department of Justice Office of Juvenile Justice and Delinquency Prevention. Revised October 1999.

... *permanent impotence.*   Burke, M. "Real Men Don't Drink." *New Scientist* November 27, 1999, as found at www.newscientist.com.

For women ...   Ibid.

p. 25   ... *forced and nonconsensual sex.* ...   Dowdall, G. W., M. P. Koss, M. Kuo, and H. Wechsler. "Non-Consensual Sex While Under the Influence: Results of the Harvard School of Public Health College Alcohol Study." Unpublished College Alcohol Study paper.

p. 25   *. . . strong measures . . .*   Wechsler H., J. E. Lee, M. Kuo, M. Seibring, T. F. Nelson, and H. Lee. "Trends in College Binge Drinking During a Period of Increased Prevention Efforts: Findings from 4 Harvard School of Public Health College Alcohol Study Surveys: 1993–2001." *Journal of American College Health* 50.5 (March 25, 2002): 203–217.

p. 27   *. . . Harvard . . . serve distilled spirits . . .*   Straus, R. and S. Bacon. *Drinking in College.* Westport, CT: Greenwood Publishing Group, 1953.

   . . . Neil Rudenstine . . .   Dembner, A. "Gore Says '60s Turned Skeptics into Cynics. *Boston Globe* June 10, 1994: page 31.

   . . . James Ewing . . .   Pace, R. F. and C. A. Bjornsen. "Adolescent Honor and College Student Behavior in the Old South." *Southern Cultures* 6.3 (Fall 2000): 9–28.

   . . . stole two horses . . .   Ibid.

Thomas Jefferson . . .   "Easters." *UVA Alumni News* Winter 2000: page 32.

p. 28   *. . . Leslie Baltz . . .*   Bromley, A. "Students Promote Healthy Behavior." Inside UVA Online. December 7–13, 2001; and "High-Risk drinking in College: What We Know and What We Need to Learn." National Institute on Alcohol Abuse and Alcoholism, as found at www. collegedrinkingprevention.gov.

   . . . Straus and Bacon survey . . .   Straus, R. and S. Bacon. *Drinking in College.* Westport, CT: Greenwood Publishing Group, 1953.

p. 29   *. . . public outcry . . .*   Ibid.

p. 30   *Student athletes . . .*   Nelson T. F. and H. Wechsler. "Alcohol and College Athletes." *Medicine and Science in Sports and Exercise* 33.1 (2001): 43–7; and Nelson, T. F. and H. Wechsler. "School Spirits: Alcohol and Collegiate Sports Fans." *Addictive Behaviors.* In press.

p. 31   *. . . fourteen million . . .*   Ketcham, K. and W. F. Asbury. *Beyond the Influence: Understanding and Defeating Alcoholism.* New York City: Bantam Books, 2000; and McGinnis, J. M. and W. H. Foege. "Actual Causes of Death in the United States." *Journal of the American Medical Association* 270.18 (1993): 2207–12.

   . . . one hundred thousand deaths . . .   McGinnis, J. M. and W. H. Foege. "Actual Causes of Death in the United States." *Journal of the American Medical Association* 270.18 (1993): 2207–12.

p. 32   *. . . increased risk for cancer . . .*   National Institute on Alcohol Abuse and Alcoholism. 10th Special Report to the U.S. Congress on Alcohol and Health. Rockville, MD: NIAAA, June 2000.

   . . . liver disease.   Ibid.

   . . . half of American adults . . .   Dawson, D. A. and B. F. Grant. "Family History of Alcoholism and Gender: Their Combined Effects on DSM-IV Alcohol Dependence and Major Depression." *Journal of Studies on Alcohol* 59.1 (1998): 97–106.

   . . . overwhelming number of Americans . . .   Wagenaar, A. C., et al. "The Robert Wood Johnson Foundation Youth Access to Alcohol Survey: Summary." Minneapolis: University of Minnesota Alcohol Epidemiology Program, 1998.

CHAPTER 2

Wechsler, H., G. W. Dowdall, A. Davenport, and S. Castillo. "Correlates of College Student Binge Drinking." *American Journal of Public Health* 85 (1995): 921–26.

Two good sources of news on college drinking are Information for Journalists on High-Risk Drinking among College Students, produced by the A Matter of Degree program, as found at www.collegedrinkingnews.net, and the Higher Education News Feed Archive, as found at www.edc.org, produced by the Higher Education Center. Many articles cited in these references can be accessed through these sources.

p. 33   *Adrian Heideman . . .*   Stannard, M. B. "Chico State Fraternity Pledge Dies After Drinking." *San Francisco Chronicle* October 10, 2000: page A17.

   . . . online diary . . .   Ibid.

p. 34   *. . . blackberry brandy.*   Vau Dell, T. "Chico Fraternity Where Pledge Died Is about Average for Alcohol Consumption." HEC/News. January 23, 2001, as found at www.edc.org.

p. 34   *... bond pledges to their big brothers ...*   Ibid.

... they found him dead.   Stannard, M. B. "Parents Sue Over Son's Death." *San Francisco Chronicle* May 23, 2001: page A22.

... .37 blood-alcohol content ...   Webby, S. "Palo Alto Couple Sue Fraternity over Son's Death after Drinking." *San Jose Mercury News* May 24, 2001.

... unfair competition ...   Andelman, K. "Frat Hazing Suit Uses 17200 Statute." *The Recorder* May 22, 2001: page 1.

"... largest unregulated industry ..."   Fierberg, D. Personal interview. April 5, 2002.

p. 35   *For college students ...*   Unpublished College Alcohol Study data.

p. 36   *The very first fraternity ...*   Sirhal, M. "Fraternities on the Rocks." *Policy Review* 99 (February and March 2000). Published by the Heritage Foundation.

Nationwide ...   About the NIC (North-American Interfraternity Conference), as found at www.nicindy.org.

p. 37   *George Kuh ...*   Kuh, G. D. and J. C. Arnold. "Liquid Bonding: A Cultural Analysis of the Role of Alcohol in Fraternity Pledgeship." *Journal of College Student Development* 34 (September 1993): 327–34.

... three-fourths of fraternity residents ...   Wechsler H., G. Kuh, and A. Davenport. "Fraternities, Sororities and Binge Drinking: Results from a National Study of American Colleges." *National Association of Student Personnel Administrators* 33.4 (1996): 260–79.

p. 38   *... twice as many fraternity residents ...*   Ibid.

p. 41   *... sorority house residents ...*   Ibid.

Scott Krueger ...   McCormick, J. "At MIT, the Party's Over." *Newsweek* September 25, 2000: page 45.

p. 42   *As early as 1992 ...*   Heimburger, D. E. "MIT May Be Criminally Liable in Scott Krueger's Drinking Death." *The Tech* 117.50 (October 14, 1997): 1; and Chacon, R. "Students Warned MIT on Drinking." *Boston Globe* October 1, 1997: page A1.

... President Vest wrote ...   Vest, C. M. Letter to the parents of Scott Krueger, September 8, 2000, as found at http://web.mit.edu.

p. 43   *... top ten risks ...*   Risk Management Manual. Alpha Chi Rho: National Fraternity. Produced by FIPG, as found at www.alphachirho.com.

... alcohol-abuse task force ...   Alpha Epsilon Pi Alcohol Abuse Task Force. Final Report. August 1, 1999, as found at www.aepi.org.

... alcohol-related insurance claims. ...   Ibid.

p. 44   *"Scott's death ..."*   Vest, C. M. Letter to the parents of Scott Krueger, as found at http://web.mit/edu.

... end its Greek system ...   Kellogg, P. P. "Santa Clara U. Says Goodbye to Greek Life." *Chronicle of Higher Education* March 26, 2001.

... Hamilton College ...   Tobin, E. M. "Don't Ban Fraternities, Embrace Them. Embrace Them Closely." *The Chronicle of Higher Education* December 14, 2001.

p. 45   *Emory University ...*   "Emory University's Greek System Thrives Under Innovative Management Plan." Emory University Office of Media Relations. September 29, 2000, as found at www.emory.edu.

p. 46   *... University of Michigan ...*   George, M. "U-M Pushes to Control Frats' Drinking, Hazing." *Free Press Ann Arbor Bureau* November 13, 2001.

Alcohol, Hazing, and the Greek Industry   Fierberg, D. Personal interview. April 5, 2002.

p. 50   *... Greek alumni donated ...*   Dungan, T. "Some Fraternities That Leave UA Come Back Stronger after Hiatus." *Arkansas Democrat-Gazette* February 25, 2001: page B3.

p. 51   *... disadvantage in recruitment ...*   McKaig, D. Personal interview. November 2, 2001.

p. 52   *... Washington State University ...*   "A Special Report: Student Rioters Demand the 'Right to Party.'" *Chronicle of Higher Education* (May 15, 1998): A46.

p. 52   ... *Dartmouth College* ...   "The Student Life Initiative at Dartmouth College," as found at www.dartmouth.edu.

CHAPTER 3

Nelson, T. F. and H. Wechsler. "School Spirits: Alcohol and Collegiate Sports Fans." *Addictive Behaviors.* In press.

Sperber, M. *Beer and Circus: How Big-Time College Sports is Crippling Undergraduate Education.* New York City: Henry Holt & Company, 2000.

Wechsler, H., A. Davenport, G. W. Dowdall, S. Grossman, and S. Zanakos. "Binge Drinking, Tobacco, and Illicit Drug Use and Involvement in College Athletics." *Journal of American College Health* 45 (1997): 195–200.

p. 54   ... *Mavericks Hockey Team* ...   "Team Picture Sends Wrong Message to Fans at University of Nebraska at Omaha!" *Booze News: Updating Advocates on Alcohol Prevention Policies* March 9, 2001, as found at www.cspinet.org.

p. 55   ... *student athletes* ...   Nelson, T. F. and H. Wechsler. "Alcohol and College Athletes." *Medicine and Science in Sports and Exercise* 33.1 (2001): 43–47.

... *80 percent of college athletes* ...   National Collegiate Athletic Association Research Staff. "The NCAA Study of Substance Use Habits of College Student Athletes." Presented to The National Collegiate Athletic Association Committee on Competitive Safeguards and Medical Aspect of Sports. June 2001, as found at www.ncaa.org.

p. 56   "... *wonderful condition.*"   Sperber, M. Phone interview. April 2, 2002.

p. 57   ... *Corey LaTulippe* ...   Lapointe, J. "Trying to Skate Past a Hazing Scandal." *New York Times* September 21, 2000: page D-2; and USCHO Staff. "Vermont, LaTulippe Reach Out-of-Court Settlement." September 14, 2000, as found at www.uscollegehockey.com.

Enrollment ...   Lapointe, J. "Trying to Skate Past a Hazing Scandal." *New York Times* September 21, 2000: page D-2.

... *Ken Christiansen* ...   Yahoo News. "Charges Filed in University of Minnesota-Duluth Death." June 27, 2001, as found at www.edc.org.

p. 58   ... *Al Bohl* ...   Associated Press. "New Athletic Director Wants Drinking Legal at Kansas Football Games." *Sporting News* August 9, 2001.

p. 59   *Alcohol and the Athlete's Body*   Adapted from "Facts for Athletes about Alcohol and Other Drugs." Mount Holyoke College's Health Services' Alcohol and Drug Awareness Project, as found at www.mtholyoke.edu.

p. 61   ... *Bacardi bat* ... *Captain Morgan* ...   Hacker, G. A. "Alcohol Advertising: Are Our Kids Collateral or Intended Targets?" *Booze News: Updating Advocates on Alcohol Prevention Policies* January 10, 2002, as found at www.cspinet.org.

p. 62   ... *Supreme Court of Norway* ...   AlkoKutt. "Supreme Court: Brewery Logos Are Alcohol Ads." January 27, 2000, as found at www.alkokutt.no.

... *"official beer sponsor"* ...   Anheuser-Busch. "Budweiser Partners with Mavericks and Stars as Flagship Sponsor at American Airlines Center." Anheuser-Busch. August 27, 2001.

... *twenty-six of thirty-one* ...   Pate, K. "Bud Scores Exclusive Deal for Invesco Field Signage." *Denver Post* June 12, 2001: page C10.

... *Invesco Field* ...   Ibid.

p. 63   ... *All-Star Game* ...   Lefton, T. "Big Bottles Key A-B's First NBA Promo." *Brandweek* 40.39 (October 18, 1999): 4.

... *ratings for commercial breaks* ...   Johnson, G. "CBS, Advertisers Banking on Hype of Super Sunday." *Los Angeles Times* January 21, 2001: page C1.

... *A-B aired* ...   Parpis, E. "Bowl Proves a Bargain." *AdWeek Midwest* February 4, 2002.

p. 64   ... *March Madness* ...   Sperber, M. Phone interview. April 2, 2002.

p. 65   ... *Earvin "Magic" Johnson* ...   Beirne, M. "OK, Just Shill Me." *Brandweek* 42.13 (March 26, 2001): 3.

p. 66 *Alcohol prevention experts . . .* Thomson, S. C. "Ad Draws Fire from Anti-Drinking Group." *St. Louis Post-Dispatch* April 3, 2002: page A1.

. . . NCAA men's basketball championship . . . Roig-Franzia, M. and H. R. Harris. "Whooping It up in College Park." *Washington Post* April 3, 2002: page A01.

Marauding drunks . . . Roig-Franzia, M. "A Tough Defeat, Then Mayhem." *Washington Post* April 2, 2001: page A01.

p. 67 *. . . "pub crawl" . . .* Washington, A. T. "'Pub Crawl' Sends Youths Wrong Message on Drinking." *Washington Times* April 6, 2001: page C2.

. . . Donna Shalala . . . Shalala, D. Guest editorial: "College Sports Must End Ties with Alcohol." *NCAA News* October 12, 1998, as found at www.ncaa.org.

Some Division I schools . . . Hacker, G. A., et al. "Letter to the Knight Commission Regarding Alcohol Sponsorship and Advertising on the NCAA Reform Agenda." *Booze News: Updating Advocates on Alcohol Prevention Policies* September 28, 2000, as found at www.cspinet.org.

Kentucky came to its decision . . . Drape, J., and M. A. Lindenberger. "Final Respects Paid as Kentucky Grieves." *New York Times* November 20, 1998.

p. 68 *The University of Wisconsin-Madison . . .* "Early Success Cited by National Effort to Reduce High-Risk Drinking Among College Students." American Medical Association and A Matter of Degree. April 9, 2002, as found at www.collegedrinkingnews.net.

. . . University of Rhode Island . . . Forliti, A. "URI Bans Alcohol at This Year's Homecoming." Associated Press. August 28, 2001.

. . . University of Dayton . . . Associated Press. "UD Cancels Homecoming Indefinitely." *Columbus Dispatch* January 9, 2001.

CHAPTER 4

Wagenaar, A. C. "Minimum Drinking Age and Alcohol Availability to Youth: Issues and Research Needs." *Economics and the Prevention of Alcohol-Related Problems.* Research Monograph No. 25. Proceedings of a Workshop on Economic and Socioeconomic Issues in the Prevention of Alcohol-Related Problems. Hilton, M. E. and G. Bloss, Eds. Bethesda, MD. October 10–11, 1991.

Wagenaar, A. C. and T. L. Toomey. "Effects of Minimum Drinking Age Laws: Review and Analyses of the Literature from 1960 to 2000." *Journal of Studies on Alcohol.* Prepared for the Advisory Council Subcommittee on College Drinking, National Institute on Alcohol Abuse and Alcoholism, March 2000. In press.

Wechsler, H., J. E. Lee, T. F. Nelson, and M. Kuo. "Alcohol and College Students below the Legal Minimum Drinking Age: Drinking Behavior, Access to Alcohol, and the Influence of Deterrence Policies." Unpublished College Alcohol Study data.

p. 71 *Groups of teenagers . . .* Wrenn, D. "'Innocent Fun,' or a 'Disgrace'? WVU Officials Take Steps to Help Alleviate Problem." *Charleston Daily Mail* January 29, 2002.

Today . . . Johnson, L., P. O'Malley, and J. Bachman. "Monitoring the Future National Results on Adolescent Drug Use." U.S. Department of Health and Human Services, 2000.

p. 72 *. . . one-third of the car-crash deaths . . .* Join Together Online. "Auto Death Stats Overshadow School Shootings." May 21, 2001, as found at www.jointogether.org.

More than 40 percent . . . Leadership to Keep Children Alcohol Free, as found at www.alcoholfreechildren.org; and Grant, B. F. and D. A. Dawson. "Age at Onset of Alcohol Use and Association with DSM-IV Alcohol Abuse and Dependence: Results from the National Longitudinal Alcohol Epidemiologic Survey." *Journal of Substance Abuse* 9 (1997): 103–110.

. . . 28 percent of suicides . . . Leadership to Keep Children Alcohol Free, as found at www.alcoholfreechildren.org.

. . . suffer depression . . . Ibid.

. . . risk of unintentional injuries . . . Join Together Online. "Doctors Play Key Role in Underage-Drinking Prevention." May 14, 2001, as found at www.jointogether.org; and Hingson, R. W., T. Heeren, S. Levenson, A. Jamanka, and R. Voas. "Age of Drinking Onset, Driving after Drinking, and Involvement in Alcohol Related Motor-Vehicle Crashes." *Accident Analysis & Prevention* 34 (2002): 85–92.

p. 72   ... $53 billion ...   Levy, D. T., T. R. Miller, and K. C. Cox. *Costs of Underage Drinking*. Pacific Institute. Prepared for the U.S. Department of Justice Office of Juvenile Justice and Delinquency Prevention. Revised October 1999.

... *the average adult drinks* ...   Leadership to Keep Children Alcohol Free, as found at www.alcoholfreechildren.org.

p. 73   ... *Cinco de Mayo* ...   Gallegos, B. "Our Culture is Not for Sale! A Campaign to Reclaim *Cinco de Mayo* from the Alcohol Industry." Case Histories in Alcohol Policy, as found at www.tf.org.

... *$350 million* ...   Elliott, S. "Slightly Sweet Malt Beverages Get Some Heavy Marketing, with Young Drinkers the Targets." *New York Times* March 2, 2002: page C10.

p. 74   ... *Jared Drosnock* ...   Nixon, J. "Man Arraigned in Bloomsburg Alcohol Death." *Morning Call* February 7, 2001.

p. 75   *The wetter the environment* ...   Wechsler, H., M. Kuo, H. Lee, and G. W. Dowdall. "Environmental Correlates of Underage Alcohol Use and Related Problems of College Students." *Journal of Preventative Medicine* 19.1 (2000): 24–29; and Weitzman, E. R., T. F. Nelson, and H. Wechsler. "Taking Up Binge Drinking in College: The Influences of Person, Social Group and Environment." *Journal of Adolescent Health*. In press.

p. 77   ... *August Busch III* ...   "Drinks Industry Moves to Thwart Prevention Strategy on Drunk Driving, Binge Drinking and Drinking Age." *The Bottom Line on Alcohol in Society* 21.3 (Fall 2000): 4–10.

p. 78   *"Society Is a Network"*   Wagenaar, A. Personal interview. February 11, 2002.

p. 79   *Car crashes are still the leading cause* ...   "1999 Youth Fatal Crash and Alcohol Facts." National Highway Traffic Safety Administration. United States Department of Transportation, as found at www.nhtsa.dot.gov.

p. 81   ... *World Health Organization* ...   Declaration on Young People and Alcohol. (Adopted in Stockholm February 21, 2001). World Health Organization. Conference on Young People and Alcohol, as found at www.youngalcohol.who.dk.

... *thirty countries in Europe* ...   European School Survey Project on Alcohol and Other Drugs (ESPAD) Report, 1995–1999. Swedish Council for Information on Alcohol and other Drugs; "Drinks, Drugs and 16 Year Olds: New Finding for 30 European Countries Announced." World Health Organization Regional Office for Europe, April 2001; and "Young Are Drunk and High." *The Globe Magazine* New Series Issue 1, 2001, as found at www.ias.org.uk.

... *forty-three thousand French* ...   Jernigan, D. "Drink Like the French, Die Like the French." *The Marin Institute for the Prevention of Alcohol and Other Drug Problems*, as found at www.marininstitute.org.

... *65 percent* ...   Riviere, C. "Alcohol: The Situation in France." *The Globe Magazine* Issue 2, 2000, as found at www.ias.org.uk.

... *five-fold increase* ...   Abramson, H. "The Flip Side of French Drinking." The Marin Institute for the Prevention of Alcohol and Other Drug Problems, as found at www.marininstitute.org.

p. 82   ... *women in England* ...   "British Women Warned to Reduce Drinking." *Booze News: Updating Advocates on Alcohol Prevention Policies* as found at www.jointogether.org.

... *Irish health workers* ...   "Celtic Myths: The Challenge for Ireland." *The Globe Magazine* New Series Issue 1, 2001, as found at www.ias.org.uk.

... *extended the free market* ...   Declaration on Young People and Alcohol. (Adopted in Stockholm February 21, 2001.) World Health Organization. Conference on Young People and Alcohol, as found at www.youngalcohol.who.dk and www.alcoholconcern.org.uk.

... *longer opening hours* ...   "Celtic Myths: The Challenge for Ireland." *The Globe Magazine* New Series Issue 1, 2001, as found at www.ias.org.uk.

p. 83   ... *Declaration on Young People and Alcohol* ...   World Health Organization. Conference on Young People and Alcohol, as found at www.youngalcohol.who.dk.

p. 84   *Fatal Crashes and the Young Driver*   Adapted from "1999 Youth Fatal Crash and Alcohol Facts." National Highway Traffic Safety Administration. United States Department of Transportation, as found at www.nhtsa.dot.gov.

p. 85   *... eleven hundred college students.*   Hingson, R., T. Heeren, R. C. Zakocs, A. Kopstein, and H. Wechsler. "Magnitude of Alcohol-Related Mortality and Morbidity Among U.S. College Students Ages 18–24." *Journal of Studies on Alcohol* 63.2 (April 12, 2002): 136–44.

    ... Laramie, Wyoming ...   "Wyoming Student Charged in Crash." September 18, 2001. CNN/Sports Illustrated online, as found at http://sportsillustrated.cnn.com.

p. 86   *... lowered the BAC limit ...*   Wagenaar, A. C., P. M. O'Malley, and C. LaFond. "Lowered Legal Blood Alcohol Limits for Young Drivers: Effects on Drinking, Driving and Driving-after-Drinking Behaviors in 30 States." *American Journal of Public Health* 91.5 (May 2001): 801-804.

CHAPTER 5

Chaloupka, F. J. and H. Wechsler. "Binge Drinking in College: The Impact of Price, Availability, and Alcohol Control Policies." *Contemporary Economic Policy* (1996): 112–24.

Weitzman, E. R., A. Folkman, K. L. Folkman, and H. Wechsler. "The Relationship of Alcohol Outlet Density to Heavy and Frequent Drinking and Drinking-Related Problems among College Students at Eight Universities." *Health and Place.* In press.

p. 89   *Tri-Eagle ...*   Tri-Eagle Sales. "The History of Tri-Eagle Sales . . . . From the President," as found at www.abwslr.com.

    ... Jeb Bush ...   "Governor Bush Announces Business Leadership Awards." September 17, 2001, as found at www.eog.state.fl.us.

p. 90   *Nearly half—47 percent ...*   "Strategic Plan to Reduce High-Risk Drinking." PAR: Partnership for Alcohol Responsibility. Final draft. January 15, 2002.

    ... 185 different establishments ...   Ibid.

p. 93   *Alcohol ads generate ...*   Erenberg, D. F. and G. A. Hacker. "Last Call for High-Risk Bar Promotions That Target College Students: A Community Action Guide." Center for Science in the Public Interest, as found at The National Clearinghouse for Alcohol and Drug Information Web site, www.health.org.

    Bar Density within 2 Miles   A Matter of Degree, Harvard Evaluation, Harvard School of Public Health, 1999.

p. 94   *... Odds Bar ...*   Parker, C. and K. C. Bender. Personal communication. April 19, 2002.

p. 95   *"This proves that ..."*   Bender, K. C. Result of Hearing Before the Alcohol Beverages Commission Board on Summary Suspension of ABC License of Odds Bar. E-mail communication to coalition members, December 6, 2000, and December 11, 2000.

p. 96   *... in the year 2000 ...*   Sperber, M. *Beer and Circus: How Big-Time College Sports is Crippling Undergraduate Education.* New York City: Henry Holt & Company, 2000.

    "The publication in general ..."   Bell, T. "We Shouldn't Tolerate Outrageous Spring Break Promotions." *Tallahassee Democrat* February 4, 2002; and Hicks, N. "Chief Fights Spring-Break Drinking." *Lincoln Journal Star* January 2, 2002.

p. 97   *A 1999 report ...*   Federal Trade Commission. "Self-Regulation in the Alcohol Industry: A Review of Industry Efforts to Avoid Promoting Alcohol to Underage Consumers." September 1999, as found at www.ftc.gov.

p. 98   *... Michael Norman ...*   Associated Press. "American Student Falls to Death During Spring Break in Mexico." MSNBC. March 20, 2002, as found at http://famulus.msnbc.com.

    ... Michael Santiago ...   Alexander, A. "Ex-Holmdel Basketball Star Slips, Falls off Motel Balcony." *Asbury Park Press* March 13, 2001: page 1.

    ... Ross Hunter White ...   Navarro, B. J., and C. Leonard. "UA Student Dies in Rocky Point." *Arizona Republic* March 15, 2001: page B1.

p. 99   *Our studies show ...*   Powell, L. M., J. Williams, and H. Wechsler. "Study Habits and Alcohol Use Among College Students." *Education Economics* February 2002. In review.

    Increasing the price ...   Williams, J., F. J. Chaloupka, and H. Wechsler. "Are There Differential Effects of Price and Policy on College Students' Drinking Intensity?" *National Bureau of Economic Research* 1 (2002): Working Paper 8702.

NOTES

p. 100 *Easy as ABC*   Holderness, B. Personal interview. February 14, 2002.

p. 102 *...51.1 percent of FSU students...*   "Strategic Plan to Reduce High-Risk Drinking." PAR: Partnership for Alcohol Responsibility. Final draft. January 15, 2002.

...noise complaints...   Meisburg, S. "Don't Let Alcohol Industry's Deception Fool You." *Tallahassee Democrat* July 8, 2001.

Crashes related to...   Bridges, T. "Drunken Driving Arrests Rise." *Tallahassee Democrat* May 9, 2001: page B1.

...killing a friend...   Skiles, D. Letters to the Editor: "Alcohol-Related Problems Should Be Taken Seriously." *Tallahassee Democrat* October 6, 2000.

...two women were allegedly raped...   Dunkelberger, R. "Two Women Raped at Clubs." *Tallahassee Democrat* December 4, 2000; and Johns, C. "Rape Victims Find Indifference." *Tallahassee Democrat* February 7, 2001.

p. 103 *...Tau Kappa Epsilon...*   "TKE Colony Under Investigation." *Tallahassee Democrat* February 8, 2001: page B3.

...Dan Skiles...   Skiles, D. Personal interview. February 7, 2002; and personal e-mail. May 1, 2002.

p. 104 *...Steve Meisburg...*   Meisburg, S. Personal interview. February 1, 2002.

...a very public debate...   Sevigny, J. "Underage Drinking Fuels Fires." *Tallahassee Democrat* online, June 10, 2001.

p. 105 *...Tallahassee's spring parade.*   Barnet, C. "Beer Bully: Anheuser-Busch Has Aggressively Forged Tight, Often Controlling Relationships with Its 'Independent' Distributors to Stay No. 1 in Florida's Big Beer Market." *Florida Trend Magazine* February 2001.

CHAPTER 6

Federal Trade Commission. "Self-Regulation in the Alcohol Industry: A Review of Industry Efforts to Avoid Promoting Alcohol to Underage Consumers." September 1999, as found at www.ftc.gov.

Villani, S. "Impact of Media on Children and Adolescents: A 10-Year Review of the Research." *Journal of the American Academy of Child and Adolescent Psychiatry* 40.4 (April 2001): 392–401.

p. 106 *According to one study...*   "Teen Tipplers: America's Underage Drinking Epidemic." The National Center on Addiction and Substance Abuse at Columbia University (CASA). February 2002.

p. 107 *...44 percent do...*   Wechsler H., J. E. Lee, M. Kuo, M. Seibring, T. F. Nelson, and H. Lee. "Trends in College Binge Drinking During a Period of Increased Prevention Efforts: Findings from 4 Harvard School of Public Health College Alcohol Study Surveys: 1993–2001." *Journal of American College Health* 50.5 (March 25, 2002): 203–217.

p. 108 *...in 1999 alone...*   "Putting Anheuser-Busch's Consumer Responsibility Campaign into Perspective." *Booze News: Updating Advocates on Alcohol Prevention Policies.* Center for Science in the Public Interest. December 14, 2000.

...at least a dozen studies...   "Stop Liquor Ads on TV." *Booze News: Updating Advocates on Alcohol Prevention Policies.* Center for Science in the Public Interest. February 2002, as found at www.cspinet.org.

p. 109 *...13.1 years of age.*   "Stop Liquor Ads on TV." *Booze News: Updating Advocates on Alcohol Prevention Policies.* Center for Science in the Public Interest. February 2002, as found at www.cspinet.org.

In our latest study...   Wechsler, H., J. E. Lee, T. F. Nelson, and M. Kuo. "Underage College Students' Drinking Behavior, Access to Alcohol, and the Influence of Deterrence Policies: Findings from the Harvard School of Public Health College Alcohol Study." *Journal of American College Health* 50.5 (2002): 223–36.

...alcohol industry data...   "Teen Tipplers: America's Underage Drinking Epidemic." The National Center on Addiction and Substance Abuse at Columbia University (CASA). February 2002.

p. 109 *...market share in beer sales.*   Anheuser-Busch Companies. "Delivering Shareholder Value." Annual Report 2000.

p. 110   ... *99.5 million barrels* ...   "Anheuser-Busch Achieves Record U.S. Beer Volume in 2001." January 8, 2002, as found at www.anheuser-busch.com.

... *one hundred nations* ...   www.beerinstitute.org.

... *Molson and Labatt* ...   McKenzie, D. "Under the Influence? The Impact of Alcohol Advertising on Youth." Alcohol Policy Network, as found at www.apolnet.org.

p. 111   ... *youth culture covets* ...   Jackson, M. C., G. Hastings, C. Wheeler, D. Eadie, and A. M. Mackintosh. "Marketing Alcohol to Young People: Implications for Industry Regulation and Research Policy." *Addiction* 95 Supp. 4 (2000): S597–S608.

... *a brand's images* ...   Saffer, H. "Alcohol Advertising and Youth." *Journal of Studies on Alcohol* Supp. 14 (2002): 173–81.

p. 112   ... *"your dad's beer."*   McCarthy, M. "Top Brewer Also Reigns as King of Marketing." *USA Today* September 8, 2000: page B1.

". . . more contemporary brand."   Ibid.

... *Tequiza.* ...   "Anheuser-Busch Launches New Ad Campaign for Tequiza," as found at www.anheuser-busch.com; Hill, J. D. "Dallas Shop Dieste Picks Up A-B's Tequiza." *AdWeek Midwest* 42.14 (April 2, 2001): 8; and Brand Builders: New Products. *Brandweek* February 14, 2000.

p. 113   ... *Latinos were binge drinkers* ...   Wechsler, H., J. E. Lee, M. Kuo, M. Seibring, T. F. Nelson, and H. Lee. "Trends in College Binge Drinking During a Period of Increased Prevention Efforts: Findings from 4 Harvard School of Public Health College Alcohol Study Surveys: 1993–2001." *Journal of American College Health* 50.5 (March 25, 2002): 203–217.

...*41 percent of teens* ...   "Teen Tipplers: America's Underage Drinking Epidemic." The National Center on Addiction and Substance Abuse at Columbia University (CASA). February 2002.

p. 114   ... *three times more likely* ...   "Alcoholic Lemonade Volume on the Rise." *Modern Brewery Age* 51.41 (October 9, 2000): 1.

In early 2001 ...   "Smirnoff Ice." *Modern Brewery Age* 52.13 (March 26, 2001): 1.

... *"gateway drugs* ..."   "National Poll Shows 'Alcopop' Drinks Lure Teens." *Booze News: Updating Advocates on Alcohol Prevention Policies* May 9, 2001, as found at www.cspinet.org.

". . . not an advertising issue."   Beer Institute. Statement on CSPI's allegation that malternatives are marketed to teens. May 9, 2001.

". . . everyday drinks."   "What Teens Are Saying about 'Alcopops.'" *Booze News: Updating Advocates on Alcohol Prevention Policies* May 9, 2001, as found at www.cspinet.org.

p. 115   *In 1997 and 1998* ...   Federal Trade Commission. "FTC Reports on Industry Efforts to Avoid Promoting Alcohol to Underage Consumers." September 9, 1999, as found at www.ftc.gov.

... *Bill Gallegos* ...   Gallegos, B. Personal interview. February 22, 2002.

p. 116   ... *"Grab a Taste of Paradise."*   "'BUD Summer 2000' Promotion Features Supermodel Daniela Pestova, \$3 Million in Prizes," as found at www.anheuser-busch.com.

... *Rolling Rock Town Fair* ...   Khermouch, G. "Marketers of the Next Generation: Rolling Rock's Darin Wolf." *Brandweek* 41.44 (November 13, 2000): 51–52; and "Brand Builders— Events: Long Live Roll 'n' Rock!" *Brandweek* 41.29 (July 17, 2000): 20.

... *major concert facilities* ...   Erenberg, D. F. and G. A. Hacker. "Last Call for High-Risk Bar Promotions That Target College Students: A Community Action Guide." Center for Science in the Public Interest, as found at The National Clearinghouse for Alcohol and Drug Information Web site, www.health.org.

... *Student Broadcasting network.*   *The Grocer.* Shorts. October 21, 2000: page 56.

p. 118   ... *complimentary beer samples.*   Anheuser-Busch. "Delivering Shareholder Value." Annual Report 2000.

... *180,000 visitors* ...   "Branding on the Net." *Business Week* November 9, 1998: 76, 84.

p. 119   ... *Center for Media Education* ...   "Alcohol Advertising Targeted at Youth on the Internet: An Update." Center for Media Education. December 1998, as found at www.cme.org.

p. 120   *Canada's Molson Breweries* ...   Summerfield, P. "Viral Marketing Effort Adds Fuel to Molson's Database." *Strategy: The Canadian Marketing Report* June 18, 2001: page D10.

p. 122   . . . *Spuds MacKenzie* . . .   "Television Alcohol Portrayals, Alcohol Advertising, and Alcohol Expectancies among Children and Adolescents." *Effects of the Mass Media on the Use and Abuse of Alcohol.* Martin, S. E., and P. Mail, Eds. NIAAA Research Monograph No. 28. NIH Publication Number 95-3743. Bethesda, MD: National Institute on Alcohol Abuse and Alcoholism, 1995.

. . . *brand spokes-characters* . . .   "Alcohol Advertising Targeted at Youth on the Internet: An Update." Center for Media Education. December 1998, as found at www.cme.org.

. . . *Smirnoff Ice* . . .   Hein, K. "'Anti-Zima' Strategy: Ice, Ice Baby." *Brandweek* 42.7 (February 12, 2001): 3.

p. 123   . . . *major tobacco companies* . . .   Kuczynski, A. "Tobacco Companies Are Accused of Still Aiming Ads at the Young." *New York Times* August 15, 2001: page A1.

. . . *Super Bowl* . . .   Hacker, G. A. "Alcohol Advertising: Are Our Kids Collateral or Intended Targets?" *Booze News: Updating Advocates on Alcohol Prevention Policies* January 10, 2002, as found at www.cspinet.org.

p. 124   *Heavy industry lobbying* . . .   Chura, H. "TV Toasts NBC Drive to Drink; Mag Publishers May be Left with Only a Hangover." *Advertising Age* December 17, 2001: page 1; and Kaplan, D. "NBC Falls Off the Wagon; Agencies Applaud Decision to Air Hard-Liquor Ads on Network." *AdWeek East* 42.51 (December 17, 2001): 1.

. . . *vodka returned to network television* . . .   Elliott, S. "Objections May Scuttle NBC's Plan to Accept Hard-Liquor Commercials." *New York Times* February 12, 2002: page C7.

CNN reported . . .   "MADD Scolds Networks over Alcohol Ads." CNN. March 21, 2002.

Even without . . .   "Stop Liquor Ads on TV." *Booze News: Updating Advocates on Alcohol Prevention Policies.* Center for Science in the Public Interest. February 2002, as found at www.cspinet.org.

p. 126   . . . *NBWA* . . .   "GM Officials Meet with NBWA Board of Directors." *Beer Perspectives* 18.9 (May 11, 2001).

Lobbying for Big Alcohol   Massing, M. "Strong Stuff." *New York Times* March 22, 1998: section 6, page 36; and "Beer, Wine & Liquor: Top Contributors." Center for Responsive Politics, as found at www.opensecrets.org.

p. 128   *Industry representatives* . . .   Rehr, D. K. "Promoting the Industry with a United Front." *Beer Perspectives* 18.1 (January 16, 2001).

Rehr himself . . .   "Rehr Takes Helm at NBWA." *Beer Perspectives* 17.1 (January 17, 2000).

. . . *campaign contributor* . . .   "Beer, Wine & Liquor: Top Contributors." Center for Responsive Politics, as found at www.opensecrets.org.

During the 2001 conference . . .   Beer Perspectives. 11th Annual NBWA/Brewers Joint Legislative Conference, as found at www.nbwa.org.

p. 129   . . . *President George W. Bush* . . .   "Rubbing Elbows with the President!" *Beer Perspectives* 18.11 (June 28, 2001).

. . . *JazzFest in New Orleans* . . .   "Lobbying Opportunity in the Heart of the French Quarter." *Beer Perspectives* 17.11 (June 3, 2000).

p. 130   "*. . . common goals* . . ."   Rehr, D. K. "Promoting the Industry with a United Front." *Beer Perspectives* 18.1 (January 16, 2001).

. . . *class action lawsuits* . . .   "Rehr Outlines Topics Unifying Beer and Wine Industries." *Beer Perspectives* 17.1 (January 17, 2000).

"*. . . Neo-Prohibitionists* . . ."   Rehr, D. K. "Promoting the Industry with a United Front." *Beer Perspectives* 18.1 (January 16, 2001).

p. 131   . . . *excise taxes* . . .   "As Alcohol Beverage Suppliers Push for Federal Tax Rollback, State Tax Battles Heat Up." *Alcohol Issues Insights* 18.2 (February 2001).

p. 131   . . . *dollar per six-pack.*   "Safety, Consumer Group, American Public Just Say No to Beer Industry's 'Roll Back the Beer Tax': Reject H.R. 1305." Mothers Against Drunk Driving. April 16, 2002, as found at www.madd.org.

p. 132   . . . *eight principles* . . .   Greener, B. "Fundamentals of Communications: Principles That Always Hold True." *Beer Perspectives* 18.6 (March 26, 2001); and Greener, B. "Fundamentals of Communications: Effective Public Speaking." *Beer Perspectives* 18.4 (February 28, 2001).

CHAPTER 7

Wechsler, H. and M. Kuo. "College Students Define Binge Drinking and Estimate Its Prevalence: Results of a National Survey." *Journal of American College Health* 49.2 (2000): 57–64.

Wechsler, H. and T. F. Nelson. "Binge Drinking and the American College Student: What's Five Drinks?" *Psychology of Addictive Behaviors* 15.4 (2001): 287–91.

Journal of American College Health 49.2 (September 2000) dedicated an entire issue to studies reviewing social norms.

Psychology of Addictive Behaviors 15.4 (December 2001) dedicated an entire issue to the debate over the term *binge*.

p. 135   ... *$16 million per year* ...   "Putting Anheuser-Busch's Consumer Responsibility Campaign into Perspective." *Booze News: Updating Advocates on Alcohol Prevention Policies.* Center for Science in the Public Interest. December 14, 2000.

   ... *$10.5 million a year* ...   Information as found at the Century Council Web site at www.centurycouncil.org.

p. 136   ... *Drew Hunter* ...   Flores, C. "Rate of Binge Drinking among Students Hasn't Budged for 8 Years, According to Harvard Study." *Chronicle of Higher Education* March 25, 2002.

p. 138   ... *Wall Street Journal* ...   Murray, S. and B. Gruley. "On Many Campuses, Big Brewers Play a Role in New Alcohol Policies." *Wall Street Journal* November 2, 2000: page A1.

   ... *Peter Cressy* ...   "Leading Industry Executives Raise Profile of Key Alcohol Policy Issues." *Alcohol Issues Insights* November 2001.

p. 141   ... *to the tune of $105,000.*   Murray, S. and B. Gruley. "On Many Campuses, Big Brewers Play a Role in New Alcohol Policies." *Wall Street Journal* November 2, 2000: page A1.

p. 143   ... *Paul Clinton* ...   "Alcohol Beverage Industry Needs to be 'Fundamentally Transformed,'" Says a Top UDV Executive." *Alcohol Issues Insights* 19.11 (November 2001).

p. 144   ... *New York Times.*   Zernike, K. "New Tactic on College Drinking: Play It Down." *New York Times* October 3, 2000: page A1.

   The Myth of Social Norms   Keeling, R. Personal interviews. November 2, 2001, and February 14, 2002.

p. 146   ... *International Center for Alcohol Policies* ...   Information about ICAP and a number of its publications are available on its Web site at www.icap.org.

p. 147   *Public health workers* ...   "Big Alcohol's Smokescreen." *The Marin Institute Newsletter* 13 (Winter 1998), as found at www.marininstitute.org.

   ... *charged that CSAP "perverted"* ...   McCreanor, T. and S. Casswell. "ICAP and the Perils of Partnership." *Addiction* 95.2 (2000). A series of commentaries follow this editorial in this special issue of *Addiction*, which features a critique of ICAP.

p. 148   *In the fall of 2000* ...   Street, S. "The Latest War on 'Binge Drinking' Is against the Term Itself." *Chronicle of Higher Education* September 8, 2000.

p. 149   ... *spent $36 million* ...   Estimate provided by the United States Department of Education.

CHAPTER 8

p. 155   ... *Bradley McCue* ...   McCue, C. Personal interview. December 8, 2000.

p. 157   ... *approximately fourteen hundred students* ...   Hingson, R., T. Heeren, R. C. Zakocs, A. Kopstein, and H. Wechsler. "Magnitude of Alcohol-Related Mortality and Morbidity Among U.S. College Students Ages 18–24." *Journal of Studies on Alcohol* 63.2 (April 12, 2002): 136–44.

p. 158   *Our data* ...   Williams, J., L. M. Powell, and H. Wechsler. "Does Drinking Reduce Human Capital Accumulation? Evidence from the College Alcohol Studies." *Journal of Labor Economics* February 2002. In review; and Powell, L. M., J. Williams, and H. Wechsler. "Study Habits and Alcohol Use among College Students." *Education Economics* February 2002. In review.

   ... *drop out of school* ...   Ochs, R. "Students Need Lesson in Alcohol Avoidance." *Los Angeles Times* September 24, 2001: page S5.

p. 159 ... *blackouts* ... White, A. M., D. Jamieson-Drake, and H. S. Swartzwelder. "Prevalence and Correlates of Alcohol-Induced Blackouts among College Students." *Journal of American College Health*. In review.

p. 160 *In our College Alcohol Study* ... Wechsler, H., J. E. Lee, M. Kuo, and H. Lee. "College Binge Drinking in the 1990s: A Continuing Problem—Results of the Harvard School of Public Health 1999 College Alcohol Study." *Journal of American College Health* 48.10 (2000): 199–210.

The White study ... White, A. M., D. Jamieson-Drake, and H. S. Swartzwelder. "Prevalence and Correlates of Alcohol-Induced Blackouts among College Students." *Journal of American College Health*. In review.

p. 162 *Watch Your BAC* Adapted from "Effects of Alcohol Intoxication" at Indiana University's Alcohol-Drug Information Center (ADIC), as found at www.indiana.edu; additional information based on personal communication with Aaron M. White, Ph.D.

p. 166 ... *Giedd used a noninvasive* ... Giedd, J. N., et al. "Brain Development during Childhood and Adolescence: A Longitudinal MRI Study." *Nature Neuroscience* 2.10 (October 1999).

p. 167 ... *shrinks the hippocampus.* .... De Bellis, M. D., et al. "Hippocampal Volume in Adolescent-Onset Alcohol Use Disorders." *American Journal of Psychiatry* 157 (2000): 737.

p. 168 *Pharmacologist Fulton Crews* ... Crews, F. T., C. J. Braun, B. Hoplight, R. C. Switzer III, and D. J. Knapp. "Binge Ethanol Consumption Causes Differential Brain Damage in Young Adolescent Compared with Adult Rats." *Alcoholism: Clinical and Experimental Research* 24.11 (November 2000).

Another set of experiments ... Pyapali, G. K., D. A. Turner, W. A. Wilson, and S. H. Swartzwelder. "Age and Dose-Dependent Effects of Ethanol on the Induction of Hippocampal Long-Term Potentiation." *Alcohol* 19.2 (1999): 107–11.

p. 169 ... *group of volunteers* ... Acheson, S. K, R. M. Stein, and H. S. Swartzwelder. "Impairment of Semantic and Figural Memory by Acute Ethanol: Age-Dependent Effects." *Alcoholism: Clinical and Experimental Research* 22.7 (October 1998).

... *long-term cognitive damage* ... White, A. M., A. J. Ghia, E. D. Levin, and S. H. Swartzwelder. "Binge Pattern Ethanol Exposure in Adolescent and Adult Rats: Differential Impact on Subsequent Responsiveness to Ethanol." *Alcoholism: Clinical and Experimental Research* 24.8 (August 2000).

p. 170 *The teens with alcohol problems* ... Brown, S. A., S. F. Tapert, E. Granholm, and D. C. Delis. "Neurocognitive Functioning of Adolescents: Effects of Protracted Alcohol Use." *Alcoholism: Clinical and Experimental Research* 24.2 (February 2000).

... *Tapert and Sandra Brown found* ... Brown, S. Personal interview. October 2000.

p. 171 *Sandra Brown's research team* ... Tapert, S. Personal e-mail. October 24, 2000.

p. 172 ... *different brain pathways* ... National Institute on Alcohol Abuse and Alcoholism. "Cognitive Impairment and Recovery from Alcoholism." *Alcohol Alert* 53 (July 2001).

... *Swartzwelder and White* ... White, A. M., J. G. Bae, M. C. Truesdale, S. Ahmad, W. A. Wilson, and H. S. Swartzwelder. "Chronic-Intermittent Ethanol Exposure during Adolescence Prevents Normal Developmental Changes in Sensitivity to Ethanol-Induced Motor Impairments." *Alcoholism: Clinical and Experimental Research* (2002). In press.

p. 173 ... *physically dependent* ... Kuhn, C., S. Swartzwelder, and W. Wilson. *Buzzed: The Straight Facts about the Most Used and Abused Drugs from Alcohol to Ecstasy*. New York City: W. W. Norton & Company, 1998.

... *four symptoms* ... "FAQ's on Alcohol Abuse and Alcoholism for the Public." National Institute on Alcohol Abuse and Alcoholism, as found at www.niaaa.nih.gov.

p. 174 ... *our survey* ... Knight, J. R., H. Wechsler, M. Kuo, M. Seibring, E. R. Weitzman, and M. A. Schuckit. "Alcohol Abuse and Dependence among U.S. College Students." *Journal of Studies on Alcohol* (May 2002).

p. 174 ... *National Epidemiologic Survey* ... Grant, B. "The Impact of Family History of Alcoholism on the Relationship between Age at Onset of Alcohol Use and DSM-IV Alcohol Dependence: Results from the National Longitudinal Alcohol Epidemiologic Survey." *Alcohol Health and Research World* 22.2 (1998): 144–47.

CHAPTER 9

Knight, J. R., H. Wechsler, M. Kuo, M. Seibring, E. R. Weitzman, and M. A. Schuckit. "Alcohol Abuse and Dependence Among U.S. College Students." *Journal of Studies on Alcohol* (May 2002).

Williams, J., F. J. Chaloupka, and H. Wechsler. "Are There Differential Effects of Price and Policy on College Students' Drinking Intensity?" Working Paper 8702. January 2002.

Williams, J., R. L. Pacula, F. J. Chaloupka, and H. Wechsler. "Alcohol and Marijuana Use Among College Students: Economic Complements or Substitutes?" Working Paper 8401. July 2001.

p. 176   ... *more problems* ...   Wechsler, H., G. W. Dowdall, G. Maenner, J. Gledhill-Hoyt, and H. Lee. "Changes in Binge Drinking and Related Problems Among American College Students Between 1993 and 1997: Results of the Harvard School of Public Health College Alcohol Study." *Journal of American College Health* 47 (September 1998): 57–68.

    About 57 percent ...   Wechsler, H., J. E. Lee, M. Kuo, and H. Lee. "College Binge Drinking in the 1990s: A Continuing Problem—Results of the Harvard School of Public Health 1999 College Alcohol Study." *Journal of American College Health* 48.10 (2000): 199–210.

p. 177   ... *drop out of college* ...   Ochs, R. "Students Need Lesson in Alcohol Avoidance." *Los Angeles Times* September 24, 2001: page S5.

    ... *economic cost of alcohol abuse* ...   Levy, D. T., T. R. Miller, and K. C. Cox. *Costs of Underage Drinking*. Pacific Institute. Prepared for the U.S. Department of Justice Office of Juvenile Justice and Delinquency Prevention. Revised October 1999.

    Problems for Students Who Drink   Harvard School of Public Health 2001 College Alcohol Study.

p. 178   ... *secondhand effects* ...   Wechsler, H., G. W. Dowdall, G. Maenner, J. Gledhill-Hoyt, and H. Lee. "Changes in Binge Drinking and Related Problems Among American College Students Between 1993 and 1997: Results of the Harvard School of Public Health College Alcohol Study." *Journal of American College Health* 47 (September 1998): 57–68.

p. 179   *Secondhand Effects of Binge Drinking on Campus*   Harvard School of Public Health 2001 College Alcohol Study; and Wechsler, H., J. E. Lee, M. Kuo, and H. Lee. "College Binge Drinking in the 1990s: A Continuing Problem." *Journal of American College Health* 48 (March 2000): 199–210.

    In our survey ...   Wechsler, H., B. Moeykens, A. Davenport, S. Castillo, and J. Hansen. "The Adverse Impact of Heavy Episodic Drinkers on Other College Students." *Journal of Studies on Alcohol* 56 (1995): 628–34.

p. 180   *A common theory* ...   Giancola, P. R. "Alcohol-Related Aggression During the College Years: Theories, Risk Factors, and Policy Implications." *A Call to Action: Changing the Culture of Drinking at U.S. Colleges*. Task Force of the National Advisory Council on Alcohol Abuse and Alcoholism. National Institutes of Health U.S. Department of Health and Human Services. National Institute on Alcohol Abuse and Alcoholism. April 2002.

p. 181   ... *students were hit* ...   Hingson, R., T. Heeren, R. C. Zakocs, A. Kopstein, and H. Wechsler. "Magnitude of Alcohol-Related Mortality and Morbidity Among U.S. College Students Ages 18–24." *Journal of Studies on Alcohol* 63.2 (April 12, 2002): 136–44.

    Testing Aggression   Giancola, P. R. "Alcohol-Related Aggression During the College Years: Theories, Risk Factors, and Policy Implications." *A Call to Action: Changing the Culture of Drinking at U.S. Colleges*. Task Force of the National Advisory Council on Alcohol Abuse and Alcoholism. National Institutes of Health U.S. Department of Health and Human Services. National Institute on Alcohol Abuse and Alcoholism. April 2002.

p. 182   ... *Atuanya Priester* ...   Geranios, N. K. "Assault on Black Student Fueled by Feud, Not Race." The Associated Press State & Local Wire. October 12, 2000; and Rivera, R. "Police Tie Booze to Violence at WSU but Minority Groups Think Race Sparked Assault Outside Frat." *Seattle Times* September 24, 2000: page B1.

p. 183   ... *Jewish menorah* ...   Crime and Justice: The District. "Vandalism of Menorah Denounced." *Washington Post* December 7, 1999: page B02; and Murphy, C. and V. Strauss. "Georgetown President to Leave Next Year." *Washington Post* March 21, 2000: page B03.

    ... *living near college campuses* ...   Wechsler, H., J. E. Lee, J. Hall, A. C. Wagenaar, and H. Lee. "Secondhand Effects of Student Alcohol Use Reported by Neighbors of Colleges: The Role of Alcohol Outlets." *Social Science and Medicine*. July 2002.

p. 184 *Washington State University* . . . Sudermann, H. "Pullman Neighborhood Still in a Froth." *The Spokesman-Review* April 9, 2001: page A1.

Pennsylvania State University . . . Short Subjects. "11 Penn State Students Arrested in Alcohol-Fueled Riot." *Chronicle of Higher Education* July 24, 1998.

p. 185 *Kent State University* . . . Levinson, A. "Campus Party Arrests Worries Schools." Associated Press Online. May 14, 2001.

University of Utah . . . Stewart, K. U. "Greeks Once Again in Neighborhood Spat." *Salt Lake Tribune* January 17, 2001.

. . . *Kurt Pydyszewski* . . . Janofsky, M. "A Suicide Draws Attention to Campus Melees." *New York Times* May 14, 2001: page A10; and Levinson, A. "Campus Party Arrests Worries Schools." Associated Press Online. May 14, 2001.

p. 186 . . . *recolonize the neighborhood* . . . Sudermann, H. "Pullman Neighborhood Still in a Froth." *The Spokesman-Review* April 9, 2001: page A1.

. . . *University of Delaware* . . . Bialey, K. "Alcohol, Noise Problems Still Plague Newark." *News Journal* September 7, 2001.

p. 187 *In our study* . . . Unpublished College Alcohol Study data.

. . . *heavy drinking and smoking* . . . Nagourney, E. "Where There's Smoke, There's More." *New York Times* July 24, 2001.

. . . *our surveys show* . . . Unpublished College Alcohol Study data.

. . . *GHB and alcohol.* "Two Men Arrested in Overdose Death of Chico Woman." The Associated Press State & Local Wire. September 10, 2001.

p. 188 . . . *linked to violent behaviors* . . . "Alcohol Linked to Violent Behavior More Often Than Use of Illegal Drugs Is Linked to Violent Behavior, Study Finds." AScribe—The Public Interest Newswire. January 23, 2002.

In our 1999 survey . . . Gledhill-Hoyt, J., H. Lee, J. Strote, and H. Wechsler. "Increased Use of Marijuana and Other Illicit Drugs at US Colleges in the 1990s: Results of Three National Surveys." *Addiction* 95.11 (2000): 1655–67.

p. 189 *The Clery Act* . . . Clery, H. and C. Clery. "What Jeanne Didn't Know." Security On Campus, as found at www.campussafety.org.

The 2000 report . . . Nicklin, J. L. "U.S. Report Shows Rise in Campus Crime: Experts Question Data." *Chronicle of Higher Education* January 22, 2001.

p. 190 . . . *failed to properly report* . . . Leinwand, D. "Campus Crime Underreported." *USA Today* October 4, 2000: page A1.

. . . *Sacramento Bee* . . . Ibid.

CHAPTER 10

Wechsler, H., G. W. Dowdall, A. Davenport, and S. Castillo. "Correlates of College Student Binge Drinking among College Students." *American Journal of Public Health* 85 (1995): 921–26.

Wechsler, H., J. E. Lee, M. Kuo, and H. Lee. "College Binge Drinking in the 1990s: A Continuing Problem—Results of the Harvard School of Public Health 1999 College Alcohol Study." *Journal of American College Health* 48.10 (2000): 199–210.

Wechsler, H., J. E. Lee, M. Kuo, M. Seibring, T. F. Nelson, and H. Lee. "Trends in College Binge Drinking During a Period of Increased Prevention Efforts: Findings from 4 Harvard School of Public Health College Alcohol Study Surveys: 1993–2001." *Journal of American College Health* 50.5 (March 25, 2002): 203–217.

p. 191 . . . *seen the videotape.* Carlson, S. "2 Heidelberg Athletes Accused of Videotaping Sexual Assault of an Unconscious Woman." *Chronicle of Higher Education* November 26, 1999.

Nearly every college woman . . . Hardy, T. and M. Barrows. "UC Keeps Sex Crimes in Shadows." *Sacramento Bee* September 24, 2000.

p. 192 . . . *74 percent of perpetrators* . . . Koss, M. P., C. A. Gidycz, and N. Wisniewski. "The Scope of Rape: Incidence and Prevalence of Sexual Aggression and Victimization in a National Sample of Higher Education Students." *Journal of Consulting and Clinical Psychology* 55 (1987): 162–70.

p. 192 ... *10 percent* ... Dowdall, G. W., M. P. Koss, M. Kuo, and H. Wechsler. "Non-Consensual Sex While Under the Influence: Results of the Harvard School of Public Health College Alcohol Study." Unpublished College Alcohol Study paper.

One study reports ... Cooper, M. L. "Alcohol Use and Risky Sexual Behavior Among College Students: Evaluating the Experience." *Journal of Studies on Alcohol* Supp. 14 (March 2002): 101–117.

p. 195 ... *national study of women's drinking* ... Wilsnack, R. W., S. C. Wilsnack, A. F. Kristjanson, and T. R. Harris. "Ten-Year Prediction of Women's Drinking Behavior in a Nationally Representative Sample." *Women's Health: Research on Gender, Behavior, and Policy* 4 (1998): 199–230.

p. 198 *For instance* ... Unpublished College Alcohol Study data; and Cooper, M. L. "Alcohol Use and Risky Sexual Behavior Among College Students: Evaluating the Experience." *Journal of Studies on Alcohol* Supp. 14 (March 2002): 101–117.

... *a survey* ... Cooper, M. L. "Alcohol Use and Risky Sexual Behavior Among College Students: Evaluating the Experience." *Journal of Studies on Alcohol* Supp. 14 (March 2002): 101–117.

p. 199 ... *implicated in more rapes* ... De la Riva, A. "Sexual Assault a Problem at U. Wisconsin." *Badger Herald* via U-Wire. October 10, 2001.

For one thing ... Wechsler, H., G. W. Dowdall, A. Davenport, and E. B. Rimm. "A Gender-Specific Measure of Binge Drinking Among College Students." *American Journal of Public Health* 85 (1995): 982–85.

p. 200 ... *university in Maine* ... Hoover, E. "U. of Southern Maine May Be Sued by Victim of Sexual Assault, Court Rules." *Chronicle of Higher Education* June 28, 2001.

Further evidence ... Wechsler, H., J. E. Lee, M. Kuo, M. Seibring, T. F. Nelson, and H. Lee. "Trends in College Binge Drinking During a Period of Increased Prevention Efforts: Findings from 4 Harvard School of Public Health College Alcohol Study Surveys: 1993–2001." *Journal of American College Health* 50.5 (March 25, 2002): 203–217.

p. 201 ... *women's self-esteem* ... Dowdall, G. W., M. Crawford, and H. Wechsler. "Binge Drinking among American College Women: A Comparison of Single Sex and Coeducational Institutions." *Psychology of Women Quarterly* 22 (1998): 706–715.

The Dartmouth Affair Graham, J. "'Animal House' in Porn Shocker." *New York Post* May 11, 2001.

p. 203 ... *satire and humor.* Gomstyn, A. "Zete Derecognized in Wake of 'Sex Papers.'" *Dartmouth Online* May 14, 2001.

"... *disrespect for women.*" "The Student Life Initiative at Dartmouth College," as found at www.dartmouth.edu.

p. 204 *Dartmouth itself recognizes* ... "The Student Life Initiative at Dartmouth College." Part G: Abuse of Alcohol on Campus. January 24, 2002, as found at www.dartmouth.edu.

p. 205 ... *national study in 1948* ... Straus, R. and S. Bacon. *Drinking in College.* Westport, CT: Greenwood Publishing Group, 1953.

p. 206 ... *tenderly join hands.* Garfield, B. "It's (Miller) Time to Explore Gender Roles Sans Hormones." *Advertising Age* June 11, 2001.

p. 207 ... *$50 million marketing blitz* ... Hein, K. "'Anti-Zima' Strategy: Ice, Ice Baby." *Brandweek* 42.7 (February 12, 2001): 3.

p. 209 ... *Central Connecticut State University* ... Associated Press. "Sexy Bar Ad Raises College President's Concern." Boston.com. September 13, 2001.

CHAPTER 11

Wechsler, H., J. E. Lee, J. Gledhill-Hoyt, and T. F. Nelson. "Alcohol Use and Problems at Colleges Banning Alcohol: Results of a National Survey." *Journal of Studies on Alcohol* 62.2 (2001): 133–41.

Wechsler, H., J. E. Lee, T. F. Nelson, and H. Lee. "Drinking Levels, Alcohol Problems and Secondhand Effects in Substance-Free College Residences: Results of a National Study." *Journal of Studies on Alcohol* 62.1 (2001): 23–31.

Wechsler, H., T. F. Nelson, and E. R. Weitzman. "From Knowledge to Action: How Harvard's College Alcohol Study Can Help Your Campus Design a Campaign Against Student Alcohol Abuse." *Changes* 32.1 (2000): 38–43.

p. 214 ... *volunteerism* ... Weitzman, E. R. and I. Kawachi. "Giving Means Receiving: The Protective Effects of Social Capital on Binge Drinking on College Campuses." *American Journal of Public Health* 90 (2000): 1936–39.

p. 215 ... *Dartmouth ... serious drinking problem* ... "The Student Life Initiative at Dartmouth College." Part G: Abuse of Alcohol on Campus. January 24, 2002, as found at www.dartmouth.edu.

p. 216 ... *students want a change* ... Wechsler, H., J. E. Lee, M. Kuo, M. Seibring, T. F. Nelson, and H. Lee. "Trends in College Binge Drinking During a Period of Increased Prevention Efforts: Findings from 4 Harvard School of Public Health College Alcohol Study Surveys: 1993–2001." *Journal of American College Health* 50.5 (March 25, 2002): 203–217.

p. 217 ... *healthy student attitudes.* Ibid.

Student Support for Tougher Alcohol Policies Wechsler, H. "Binge Drinking on America's College Campuses. Findings from the Harvard School of Public Health College Alcohol Study." *Research Monograph* 2000.

p. 218 ... *equity and globalization* ... World Health Organization. A Summary of Global Status Report on Alcohol. Management of Substance Dependence, Non-Communicable Diseases. World Health Organization. June 2001.

p. 219 ... *NU Directions* ... Major, L. and T. Workman. "Campus-Community Solutions to Collegiate High-Risk Drinking." *Metropolitan Universities: An International Forum* 11.2 (2000): 63–70.

p. 220 *"We Exist to Not Exist"* McEvily, J. Personal interview. March 6, 2002.

p. 225 ... *CIRCLe Network* ... Dungy, G. J. and J. C. Michael. "Leadership Development for Social Change: A Campus-Wide Strategy." *Campus Drinking 2002: A New Framework and Call to Action.* Richard P. Keeling & Associates. NASPA Center for Student Studies and Demographics and Outside the Classroom. March 2002.

p. 228 *Building a New Culture for Learning* Carothers, R. Personal interview. February 14, 2002.

p. 233 ... *alcohol-free living arrangements* ... Wechsler, H., J. E. Lee, M. Kuo, M. Seibring, T. F. Nelson, and H. Lee. "Trends in College Binge Drinking During a Period of Increased Prevention Efforts: Findings from 4 Harvard School of Public Health College Alcohol Study Surveys: 1993–2001." *Journal of American College Health* 50.5 (March 25, 2002): 203–217.

p. 235 *The University of Colorado* ... Bormann, C. A. and M. H. Stone. "The Effects of Eliminating Alcohol in a College Stadium: The Folsom Field Beer Ban." *Journal of American College Health* 50.2 (September 2001).

... *alcohol dependent* ... Knight, J. R., H. Wechsler, M. Kuo, M. Seibring, E. R. Weitzman, and M. A. Schuckit. "Alcohol Abuse and Dependence among U.S. College Students." *Journal of Studies on Alcohol* (May 2002).

CHAPTER 12

p. 239 ... *"Let's Talk Over a Beer"* Pamphlet: "Description of Beer Industry Programs." The Beer Institute. Distributed to Congress. September 27, 2000.

p. 241 ... *risk scores for substance use* ... "Teen Tipplers: America's Underage Drinking Epidemic." The National Center on Addiction and Substance Abuse at Columbia University (CASA). February 2002; and "Back to School 1999—National Survey of American Attitudes on Substance Abuse V: Teens and Their Parents." The National Center on Addiction and Substance Abuse at Columbia University (CASA).

p. 243 ... *delay the first drink* ... Hingson, R. W., T. Heeren, S. Levenson, A. Jamanka, and R. Voas. "Age of Drinking Onset, Driving after Drinking, and Involvement in Alcohol Related Motor-Vehicle Crashes." *Accident Analysis & Prevention* 34 (2002): 85–92; and Hingson, R., T. Heeren, and R. Zakocs. "Age of Drinking Onset and Involvement in Physical Fights after Drinking." *Pediatrics* 108.4 (October 2001): 872–77.

p. 243   . . . *all illicit drugs combined.*   Rogers, J. D. and T. K. Greenfield. "Beer Drinking Accounts for Most of the Hazardous Alcohol Consumption in the U.S." *Journal of Studies on Alcohol* 60.6 (1999): 732–39.

p. 244   . . . *obtain alcohol from a parent* . . .   Wechsler, H., J. E. Lee, T. F. Nelson, and M. Kuo. "Underage College Students' Drinking Behavior, Access to Alcohol, and the Influence of Deterrence Policies: Findings from the Harvard School of Public Health College Alcohol Study." *Journal of American College Health* 50.5 (2002): 223–36.

. . . *sixth- and ninth-graders* . . .   "Teen Tipplers: America's Underage Drinking Epidemic." The National Center on Addiction and Substance Abuse at Columbia University (CASA). February 2002.

p. 245   . . . *less inclined to drink.*   Ibid.

. . . *23 percent of parents* . . .   Ibid.

p. 246   . . . *two thousand* . . . *commercials* . . .   "Stop Liquor Ads on TV." *Booze News: Updating Advocates on Alcohol Prevention Policies.* Center for Science in the Public Interest. February 2002, as found at www.cspinet.org.

p. 248   *The Proactive Way to Pick a School*   DeJong, W. and K. L. Zweig. "Checking out Colleges: Questions to Ask School Officials about Alcohol and Other Drug Prevention." *Driven.* Mothers Against Drunk Driving. Spring 1998.

p. 249   . . . *a high-binge college.*   Weitzman, E. R., T. F. Nelson, and H. Wechsler. "Taking Up Binge Drinking in College: The Influences of Person, Social Group and Environment." *Journal of Adolescent Health.* In press.

CHAPTER 13

p. 261   *Iowa City, Iowa* . . .   Solow, C. Personal interview. March 18, 2002; Langenberg, S. "Six Months Later: Officials, Bar Owners Give Ordinance Mixed Reviews." *Iowa City Press-Citizen* February 1, 2002; and Iowa City Ordinance No. 01-3968.

p. 262   *Lincoln, Nebraska* . . .   Casady, T. Personal interview. March 6, 2002; and Hain, C. J. "Council Dries out Football Gamedays." *Lincoln Star Journal* August 21, 2001.

p. 264   *Salinas, California* . . .   Mosher, J. F. and B. Reynolds. "How to Use Local Regulatory and Land Use Powers to Prevent Underage Drinking." Pacific Institute for Research and Evaluation. Prepared for the U.S. Department of Justice Office of Juvenile Justice and Delinquency Prevention, Rockville, MD.

p. 265   *Annapolis, Maryland* . . .   Babington, C. "Maryland's Grassroots Effort to Reduce Underage Drinking. *Case Histories in Alcohol Policy.* Editor Joel Streicker. The Trauma Foundation, as found at www.tf.org.

. . . *one-quarter of all states* . . .   Wagenaar, A. C. "Alcohol Policies in the United States: Highlights from the 50 States." Alcohol Epidemiology Program. Minneapolis: University of Minnesota, 2000.

p. 266   *Los Angeles* . . .   Gallegos, B. Personal interview. February 22, 2002; and Gallegos, B. "Chasing the Frogs and Camels out of Los Angeles: The Movement to Limit Alcohol and Tobacco Billboards." *Case Histories in Alcohol Policy.* Editor Joel Streicker. The Trauma Foundation, as found at www.tf.org.

p. 267   *The bottom line* . . .   Skiles, D. Personal interview. February 7, 2002.

p. 269   . . . *tax-exempt status.*   Keeling, R. P. "Next Steps: Rethinking Campus Drinking." *Campus Drinking 2002: A New Framework and Call to Action.* Richard P. Keeling & Associates. NASPA Center for Student Studies and Demographics and Outside the Classroom. March 2002.

. . . *cultural heritage.*   Mosher, J. F. "Alcohol Policy and the Young Adult: Establishing Priorities, Building Partnerships, Overcoming Barriers." *Addiction* 94.3 (1999): 357–69.

INDEX